# JANE CAMPION

Jane Campion is one of the most celebrated auteurs of modern cinema and was the first female director to be awarded the prestigious Palme d'Or. Throughout her relatively short career, Campion has received extraordinary attention from the media and scholars alike and has provoked fierce debates on issues such as feminism, colonialism, and nationalism.

In the first detailed account of Jane Campion's career as a filmmaker, Deb Verhoeven examines specifically how contemporary film directors "fashion" themselves as auteurs – through their personal interactions with the media, in their choice of projects, in their emphasis on particular filmmaking techniques and finally in the promotion of their films.

Through analysis of key approaches to Campion's films, such as *The Piano*, *In the Cut*, *Sweetie*, *An Angel at My Table*, and *Holy Smoke*, Deb Verhoeven introduces students to the passionate debates surrounding this controversial and often experimental director.

Featuring a career overview, a filmography, detailed analysis and an extended interview with Campion on her approach to creativity, this is a great introduction to one of the most important directors of contemporary cinema.

**Deb Verhoeven** is Associate Professor of Screen Studies in the School of Applied Communication at RMIT University, Australia.

# Routledge Film Guidebooks

The Routledge Film Guidebooks offer a clear introduction and overview of the work of key filmmakers, schools or movements. Each guidebook contains an introduction, including a brief history, defining characteristics and major films; a chronology; key debates surrounding the filmmaker or movement; and pivotal scenes, focusing on narrative structure, camera work and production quality.

Bollywood: a Guidebook to Popular Hindi Cinema
*Tejaswini Ganti*

James Cameron
*Alexandra Keller*

Jane Campion
*Deb Verhoeven*

# Jane Campion

*DEB VERHOEVEN*

Routledge
Taylor & Francis Group

LONDON AND NEW YORK

First published 2009
by Routledge
2 Park Square, Milton Park, Abingdon, Oxon, OX14 4RN

Simultaneously published in the USA and Canada
by Routledge
270 Madison Ave, New York, NY 10016

Routledge is an imprint of the Taylor & Francis Group, an informa business

© 2009 Deb Verhoeven

Typeset in Joanna by
Swales & Willis Ltd, Exeter, Devon
Printed and bound in Great Britain by
TJ International, Padstow, Cornwall

British Library Cataloguing in Publication Data
A catalogue record for this book is available from the British Library

Library of Congress Cataloging in Publication Data
Verhoeven, Deb.
Jane Campion/Deb Verhoeven.
     p. cm. – (Routledge film guidebooks)
   Includes bibliographical references and index.
   1. Campion, Jane, 1954– Criticism and interpretation.   I. Title.
PN1998.3.C3545V47 2008
791.4302'3092–dc22                                    2008032506

ISBN10: 0–415–26274–7 (hbk)
ISBN10: 0–415–26275–5 (pbk)
ISBN10: 0–203–88596–1 (ebk)

ISBN13: 978–0–415–26274–3 (hbk)
ISBN13: 978–0–415–26275–0 (pbk)
ISBN13: 978–0–203–88596–3 (ebk)

# CONTENTS

# LIST OF ILLUSTRATIONS

**FIGURES**

## TABLES

# ACKNOWLEDGEMENTS

It sometimes feels as if both this book and its author have lived a multitude of lives before arriving at the pause that comes with publication. And as with any project that traverses a period of time, this one has faced its share of dramas – calamitous change, sudden illness, a near death experience followed by a miraculous resuscitation. And that was just the computer. So, first and foremost, I would like to thank the various technicians who rescued this manuscript from the brink of erasure on more than one occasion. If it weren't for the heroic efforts of Mark, Remi and Pete, it is doubtful this book would have been published at all.

Other people have contributed to the ongoing lives of this work. The team at the AFI Research Collection deserve special mention: Aysen Mustafa, Sarah Sanderson, Michelle Carey and Olympia Szilagyi have all at one time or another worked with me. But, in particular, I want to thank the current AFIRC Librarian, Alex Gionfriddo, for his imaginative research assistance and outstanding support. Laurene Vaughan, Peter Kemp and Cynthia Troup have also expended research effort.

Different aspects of the manuscript were discussed with colleagues: many thanks to Brian Morris, Alistair Fox, Ian Henderson, Cathy

Greenfield, John Berenyi and Lisa French for their input as well as Adrian Danks and Lino Caputo for their encouragement. Jane Campion and her agents at HLA have been extremely helpful as was Andrew Pike from Ronin Films. Alan Finney was extremely obliging, providing colour and detail to my understanding of the promotion of *The Piano* in Australia.

From Routledge, at various times, I can thank a succession of reassuring and unfailingly patient editors, in particular Aileen Storrey but also Natalie Foster and Katrina Chandler.

More broadly, I would like to acknowledge the Campion authors and commentators who precede me and who have set the benchmark for anyone attempting to write on this filmmaker: Dana Polan, Sue Gillett, Harriet Margolis, Gail Jones, Kathleen McHugh (to name but a few) have made the exercise of writing on Campion as invigorating as it has been gratifying.

Finally I want to offer my appreciation to Ryder and Tilde who have always lived with this book lurking somewhere in the background and especially to Robyn who can still remember a time 'BC' ('Before Campion').

# INTRODUCTION

## Being Jane Campion in a Post-Campion World?

This isn't my life. This is the book I wrote about my life.

Janet Frame[1]

Jane Campion is one of the world's most recognised and celebrated filmmakers, the winner of innumerable awards and critical acclaim. That Campion has arrived at these accomplishments with only a handful of feature films to her name makes them seem all the more remarkable. She was the first woman (and not incidentally the first New Zealander) to earn a coveted Palm d'Or at the Cannes film festival, doing it with just her fourth feature film, *The Piano* (1993), previously having won the festival's equivalent short film award with her student film *Peel* (1982).[2] By any standards she is the most successful woman working in the contemporary film industry.

In 2007, the Cannes film festival, the scene of so many Campion triumphs, recognized her achievements by inviting her to join thirty-five of the world's leading auteurs to celebrate its sixtieth anniversary. Each filmmaker was asked to contribute a short film that expressed 'their state of mind of the moment as inspired by the motion picture theater', the sum of which were then compiled as *Chacun Son Cinéma* (*To*

*Each His Cinema*, 2007). Of the thirty-five directors who participated, Campion was the only woman, a disturbing fact she commented on frequently. Her concerns were further elaborated in the film she produced for the festival, *The Lady Bug* (2007), which also provided a commentary of sorts on the under-representation of women in the film industry. In the film a woman dressed in an insect costume tries to extend her wings and dance centre-stage but is ignominiously squashed by an annoyed cleaner. Campion was quick to point out that the film was a metaphor for women in the film industry: 'I just think this is the way the world is, that men control the money, and they decide who they're going to give it to'.[3] Photos taken at the launch of the film show her as a striking figure, a singular woman surrounded by a multitude of suits (see Figure 0.1). In part through sheer attrition, Jane Campion has become a heightened emblem of the plight of the female auteur in contemporary filmmaking, a figure to be celebrated and criticized for what she has come to represent as much as for what

FIGURE 0.1 Cannes 2007: lone woman in a sea of suits
Anne-Christine Poujoulat/AFP/Getty Images

she does. Jane Campion's success is exemplary both in the sense that it is admirable and also in the sense that her career serves to epitomize many aspects of the contemporary experience of auteur cinema.

## AUTEUR AS EMBLEM: THE CAMPION COMPARISON

Over the years Campion's stellar career has been used emblematically by industry observers, members of the media and academics alike to illustrate various aspects of the film industry; she is for instance the consummate early success story, a handy signifier of nascent talent poised on the verge of international recognition; she has been embraced as the figurehead for women's cinema by critics and commentators; and she has been claimed as the representative of more than one national cinema (see Figure 0.2). It is Campion's symbolic value that is immediately striking in many accounts of her career.

In particular the rapid elevation of Campion to 'auteurdom' has been a recurring theme for the press who like to draw on her successful

FIGURE 0.2 A national emblem no mater what the outcome
Courtesy Mark Knight/Herald & Weekly Times

history as a short filmmaker in describing rising industry talent. Campion's role as the media exemplar of early promise has given rise to the 'Campion comparison' in which emerging directors (invariably women) measure themselves or are measured by others against Campion's precocious career prominence. Cate Shortland, a filmmaker with a string of successful short films, remarked on the occasion of the Cannes screening of her first feature film, *Somersault* (2004): 'Growing up in Australia, it wasn't unusual to want to be a director because we had Gillian Armstrong and Jane Campion.'[4] Similarly Ana Kokkinos (*Head On, Book of Revelations*) describes the enabling impact of Campion's presence on her own choice to be a director in the early-1990s. For Kokkinos, directing was her second career and involved;

> a very active conscious decision to say, "I now feel stronger and in a better position to launch into something like this". And there was no doubt that for me, particularly in that period, Jane Campion's work was very inspirational, because, again, another very strong woman director was emerging. In my late twenties that was a terrific impetus.[5]

For Shortland and Kokkinos, 'Campion' is kind of handy reference for their own emerging sense of agency as filmmakers.

However, not all Campion comparisons have been generated by filmmakers anxious to footnote their debt to a successful precursor. In 1994 shortly after the release of *The Piano* and in the wake of her own film *Orlando* (1992), British director Sally Potter related a curious confusion on the part of both the media and audience members:

> When I was first being interviewed about *Orlando*, a lot of people would ask what I thought of *The Piano*. Or people would come up to me and say, "You're Sally Potter! I just saw *The Piano*!" as if there was some connection. Maybe there's something in the films themselves that causes people to link them, beyond the fact they happened to be made at the same time, by women directors. I don't find it worrisome. I'm an enormous fan of Jane Campion's work and of her as a person, and I'm

happy about being bracketed with her, rather than with many others, and I hope she would feel the same. It's an exciting moment for both of us; we've become visible in a way that transcends the ghetto principle.[6]

Potter presents the public confusion between *Orlando* and *The Piano* as if it arises from a belief that she and Campion have surpassed the 'ghetto principle' that would otherwise confine them to the margins of the cinema. Notwithstanding the evident success of both these films, it is just as easy to interpret the public confusion between the two directors and their films as reiterating their marginality, such that their unique status as female directors of period films is all that needs to be known about them and their individual talents and achievements are subsumed by this summary knowledge as if to say that any given female auteur is interchangeable with another.

It is not only established feature directors that are matched to Campion in the media. Graduates of Campion's *alma mater*, the Australian Film Television (and later, Radio) School (AFTRS) are particularly singled out for comparison. Ivan Sen's pre-feature success was painted by the School's director Rod Bishop in terms defined by Campion's record of achievement;

It's a bit like when you see somebody act for the first time and they're acting at a level which clearly demarcates them from the rest. Jane made films that way. Her control over technique, her control over the subject matter and the balance between those two things was so exceptional it took your breath away. And Ivan's films, I feel, are the same.[7]

Finally, the 'Campion comparison' is not always deployed for the purpose of revealing the career possibilities for film graduates. In an article titled 'The Next Campion?' AFTRS graduate Kim Farrant gave a less than enthusiastic response to suggestions that she would follow in Campion's footsteps; 'I hope to be the next Kim Farrant' she averred, 'I hope to be me'.[8] Given that, by her own admission, Campion failed to impress her teachers at AFTRS ('I was not a student most likely to succeed in the eyes of almost all the staff'), these comparisons must seem equally galling to her.[9]

Campion has spoken in several interviews about her disappointing experiences at film school particularly with what she viewed to be the conservatism of the staff and curriculum. Instead she turned to other students, drawing inspiration from collaborators such as Gerard Lee, Sally Bongers (both of whom collaborated with her on *Sweetie*) as well as Laurie McInnes and Alex Proyas. Reminiscing with Sally Bongers on the production of their first feature film *Sweetie*, they recalled their unpopularity at the school as being something of an advantage: 'There was no way they were going to like what we did. We knew that from the beginning. And in a way that creates a kind of freedom because you're not trying to please the staff'.[10] Campion's comment here, that there is a freedom in not having to live up to other people's expectations is an early pointer to her later career-defining frustrations with this sense of obligation to honouring one's career, that comes with success.

Early in her career Campion wore her rebellion like a badge. In the program notes for her graduate screenings she described herself in a series of pithy and sharply pretentious statements:

> In film I am committed to quality and innovation. While at School I subverted the workshop system by gaining skills in many areas. I wrote three scripts, did camera, 1st Assisted; directed and also edited [. . .]
>
> Hobbies: Tightrope walking; habits of the Lactrodectus Mactans[11]
>
> Speaks: Cappocino (sic) Italian
>
> Reads: All the time.[12]

No doubt it was pointed humour like this that gave heart to some feminists in search of a filmmaker who would encapsulate their hopes for a Women's Cinema defined by an irreverent approach to film style and working method. Campion's preference for working closely with other women, her thematic preoccupation with women's narratives and her frequent assertion that her work was infused with the personal gave many feminist film commentators hope that they had found 'their' auteur. Campion however hasn't always been entirely at ease with this assignment and at different times in her career has sought to distance herself or her films from a feminist ascription. The use of Campion's name as a metonym for larger industry categories has not been limited to advocates of a 'women's cinema'. Also, throughout her career, Campion's name has been used as an indication of the state of either the Australian or New Zealand film industries, a matter on which she has been equally evasive.

Campion's equivocation on these ascriptions is understandable given the way in which they have been used on occasion to undermine the authenticity of her achievements. For example, in assessing *In the Cut*, Australian film reviewer Jim Schembri measures the film against the elevated anticipation he associates with the Campion credit:

> But *In the Cut* is meant to be a major motion picture event, isn't it? After all Jane Campion directed it, right? Due to the fact she's one of the few women directors of note working the mainstream and because her 1993 triumph, *The Piano*, was so deeply loved across the globe, Campion has achieved an iconic status, as though she carries the torch for all female directors. But it's a reverence her body of work simply cannot support. Yes, *The Piano* was lovely, but since then Campion hasn't exactly redefined cinema or endeared audiences with The *Portrait of a Lady* (1996) or *Holy Smoke* (1999).[13]

Like Schembri, Adrian Martin, in his review of the same film, describes it as raising 'serious, retrospective questions about how "top form" Campion ever was, even at her best.'[14]:

> Campion is a director whom moviegoers and critics along the Australia-New Zealand axis have trouble judging with any clarity or equanimity. The commendable aspects of her work have been systematically exaggerated by stoked commentators keen to enshrine her career as a shining beacon of antipodean women's cinema. This has given rise to a myth of Campion

an all-time 'great artist' which creates great expectations that even the director herself must now surely find burdensome.[15]

For Martin, Campion's elevation to emblem by well-meaning but misguided moviegoers simultaneously undermines her standing as an authentic auteur and underscores the crucial role of critical expectation in the development of Campion's career, key observations for understanding the dynamics of contemporary auteurism.

## CAMPION AND CONTEMPORARY AUTEURISM

Despite Campion's evident success, as this book goes to press she has not actively worked as a feature director for some years and is only just re-entering the filmmaking fray with the production of *Bright Star*. In November 2003, during the promotion campaign for her new feature *In the Cut*, Jane Campion unexpectedly announced that she would be taking a four-year break from filmmaking.[16] A recurrent theme in Campion's media interviews at this time was her express wish to be free from any sense of obligation. In her words, 'I want to do nothing'.[17] Sharp-eyed observers would recognize in Campion's statement an echo from her earliest years as a filmmaker. Interviewed in 1989 about her personal ambitions she listed several imagined career paths before suggesting; 'Other fantasies just involve walking along beaches and doing nothing . . . I just hate the idea of a life of just endless work in front of me'.[18]

What is most interesting about Campion's announcement is its declaratory intent. Many filmmakers spend years in hiatus, 'between productions' or 'in development'. Few go so far as to deliberately advance their absence or give glimpse to their ambivalence.

Across several media interviews Campion provides a slew of different explanations for her withdrawal ranging from the personal, 'to be with my daughter' to the professional, 'I've had a great time with my life in film but it's not the only life I'm able to lead or know'.[19] Her lengthiest reflections identify the difficulties of combining both

FIGURE 0.3 On the set of *Portrait of a Lady* with her daughter
Polygram/Propaganda/The Kobal Collection/Teller, Jurgen

family-making and filmmaking in which she describes how directing films is an, 'obsessive, full-on job, and if you want to have family and kids as well, for women, it's really impossible'.[20]

Given these already apposite accounts there would seem no need for even further explanation. But Campion added an extra detail, acknowledging that her departure, her desire to 'do nothing' was not just a response to a set of immediate concerns but had something to do with the trajectory of her own course as a filmmaker: 'I actually think I've satisfied myself enough career-wise to really love doing nothing'.[21] Or as she put it in another interview, 'The nature of the job is pure commitment and I don't have that much ambition. Life's not forever and I want to experience it in different ways, not just through a career'.[22]

It is a rare filmmaker that is so bold as to suggest that she has fulfilled her own expectations and no longer hungers for filmmaking (especially in a trade ordinarily renowned for its ethos of insatiable consumption). But perhaps it is also possible to see in Campion's statement another underlying motivation that tells us something about the options available to many contemporary filmmakers for conducting their careers. Perhaps Campion's comments relay to us her frustrated sense of her own agency as a filmmaker at this particular point in time. Campion's announcement of a short-term retirement suggests that she felt the alternatives available to her as a director were simply put; to make films . . . or not. To do 'something' out of a sense of obligation . . . or to choose 'nothing'. And 'nothing' seemed to her the most viable and liberating option at the time. Some months after these announcements Campion speculated about whether she would return to film-making:

> I probably will, but what I want to do is create a space in which I don't know what's at the end. When I get to the end of it I can say, 'Maybe I won't do that, I'll do something else.'[23]

Here, Campion is strongly suggesting that what is missing in her life as a filmmaker is a sense of space that isn't already earmarked for some other function, a space without a prior sense of purpose or value.

In what has become an increasingly precipitant critical environment for filmmakers, in which films (and their directors) are frequently evaluated well before their cinema release, Jane Campion's express desire to do 'nothing' can be seen as her own pre-emptive strike, a strategic attempt to set her own agenda as a filmmaker irrespective of the encompassing commercial and critical context for her films. It's a choice that in an unexpected way actually underlines her status as an uncompromising auteur rather than detracts from it.

Woven through Campion's explanations it is possible to discern a more contemporary figuring of the auteur. Taking time-out might once have been seen as representing a loss of 'self' (the sign of a broken or failed auteur), or alternatively it might have been taken to signal a 'recuperation of self' (time-out as a form of personal and creative renewal). But a strategic retirement like Campion's might equally be seen as a recognition that making films (or not) bears little relation to the filmmaker's status as an auteur. For some commentators such as Timothy Corrigan, auteurism has come to constitute a form of film consumption which no longer involves the viewing of a film: 'An auteur film today seems to aspire more and more to a critical tautology, capable of being understood and consumed without being seen.'[24] If, as Corrigan suggests, a film can be granted 'auteur' status more or less sight unseen we might also consider how the very being of the 'auteur' is no longer *entirely* reliant on the production, consumption and appraisal of films (if it ever was) but an intricate set of industrial processes (from project selection to publicity and advertising) that impinge on a filmmaker's career, processes in which the film itself (the text) is only one component. That in Jane Campion's mind, 'nothing' is just as valid a career choice as 'something', strongly suggests that for her, at this point in time, there might as well not be a film text either.

The extent of this environment of anticipation in the contemporary film industry cannot be underestimated. And it seems to have been a particularly potent dimension of Jane Campion's experience as a film director. Take for instance an anecdote relayed in 1997 by Michel Ciment editor of the influential French film magazine *Positif*:

> With a friend of mine last June, without having seen one still from *The Portrait of a Lady* by Jane Campion, we wrote together the reviews that were going to appear. We knew in advance, without having seen one shot of the film, that it would be lambasted by the cinema press in France. What was our reason for this? The director was young, extraordinarily successful, the previous winner of a Golden Palm at Cannes and an Academy Award in Hollywood. And after this extraordinary success, instead of doing a simple, small film with a crew of five, she accepted 25 million dollars to make an adaptation of Henry James, with John Malkovich and Nicole Kidman in the leading roles. This insolence of such a successful woman making a huge production in the wake of all the heritage films (the Jane Austen, Joseph Conrad and E.M. Forster adaptations) would mean, we believed, that negative reviews would flourish.
>
> And without boasting, it happened exactly as we thought.'[25]

The backlash against *Portrait of Lady* was by no means limited to French critics. Many reviewers around the globe responded unfavorably to the film (and Campion's next, *Holy Smoke*). Todd McCarthy's review in *Variety* was headlined, 'Campion's elegant, chilly Portrait' and many critics imputed this interpretation of the film's aesthetic onto Campion's own motivations, asserting that her film was a triumph of hollow art over content and that the director had made an empty middle-brow costume drama in order to cash-in on a conspicuous trend for historical adaptations. The film did appear in the wake of a series of British and American adaptations: *The Crucible*, *The English Patient*, *Hamlet*, *Romeo and Juliet*, *Orlando*. But the accusation of cynicism is seldom leveled at other more prolific producers of this genre such as Merchant Ivory.[26] For these reviewers it is the literary nature of *Portrait* that they object to. Some critics explained their disappointment by noting that Henry James novels are notoriously difficult to adapt.[27]

Other reviewers also found fault in Campion's reading matter, though for different reasons. For Adrian Martin, *Portrait* was an early sign that Campion had 'lost her way' and that she had started to believe her own publicity: 'Like so many directors in global cinema culture today Campion probably became a self-conscious auteur too quickly, read and heard too much about herself and her "vision".'[28] For traditional auteurists, filmmakers should be unfettered or 'pure' producers of films, not readers or consumers (especially of publicity patter), their careers unfolding in a singular direction without deviation (i.e. without 'losing her way').

Ciment's explanation for the media's negativity lies with the idea that Campion was becoming 'a new James Ivory'; a stance he is unable to share on the basis of his own viewing of the film which he finds to be 'mostly about personal conflicts'.[29] Instead, for Ciment it is actually an underlying prevalence of preconception that is at the heart of the critical reaction against Campion's *Portrait*. The particular qualities of the film itself are not the issue for the media, it is Campion's choice of project that apparently offends. As Ciment would have it, Campion was blind to the implications of this choice and therefore to her film's future

FIGURE 0.4 Isabel Archer (Nicole Kidman) thinks things over in *Portrait of a Lady*

Polygram/Propaganda/The Kobal Collection

reception, which she had not foreseen. In his reckoning, the critical audience was already 'prefigured' for *Portrait* based on a larger set of expectations that surrounded Campion herself and which are generated not only by the director's previous films but by the vast amounts of PR and film journalism designed to excite advance awareness of movies in production.

It's likely however that Ciment's account does Campion a slight disservice and that she did anticipate something of the heightened expectation around her film. Interviewed on the set of *Portrait of a Lady* she speculated about the film's reception in terms which strongly suggest her own sense of uncertainty and hesitation in the face of widespread expectation:

> People might say things to me like, "Oh you know, its so good you're doing *Portrait of a Lady*. I can't wait to see what you do with it." And I'm thinking, "Yeah, I wonder what they mean." I gather that they are expecting me to do something kind of very surprising. And I'm not thinking anything surprising. And now I'm thinking maybe I should be thinking something surprising. I don't know. I guess I should be thinking about it in a slightly more serious way.[30]

Campion's worried recognition of a prevailing current of preconception is also present in the film's script. Isabel, the central figure in the film, confronts her cruel husband Osmond, accusing him in terms which might just as easily be describing the media's treatment of Campion: 'You like nothing I do or do not do. You pretend to think I lie . . . I can't tell you how unjust you seem to me. It's your own opposition that's calculated . . . It's malignant.'[31] Rather than being completely powerless in the face of media opinion, as Ciment imagines, both Campion and to some extent the film itself also provide commentary on these issues.

The implications of Ciment's observations for how we understand and receive the contemporary auteur are far-reaching and form the basis for much of the discussion of Jane Campion's career in this book.

Ciment suggests there are ways in which select filmmakers themselves now have audiences, that they, like other film industry celebrities such as high-profile actors, are the subject of intense public expectation irrespective of the perceived value of their films. In revealing the ways in which filmmakers such as Campion are assessed on their choice of project, prior to and rather than, the perceived quality of their films, Ciment's anecdote of a 'criticism with intent' loosens auteurist studies from an over-dependence on textual analysis in which, as Peter Wollen, described it, the auteur is constructed a *posteriori*, an outcome of the reading of their films.[32] Instead we might recognize how the contemporary film industry addresses the auteur as an integral part of its operations, as a crucial component of the ways in which films are financed, in which key personnel (crew, stars) are recruited to particular projects and in which films are marketed to audiences.

From Campion's perspective the opportunity to work on *Portrait* brought with it several developments previously not possible in her career but enabled by the staggering success of her prior film, *The Piano*; experience in directing A-list actors, working on a (relatively) big-budget production in a range of international locations and dealing with a dramatically elevated media profile. There is a curious disconnection between what Campion might have viewed as her expanded capacity in career terms and what Ciment tells us the French cinema press saw as her 'proper place'.

The idea that Campion is somehow improperly 'placed' is actually quite useful. It helps us to make sense of Campion's situation if we accept that the contemporary author is a composite figure, both personified and projected, occupying a 'place' at the intersection of sometimes competing and sometimes complementary aspirations and interpretations.[33] The author-ised 'Jane Campion' is formed at the intersection of many discursive and material events (including those involving the director). There is for instance the media's Campion, the film critic's Campion, the festival director's Campion, Campion's Campion and so on each bearing on the other. So if 'Campion' is the name of a constellation of cultural and individual investments of varying intensities then the changeability of what 'Campion' signifies is not simply the result of personal capriciousness (McCarthy) or a lack of self-awareness (Ciment) or too much self-awareness (Martin) but also arises sometimes unpredictably from historical changes in context. The practice of contemporary auterism can be understood both as a name for whatever it is that is 'enabling' for the individual filmmaker within a set of industrial circumstances or constraints, and as the commercial creation and circulation of the 'auteur-name'. The idea that an auteur's career unfolds in a neat linear progression, one film at a time, each adding to the next, does not do justice to the circuitous, contradictory, distorted, exposed and uneven experiences that characterise a career in filmmaking; a career that is less about the consistent performance of personal expressivity than it is about creating the optimum conditions for consistent commercial performance.

There is also an evident contradiction between the retrospective nature of career assessments (including those in the form of auteurist accounts) and the predictive momentum in which the film industry operates. In the film industry, forecasting is a fine art, from predicting total box-office takings on the opening weekend of a release, to betting on a star's bankability when negotiating their contract. The idea that the industry operates with a forward-looking focus, that it is 'out of synch' with its audience, is underlined by the long window between production and release so that filmmakers might already be engaged in pre-production on a future film whilst publicly promoting their previous. Furthermore the audience's experience of a filmmaker's career doesn't usually occur in the same sequence as an auteur's own experience. Campion for example began working on *The Piano* many years before it was realized, and she optioned Janet Frame's autobiography (with a view to producing her second feature *An Angel at My Table*) when she was still in film school, approaching producer Brigid Ikin after she completed her student film *Peel*. Many filmgoers outside Australasia were unable to see Campion's pre-*Piano* films until they were re-released in cinemas and on DVD in the wake of her later success. Her first feature *Two Friends* for example, was made in 1986 but not released in the US until 1996.

Auterist assessments, on the other hand, usually present films in the order in which they were first released, as evidence of the author's expressive development (or regression). The connection or disjuncture between one employment choice and another in the form of film productions is usually only understood in the mode of retrospection. But films are not necessarily conceived in that order and many other industrial and personal factors determine when, or even if, films are realized. Campion has proposed over the years several ideas for films that did not come to fruition.[34] Furthermore, the hindsight of auteurist appreciation can make it blind to other assessments at work in the inception of a career such as early criticisms and dismissals, or in Jane Campion's case her evident ambivalence about her career choice.

Indeed, for some critics and academic commentators, Campion has herself come to represent the end of traditional auteurism itself and the flourishing of a new auteurism. Right at the end of his extended survey of Jane Campion's work, Dana Polan sounds a culminating note of caution; 'to study her is to study the cinema differently, to rethink the very terms of analysis of the film director'.[35] Polan himself goes some way towards this rethinking. Rather than presenting Campion as the irreducible source of a singular vision, he emphasizes throughout his book Campion's creative collaborations, the evident textual contradictions and stylistic divergences between her films, the differing interpretations of her works by academics, critics and fans. For Polan, 'Campion's career bears no unity of theme and style but is marked rather by shifts of direction and changes of emphasis'.[36] Polan's book in large part however remains committed to the analysis of Campion's films (the texts) as the key site for understanding the auteur though this commentary is not expressly written within the mode of auteurist connoisseurship.

Polan's focus on Campion's *oeuvre* as one characterized by change and variation has also been noted by other critics but to different ends. Several auteurist critics, upset at the course of Campion's career and what they perceive to be the inconsistent calibre of her films, have rejected her title to genuine auteurism and set aside her later works from the canon. Stuart Klawans for example found *The Piano* did not live up to the precedent of her early work:

> Compared with *Sweetie*, her extraordinary first film, *The Piano* seems to me contrived, allegorized, rhetorical and altogether too eager to tell people what they want to hear. It's not so much an outburst of wild talent as it is the performance of wildness before an audience.[37]

But perhaps the most astonishing of these critical reversals belongs to the Australian writer, broadcaster and occasional filmmaker, Phillip Adams, who responded with furious prose to Campion's *Holy Smoke*:

> Where *Attack of the Killer Tomatoes* was bad, *Holy Smoke* is ostentatiously, pretentiously, arrogantly bad. Some may think it the work of a director of genius. But others will see it as the work of a director who thinks she's a genius.[38]

Like Martin and Klawans, Adams sees Campion's self-consciousness as the cause of her difficulties. For this he also blames the uncritical praise of the 'Campion cognoscenti' and the 'sad fact that many of our reviewers lack critical faculties and are little more than obedient cogs in the publicity machine.' Adams concludes:

> Over-praise has led to self-indulgence, early promise to calamitous decline. If Campion is to redeem her reputation, she'll have to stop parading infantile philosophies in Panavision. I wouldn't swap all the hours Campion has spent with Holly Hunter, Nicole Kidman and Winslet for 10 minutes with Sweetie or Janet Frame. Now, there were women worth the effort.[39]

What seems to be at stake for Adams is Campion's celebrity status, all the hours she has spent with movie stars, and the media's complicity in promoting her as such. She is, according to Adams, a victim of her early success. His criticism echoes one often made of 'bad' celebrities; that they have lost their humility and hunger ('good' celebrities constantly point out that they are still 'just like us' even when they are simultaneously demarcated as somehow 'special'). Instead, 'bad' stars are the executors of a type of public gluttony characterised by an inward and downward spiral of excessive consumption that in Campion's case ultimately results in the celebrity swallowing their own publicity (her apparent 'self-indulgence'). Celebrities, it seems, should be consumed and not revealed to be consumers themselves (let alone consumers of themselves).

FIGURE 0.5
Toronto 2003:
Jane Campion and
Meg Ryan at the
première of
*In the Cut*
Photo by Donald
Weber/Getty Images

Whereas Phillip Adams condemns the inconsistency of Campion's later films, Polan recuperates Campion from this dismissal to some extent by describing her work as being characterised by 'ellipsis' and 'dispersion' (rather than reading her career as subject to their vicissitudes). But most importantly Polan also suggests that instead of focusing on the canonical aspects of Campion's films (or the lack thereof), it might be more interesting to try and imagine what being an 'auteur' might mean to an Australasian director working within and between national, antipodean, international audiences and art-house, government, indie and studio industries. Perhaps, as Polan proposes, there is something about contemporary auteurist practice that needs to be reconsidered, and perhaps we should also therefore be looking for new configurations in the existential parameters of the auteur. Perhaps we can conceive of a version of the auteur that supports rather than reproaches her fluid crossings over traditional identity boundaries, one that might, for example, afford her the capability of forging a consciously interpretive sense of her 'self'.

Bearing this in mind, it is possible then to see that Adams' dismissal of Campion lies not so much in the seismic shift he sees in the quality of her films but rather in what he sees as a shift in her industry practice as a celebrated auteur. In the terms of Chris Rojek's taxonomy of celebrity, a critic such as Adams would have Campion changing from being an 'achieved' auteur in her early career (in which her fame as a director is linked to her talents and achievements and which are specifically manifest in her films) to being an 'attributed' auteur later on (in which her celebrity emerges from concentrated media attention and which may or may not be reliant on the success of her films).[40] This is especially challenging for a traditional auteurist like Adams because it would seem to nag away at the underlying conception of self at the heart of the auteur's being; the belief that they are great because of an indefinable, internal quality of self which pre-destines them to fame (rather than their celebrity as auteurs being purposefully 'manufactured' through the publicity process).

FIGURE 0.6 **Inappropriate consumption: Sweetie (Genevieve Lemon) chews the china horses**
Arenafilm Pty Ltd

Contemporary filmmakers negotiate a complex position in relation to their perceived status as authors, frequently required to draw on traditional auteurist verities as well as newer industry configurations and the expectations they produce. Corrigan's view that the art-cinema market might find a use for discourses of 'personal vision' in marketing particular directors is a good case in point. As Corrigan sees it, rather than being 'absorbed as a phantom presence within a text' the auteur has now rematerialized 'as a commercial performance of *the business of being an auteur*'.[41] This observation needs to be further refined as Jane Campion's case indicates, since changes in industry structure, personal practice and critical or audience reception are not always in alignment. So for example, those who continue to adhere to the idea that the auteur is a uniquely talented, authentically expressive individual may react less favourably if the auteur is seen to be 'performing' overtly, or if the actions or agency of the auteur are too obviously based on self-reflection or interpretation.

## TOWARDS A THEORY OF POST-AUTEURISM

Perhaps then it's not surprising to find Campion herself being used as the basis for reconsiderations of authorship. Campion is the auteur you have when you have the idea of an auteur (rather than a belief in 'pure' expressivity). Classic auteurism assumes the auteur doesn't really understand the meanings of her own creations, which are for critics and connoisseurs to best determine. There is an emphasis in old auteurism on mystical creativity and deep thematics rather than on craft or pragmatism; on what Dana Polan calls an 'auteurism of metaphysics' (in which the director's artistic vision emerges from 'ineffable deep wells of creativity') rather than an 'auterism of energetics' (in which directorial activity is seen as a material activity).[42] Some filmmakers prop up this belief in their own 'truthfulness' to cinematic expression by deflecting interview questions about the meaning of their films onto others, and either implying or proclaiming their approach to be intuitive or unreflected. In teaching film production students over many years I am myself more than familiar with their fear that talking about the structure and meaning of their films (and also those by others) will somehow 'spoil' their pleasure in the cinema; that knowing how the cinema is performed will reduce its magic to mere trickery. For many filmmakers and filmgoers it seems, films are like hot dogs – if you really love them, you don't want to know how they are made (or what they might 'mean' for you).

This creates an interesting problem given the expectations of the modern media for filmmakers to provide 'added value' in talking about their films. Contemporary directors are expected to fully participate in the publicity process for their films, which inevitably includes copious media interviews, but might also consist of festival appearances, the production of 'making-of' documentaries, additional commentary tracks on DVD releases and so on. It is their 'unique' insights that give filmmakers special status as auteurs in the contemporary industry and which in turn is part of what Polan describes as, 'the building up of a useable image of the director'.[43] But this is also a form of auteurist expression that is out of synch with the production of the text itself and the likelihood is that the auteur will not be coherent, nor consistent, nor canonical in her every iteration.

At the risk of fixing yet another paling to an already long line of 'posts', it might be possible to see Jane Campion as practising a form of 'post-auteurism'. Although it hazards being hackneyed even before it has been coined, the 'post' in 'post-auteurism' is useful for a number of reasons. Firstly it suggests the posthumous nature of contemporary authorship – exhumed from the early announcement of its demise, usually and somewhat erroneously attributed to Roland Barthes and Michel Foucault, but also to be found in popular media reports about art cinema.[44] For instance Geoffrey Macnab has suggested that the almost coincident deaths of Ingmar Bergman and Michaelangelo Antonioni in 2007 were a portent of a larger termination: 'There is a dispiriting sense that the two deceased directors were among the last of a breed. The old-style "auteurs" are fast disappearing.'[45] Secondly, the 'post' in 'post-auteurism' implies that the persistence of the auteur for contemporary film audiences needs to be distinguished from previous understandings of the expressivity of the filmmaker. And finally, the 'post' in 'post-auteurism' invites us to retrospectively reconsider the precepts of classical auteurism itself; to look differently on past auteur and auteurist practice and to acknowledge a pluralism of approaches to authorship. The practice of contemporary film production seems to allow the author to be many things in different industry contexts; an expressive individual, a social subject, a 'name' established across a series of film texts and through their promotion to the public.

If post-auteurism shifts the emphasis from the single image of the individual author, a driven artist struggling to overcome a variety of institutional obstacles in order to find an outlet for their expressions, to a composite picture that emphasises instead the director's collaborative relationships, their industrial context and their artistic ascriptions, then a whole new series of questions might be proposed. These questions are as informed by contemporary media experiences such as the social framework of Web 2.0 or the endless possibilities entailed in culture jamming or in the production of mashups, as they

TABLE 1.1 **Some features of post-auteurism**

- Proposes processes of 'authorisation' rather than a belief in 'pure' expressivity *per se*
- Understands that policy initiatives or commercial imperatives are as influential in establishing the auteur as her own individual endeavour or talent and that the system is not inherently 'opposed' to auteurs
- Focuses on the industrial context and on 'factors' rather than causes or intentions
- Emphasises the extent to which the auteur's 'author-name' operates like a commodity in the film industry
- Recognizes contributions made by personnel other than the director (the DOP or producer as auteur for instance), or the contributions made by directors previously marginalised (women for example)
- Emphasises the importance of collaborations – including the actor-director relationship – and contestation in contemporary auteurist practice
- Calls attention to intertextuality in the work of contemporary auteurs rather than seeing the director as a singular point of origin (as in adaptations for instance, but also finding intertextuality in films that less obviously reassign sources)
- Reveals the duality of the director as both an enunciator and a 'reader'
- Proposes the auteur as a multivalent identity, best understood from a plurality of approaches
- Does not regard the film text as either conceptually or industrially discrete, displacing its importance as the principle basis for understanding auteurist practice

are by the specific demands of the cinema itself. What for example, might constitute creativity and originality in expressive formats based on acts of quotation, re-editing and characterised by familiarity, repetition, borrowing or collaboration? What obligations do filmmakers owe to those who have inspired and informed their work and how much creative freedom should they exercise over their shared materials? To greater and lesser extent these questions have dogged Jane Campion throughout her career as she has negotiated both conventional and contemporary expectations of her role as an auteur. How influential was cinematographer Sally Bongers in defining Campion's early sense of film style? Or Veronika Jenet who has edited almost all of Campion's films.

What, if any, are Campion's obligations to novelist Jane Mander whose *The Story of New Zealand River* is said by some to have inspired *The Piano*? How might a contemporary auteur like Campion construct their career in terms of scalability (a ready capacity to shift approach and genres from one film to the next) rather than from a singular evolutionary path?

## ABOUT THIS BOOK

Although approaching the career of Jane Campion from a revisionist perspective, this book shares with classic approaches to auteurism an interest in understanding the director's way of seeing, especially in terms of thinking about how creative matters (such as auteur style) often arise from hands-on problem-solving. William D. Routt describes this concern with the materiality of creative and industrial processes as a form of 'cine-pragmatics' which he explains as, 'the recognition that what is shown on the screen is the result of countless apparently minute or trivial practical decisions'.[46] What stylistic constraints and possibilities arise when a specific film stock or a particular location is chosen for instance? Many directors, Campion included, are discursive on the day-to-day practical problem solving involved in film production. Film director Paul Schrader memorialised this approach to the craft of directing in a single line: 'Inspiration is just another word for problem-solving'.[47] Campion goes to some detail, describing how the script of *In the Cut*, presented a series of challenges:

> By taking over the writing I felt like I had passed into a chamber of secrets such that I would solve one set of problems only to discover another equally complicated set of problems that I couldn't previously see . . . finding my way through was somehow not only solving the story issues but also illuminating my own thinking about self, romance, relationships and erotic love.[48]

But there are larger, less finicky ways of thinking about problem-solving too. How do policy and funding regimes, commercial concerns and critical expectations also present 'problems' that the filmmaker needs to address creatively.

Post-auteurism establishes a complexity between auteurism, industry and commerce. Justin Wyatt suggests that textual style is not simply the result of processes of authorship (including pragmatic problem solving) but of economic and industrial circumstances also (size of budget for instance).[49] Wyatt proposes a process of 'authorisation', to describe the ways in which films are constructed into a coherent framework under the name of the director. These nominal groupings also occur for commercial purposes: as a pro-gramming method for film festivals for example (Campion's collected short film screenings being a notable case in point) and as a special focus for critical writing (on women in the cinema for instance). For Wyatt, industrial issues or 'commerce' influence filmmakers and their artistic choices and are also a process of constructing auteurs. On this basis Wyatt suggests that in order to begin to understand the contemporary auteur a multitude of interconnected vantages need to be considered, each of which help to constitute and circulate an 'auteur-name'.[50] To historicize effectively Campion as a notable contemporary auteur then, equal weight needs to be given to her relationship with the various industrial structures within which she worked (for example identifying the shifting relationship between government subsidised national cinemas, the 'major' independents and the auteur herself); to the changing degree of autonomy she experi-enced; and to the critical association of the textual and extra-textual (such as publicity, promotion, advertising) in the public presentation of her work a director. If authorship, as Rosanna Maule describes it, is 'a tactic of enunciation and appropriation' for contemporary filmmakers, then it may be expressed in many places and in many forms, for example through films themselves but also through the media and most particularly in media interviews with directors.[51] It might equally be observed then that by breaking with production altogether, Campion is also deploying these 'tactics', disrupting emblematic narratives about her career. In removing herself entirely from the plot she ensures these storylines, which presuppose a continuous relationship across successive films, do not easily 'stick'.

By taking a multi-faceted approach to the auteur it is possible to see how filmmakers, studios, distribution companies, funding agencies, media, critics and academics are all engaged in a process of authorising (or actively de-authorising) film directors. Each plays a role in elaborating frameworks for understanding the contributions of particular auteurs. This book is structured around four such lines of 'authorisation' in Campion's career, firstly as they persist in the media (dealt with in chapter one); in industry (chapter two); in academic scholarship (chapter three); and in the domain of personal reflection and self-promotion (chapter four) to the extent that these four industry practices can be distinctly delineated (for instance many members of the media are familiar with academic writing, many industry players are also academics, each informing and at times undermining the other and so on). These are of course, not the only ways in which Campion's career has been appreciated and expanded and represent a modest start in rethinking how we might talk about contemporary auteurist practice. In this way, this book explicitly takes a step back to provide some sense of perspective and context to Jane Campion's representation and role as an auteur, rather than aspiring to be yet another voice in the chorus of connoisseurship that has emerged around her films. The next chapter takes a detailed approach to Campion's furrowed relationship with the media, identifying a series of interrelated and yet often contradictory 'modes of auteurism' that preoccupy media assessments of Campion and her films.

## NOTES

1   In the commentary for *An Angel at My Table* (Criterion).

2   There is considerable disagreement as to how Campion's feature films are counted. Should for example her tele-feature, *After Hours* be considered a feature? Or her three-part TV series *An Angel at My Table* which was repackaged for theatrical release but was not originally intended as a

feature film? If they are not then it can be said that Campion secured the Palm d'Or with only her second feature film, an even more extraordinary achievement. These calculations become especially significant given the difficulties experienced by film directors in making multiple productions in Australasia. For example in the 1990s only 7% of film directors based in Australia had worked on three or more feature films. Even without festival awards and critical accolades to have made four feature films as an Australasian is a significant accomplishment in and of itself.

3   Angela Doland, 'Campion laments lack of female filmmakers', *The Age*, May 22, 2007, p. 15. The Cannes invitation was extended to 33 directors from 5 continents and 25 countries, emphasizing a certain commitment to diversity but significantly the title of the resultant film was translated 'to each his own cinema'.

4   Gary Maddox, 'Cannes Opening a Snow-capped Peak for Director', *Sydney Morning Herald*, 8 May 2004, p. 3.

5   Lynden Barber, 'Reel Women', *The Weekend Australian Review*, 25 April 1998, pp. 4–6.

6   Scott MacDonald (ed.), *A Critical Cinema 3: Interviews with Independent Filmmakers*, Berkeley: University of California Press, 1998. Campion is also complimentary about Potter's *Orlando*: 'People say making movies isn't a cure for cancer. I disagree; filmmaking is a cure. It gives you a reason for living. When my son died, on the third day I was devastated, I didn't know what to do with myself. I went to see *Orlando*. It was so beautiful. This earth can be transformed. There are moments of extreme wonder . . . and that's all worth living for. In the act of making a movie you are involved with those moments, those transformations, For me it's been a way of life, totally fulfilling'. See Kathleen Murphy, 'Jane Campion's Passage to India', *Film Comment*, vol. 36, no. 1, 2000, pp. 30–6.

7   Gary Maddox, 'Young Gun a Shooting Star', *Sydney Morning Herald*, 9 September 1999, p. 19.

8   Peter Gotting, 'The Next Campion? Just Me, Myself, I', *Sydney Morning Herald*, 6 May 2000, p. 7.

9   Meredith Quinn and Andrew L. Urban (eds), *Edge of the Known World: The Australian Film Television and Radio School. Impressions of the First 25 Years*, Sydney: AFTRS, 1998, p. 54.

10    Campion speaking on the alternative soundtrack to Sweetie, *Sweetie: Criterion Collection DVD* (2006).

11    Lactrodectus Mactans is the scientific name for the Black Widow spider that is known for its especially potent defensive bite and the female's occasional tendency to poison its mate after breeding.

12    As given in the *Program Notes*, Australian Film and Television School Graduate Screenings, 1984, p. 7.

13    Jim Schembri, 'New Releases' *The Age*, 14 November 2003, p.10.

14    Adrian Martin, 'Master or Myth?' *The Age – Metro* (A3), 13 November 2003, p. 6.

15    Martin, 'Master or Myth?', p. 6.

16    Since 2003 Campion has completed several short films and worked as a documentary producer (*Abduction: The Megumi Yokota Story*, 2006). In 2007, four years after she announced that she would take a break from feature filmmaking, she began production on a new feature, *Bright Star*, due for release in 2009.

17    Lizzie Francke, 'Jane Campion: dangerous liaisons', *Sight and Sound*, v. 13 n. 11 (Nov. 2003), p. 19.

18    Campion speaking in the 1989 filmed conversation with critic Peter Thompson, *Jane Campion: The Film School Years*; this interview piece is amongst the special features available on *Sweetie: Criterion Collection DVD* (2006).

19    Gary Maddox, 'For Film-maker Campion, it's a Wrap – For Now', *Sydney Morning Herald*, 7 November 2003, p. 3; see also David Konow, 'Rough Cut: Jane Campion and Susanna Moore on *In the Cut*', *Creative Screenwriting*, vol. 10, no. 5, 2003, p. 73.

20    Kunow, 'Rough Cut', p. 73.

21    Maddox, 'For Film-maker Campion, it's a Wrap', p. 3.

22    No author, 'Jane Walks Away', *Sunday Herald Sun*, 19 October 2003, p. 115.

23    No author, 'New Act for Director, *Sunday Herald Sun*, 14 March 2004, p. 29.

24    Timothy Corrigan, *A Cinema Without Walls: Movies and Culture after Vietnam*, New Brunswick: Rutgers University Press, 1991, p. 106.

25    Michel Ciment, 'The Function and State of Film Criticism', in John Boorman and Walter Donohue (eds.), *Projections 8: Film-makers on Film-making*, London: Faber and Faber, 1998, p. 41. In the introduction to the

English translation of an interview between Ciment and Campion, Ciment's critical role in the development of Campion's career is described by the editors as follows: ' . . .were it not for *Positif*, and particularly its editor-in-chief Michel Ciment, Campion's daring artistry would likely have been relegated to the dustbin'; see 'Jane Campion and *Positif*', Part II in Raffaele Caputo and Geoff Burton (eds.), *Second Take, Australian Film-makers Talk*, St Leonards NSW: Allen & Unwin, 1999, p. 45.

26    Todd McCarthy, 'Campion's Elegant, Chilly *Portrait, Variety*, 9–15 September 1996, p. 114. A case in point: directly opposite McCarthy's review of *Portrait* is a glowing assessment of the Merchant Ivory production *Surviving Picasso* (Ivory, 1996).

27    There is an historical precedent for the assertion that James is difficult to adapt which goes back to David O. Selznick's disastrous attempt to mount a stage adaptation of *Portrait* on Broadway in 1954.

28    Adrian Martin, 'Losing the Way: The Decline of Jane Campion', *Landfall*, vol. 200, no. 2, 2000, p. 101.

29    Ciment, 'The Function and State of Film Criticism', p. 42.

30    Campion speaking in *Portrait: Jane Campion and The Portrait of a Lady* (1996).

31    See Laura Jones, *The Portrait of a Lady: Screenplay Based on the Novel by Henry James*, London: Penguin, 1997, p. 404.

32    Peter Wollen, *Signs and Meaning in the Cinema*, London: Secker and Warburg, 1974, p. 78.

33    Jean-Jacques Lecercle, *Interpretation as Pragmatics*, London: Macmillan, 1999, p. 150.

34    Examples include *Ebb*, referred to by Campion in Thomas Bourguignon and Michel Ciment, 'Interview with Jane Campion: More Barbarian than Aesthete', published in Virginia Wright Wexman (ed) *Jane Campion Interviews*, Jackson: University Press of Mississippi, 1999, p. 102 and *My Guru and His Disciples*, based on the life of Christopher Isherwood. This film went some distance down the pre-production path. Campion refers to the project in a 1991 interview with Heike-Melba Fendel (republished in Wexman, p. 89) prior to making *The Piano*. By early 1993 she seems to be tossing up between this project (to be financed by CIBY 2000) and *Portrait* (see her interview with Bourguignon and Ciment in Wexman p. 112). And at the end of 1993 she was hard at work on the script with Philip

Lopate and had every intention of making both films. It is quite possible that some of the material developed for My Guru eventually found its way into Holy Smoke though this remains speculation.

35    Dana Polan, Jane Campion, London: British Film Institute, 2001, p. 167.

36    Polan, Jane Campion, p. 167.

37    Stuart Klawans, 'The Piano', The Nation, v. 257, n. 19 (6 December, 1993), pp. 705.

38    Phillip Adams, 'Holey Smoking Reputation', The Australian, 5 February 2000.

39    Adams, 'Holey Smoking Reputation'.

40    Chris Rojek, Celebrity, London: Reaktion Books, 2001, p. 17.

41    Timothy Corrigan, A Cinema Without Walls: Movies and Culture after Vietnam, p. 104.

42    Dana Polan, 'Auteur Desire', Screening the Past, no. 12, 2001, http://www.la trobe.edu.au/www/screeningthepast/firstrelease/fr0301/dpfr12a.html

43    Polan, 'Auteur Desire'.

44    Roland Barthes, 'The Death of the Author', in Stephen Heath (ed. and trans.), Image, Music, Text, New York: Hill, 1977, pp. 142–48; and Michel Foucault, 'What is an Author?', translation Donald F. Bouchard and Sherry Simon, in Language, Counter-Memory, Practice, Ithaca, New York: Cornell University Press, 1977. pp. 124–127.

45    Geoffrey Macnab, 'Following the deaths of Bergman and Antonioni, is this the end of the auteur?', The Independent, 3 August 2007, http://www. independent.co.uk/arts-entertainment/film-and-tv/features/following-the-deaths-of-bergman-and-antonioni-is-this-the-end-of-the-auteur-460001.html

46    William D. Routt, 'Misprision (note version), Screening the Past, no. 20, 2006, http://www.latrobe.edu.au/screeningthepast/20/misprision.html.

47    Paul Schrader speaking at the Ebertfest screening of his Mishima: A Life in Four Chapters (1985), http://blogs.suntimes.com/scanners/2008/05/mishima_blood_cult.html

48    Jane Campion, 'Directors Speak: In the Cut', InsideFilm, no. 60, November 2003, p. 14 (originally published in USA Today).

49    Justin Wyatt, 'Economic Constraints/Economic Opportunities: Robert Altman as Auteur', The Velvet Light Trap, 38, 1996, pp. 51–67.

50    Wyatt, 'Economic Constraints/Economic Opportunities: Robert Altman as Auteur', p. 64.

51    Rosanna Maule, 'De-authorizing the *Auteur*' in Cristina Degli-Eposti (ed.) *Postmodernism in the Cinema*, New York: Berghahn Books , 1998, p. 113–130.

# 1

## BECOMING JANE CAMPION

### Modes of auteurism and the media

Something happens to people when they meet a journalist . . .

Janet Malcom[1]

Meeting her is like watching her films: you tend to be swallowed up whole.

Fiona Morrow[2]

Authorship is a critical component of the way many films are marketed in the media. In the case of art or 'indie' cinema such as that produced by Jane Campion there is a demonstrable commercial need to continue with the idea that the creative artist is the principal source of cinema expression and communication. Throughout her career there have been many different ways in which Campion has been described in the media as an auteur. These ways of understanding Campion's auteur status are not mutually exclusive and often run alongside each other or up against each other in ways that are not always logical. Consider for example that Campion is the director of one of the industry's most profitable crossover films (*The Piano* moving successfully from art cinemas to multiplexes) and yet in many media accounts she continues to be described in terms that paint her at the margins of mainstream cinema, as an oppositional voice to the vagaries of studio production. These methods of presenting Campion might vary according to the inclination of the journalist, the anticipated audience for the media outlet, the particular film Campion is being interviewed about and so on. They may be invoked by, or attributed to, Campion herself. They circulate at different intensities, ebb and flow at different moments in her career.

In particular, media interviews provide useful insights into how a filmmaker understands their capacity to work and be creative, revealing what Janet Staiger calls their 'technique of the self'.[3] The presentation of filmmakers in these interviews speaks to wider concerns about how media consumers are expected to appreciate the filmmaker's evident display of creative agency as an elaboration of their individual self or as the outcome of a divergence between authenticity and performance. Rather than simply providing access to the filmmaker as an authoritative or uncomplicated source, interviews are a valuable place in which to identify how filmmakers participate in a system of film promotion that places enormous value on their presence. And yet even the value of the filmmaker's attendance is not so simple. What becomes evident through the course of many of Campion's media interviews for instance is a kind of double purpose: in which the journalist locates Campion within the tenets of traditional auteurism (as the straightforward source of creative inspiration and the authoritative interpretation of the films under discussion) often *against* the filmmaker's own attempts to speak differently, to tell of commercial realities and personal ambivalences. And in specific circumstances, for example, in defending her 'self' against media criticism (that she is inauthentic or somehow 'absent' from her works), Campion has alternatively drawn on the image of the filmmaker as a continuous, fully present and coherent creative agent.

Interviewing filmmakers seems to be important for media outlets in order to provide an additional step in the imposition of authorial will, guaranteeing the film text's meaning or the correctness of particular interpretations. Many interviewers and interviewees reiterate the traditional auteurist idea that authorial intention occurs prior to expression (in showing this, I meant that) particularly when filmmakers in promotional media interviews conducted at the time of a film's theatrical release usually speak after the text not in advance of it and are therefore able to very neatly, retrospectively confirm their objectives.

Campion herself is also discursive on the process of being interviewed and has on occasion expressed her discomfort at the conventions of this form of industry promotion and enquiry. In a notable interview for the LA Weekly, Campion pointedly asks her interviewer, Judith Lewis, if she has ever read The Journalist and the Murderer, Janet Malcolm's reflection on the exploitative ethics of media interviews and to which Campion likens their situation. Campion then goes on to describe her growing disenchantment with her own media performances:

> [I]n the beginning you're kind of chuffed that people are interested in you, and you believe it. It's all so simple, really, so childish: Very simply and babyishly you trust them all and you say things thinking it all sounds so cute. And then you read it.[4]

But even armed with a newfound sense of distrust she realizes there are further problems in her dealings with the media: 'I'm an idiot, because as soon as I say something I think I can stick with, I immediately realize the opposite is true.'[5] Campion's description of an internal contradiction goes some way toward thinking of the auteur as someone less than constant, instead troubling and dispersing her own agency as the organizing principle for understanding her films (and her relationship to them).

Earlier, Campion had described her reluctance to participate in the publicity process, preferring not to be photographed for one interview: '[B]ecause it doesn't fit with what I perceive as my role. It's alright for the actors, they have to promote their image, but I am just a maker of products.'[6] The idea that directors are not in the image business but are simply engaged in the production of films as 'products' sounds at first like a world-weary assessment of the grim realities of the film industry. But in fact these self-effacing sentiments do not attend to so much of what is involved in contemporary film production and pro-motion. Michael Budd has written on the pervasive way in which art cinema, in particular, differentiates its products as prestigious, cultured and individualistic and how it transforms the 'artistic personality' of the art film director into an exchangeable commodity.[7] But Budd also notes that, 'the commodification of art cinema is always uneven and incomplete' describing instead, 'a tension, largely invisible to viewers, between standardization and novelty.'[8] The picture of Jane Campion that emerges in English-language media reviews, interviews and promotional campaigns traces this uneven tension through a series of overlapping, sometimes contrary approaches to her practice and status as a filmmaker from the very inception of her working life.[9]

## THE AUTEUR OF EARLY PROMISE OR 'L'ENFANT AUTEUR'

Jane Campion's career has been characterized from the outset by a climate of fervent expectation. Citations for her student films at the 1984 Melbourne international film festival acclaimed her 'compelling stylistic innovation'. Fresh out of film school, with no feature film in sight she was already vaunted as 'one of our most significant talents' in the Australian media.[10] One year later, in 1987, Freda Freiberg published an extraordinarily prescient article solely on Campion's short film efforts in which she described her as an 'unusual talent' possessed with a 'powerful visual style'.[11] By January 1988 she was one of six filmmakers predicted by an Australian media outlet to be a 'film high flyer'.[12]

   This early recognition of Campion's promise also very consistently claimed for her a distinctive signature. An article on upcoming Australian women directors published in the late 1980s anoints her as someone 'rapidly achieving auteur status'. It continues, describing how her 'black comic vision and quirky use of *mise en scène* mark her films with a distinctive personal style which hovers somewhere between surrealism and absurdism'.[13] That such an inexperienced director could be announced as an auteur after only a handful of short films strongly suggests that, for these commentators at least, the definition of the auteur had shifted from its classical incarnation in which particularly accomplished directors are singled out for their expressive technique and intentions to the idea that there is a semiotic shortcut to identifying a generic auteurism, an on-screen taxonomy that simply cautions 'author at work'. Thomas Elsaesser, writing in the mid-1990s identified a shift in what the auteur was understood to mean, away from a traditional reliance on the textual presence of self-doubt or self-expression, metaphysical themes or the particular 'indeterminacy of reference' critics prized as 'realism'. Instead, he argues, contemporary auteurs dissimulate or disguise the signatures of their selfhood, demonstrating authority and authenticity through their command of, 'the generic, the expressive, the excessive, the visual and the visceral'.[14]

While for many this observation of a newfound emphasis on performative signature moments has been a cause for celebration of Campion's filmmaking prowess, it has also been a cause of criticism especially as her career has advanced. For film critic Adrian Martin, her films have become 'immobile, leached of life, fixed in compulsive repetitions of signature-effects'.[15] And more recently, in a review ominously titled 'Master or myth?', he notes that, 'Campion is too fond of symbolic inserts' and in relation to her use of camera style he describes the 'look' of the film as, 'laid on . . . without development or modulation' causing it to become 'tiresome and its aesthetic returns diminish'.[16] By way of contrast, Todd McCarthy in *Variety* describes that same film's visual approach as 'emotionally effective', noting how Campion layers the film with, 'innumerable visual details that combine for an almost palpable atmospheric density'.[17] Both critics and fans alike are in agreement that Campion's films strive for stylistic distinction, irrespective of their belief in her success or failure at achieving this.

Much earlier in her career it is possible to see how the commentary around Campion's signature film style methodically weaves an image of her in terms of the classical auteurist precepts: 'originality', 'authenticity', 'non-commercialism' and so on. Film journalist Lynden Barber, writing about the 1990 mini-series-turned-movie *An Angel at My Table* described it as 'instantly recognizable as Campion – economical, feminine and full of shots that set the eyes whirring'. Campion herself he calls 'eccentric and original'.[18] Writing on the same film in the *LA Times*, Mark Chalon commends the film which he says, 'never seems less than genuine, it's consciously anti-commercial'.[19]

In order to sustain their claims for Campion's distinctive signature at this early stage of her career, film critics appeared determined to demonstrate a stylistic and thematic connection between her two early features, *An Angel at My Table* and Campion's previous film *Sweetie*, despite their evident differences. This is in part an extension of traditional auteurist approaches to individual films in which the critic's role is to scour the film for signature moments and motifs that reveal the text's reliance on an individual author, stitching a sequence of films together with the threads of biography. The laboured work these critics make of connecting Campion's films might also be a way of avoiding a direct evaluation of the film at hand, in this case *Angel*, preferring instead the pleasures of a predictive reading that arises from the critic's prior knowledge of its 'author'. In this way, the critic is not reading the films per se but the reputation of the auteur. Jonathon Rosenbaum's droll summary of contemporary authorship: '[A]uteurism exists largely for the convenience of critics and other packagers. It's mainly a way of reading movies, not of explaining how they're made', might just as easily be rewritten to suggest instead that auteurism is mainly a way of reading filmmakers, not of explaining how they make films.[20]

In her interviews with the media, Campion herself was quick to point out the industrial reasons for the stylistic divergence between these two works – *Angel* an adaptation originally made for television and then later released to cinemas; *Sweetie* an original screenplay made specifically for cinema release: 'With the subject matter of *Sweetie* I always imagined it as having a very adventurous visual style – looking at the exoticness of suburban life. With *An Angel at My Table* I felt any treatment that interfered with your relationship to Janet Frame would feel like a filmmaking conceit. You needed to keep it very simple.'[21] Here Campion reiterates a distinction between film and television that underscored the historical emergence of auteurism as an industrial category designed to elevate cinema from the wash of other media images emerging in the 1950s and beyond. Cinema would be associated with creative and personal visions whereas the mass entertainment of TV would not. In talking about the film some years later Campion restated these associations: 'I guess I'm a kind of a film snob and even though I think the Janet Frame story as you'll see here is very touching and very affecting, to me its still like a TV series and I like film that's a little more risk taking or bold.'[22] And yet, some years later again, in thinking about what she might do after her long break from filmmaking Campion seems to have reconsidered the value of television production, no doubt inspired by the emergence of the highly successful, prestige production models offered by cable channels such as HBO: 'I think that's actually a more radical medium. You can do things quickly and interestingly with stories that are so hard to do in feature films.'[23] (See Figures 1.1 and 1.2.)

Film critic Steve Weinstein looked further afield for an explanation for what he saw as the formal deviation between *Angel* and *Sweetie* suggesting that Campion's change of tack was prompted by the negative attention received by the earlier film. In response, Campion reiterates her concern for delivering Janet Frame's story with a minimum of personal embellishment but admits that the shift in tone had unanticipated benefits for her own career:

> Janet's story is very emotionally based, and I felt that to be real theoretical about it or to make it a vehicle for my own quirky style was to disempower her story . . . It's not a signature piece. It's a story that I loved and, and I was happy just to be a loving and honest custodian for it. I am committed to experimenting further, but I enjoyed doing Janet Frame because it destroyed the opportunity for people to categorize me.[24]

FIGURE 1.1 The young Janet Frame (Karen Fergusson) in *An Angel at My Table*
Courtesy Hibiscus Films Ltd

FIGURE 1.2 The young Sweetie (Emma Fowler) in *Sweetie*
Arenafilm Pty Ltd

Despite Campion's careful distinctions, Weinstein manages to find a further basis to connect the films, asserting that *Angel* 'mines much of the same emotional territory Campion has explored previously: family, the artistic temperament, sex, madness, superstitions and the unconscious mind'.[25] So, should a stylistic distinction unravel the fabric of authorial coherence then a thematic preoccupation will surely sew it back together again.

Like Weinstein, many other critics found reason to link the two films through the prism of Campion's authorship. The influential *Variety* review of *An Angel at My Table* by David Stratton noted:

> One of the many remarkable elements of this beautiful film is the way the characters, though all based on real people . . . seem to have stepped from other Campion pics. They have the same sweet eccentricities and sexual and emotional hang-ups as the characters in *Sweetie* and the director's short films. Family scenes are also instantly recognizable as Campion's work . . . Campion demonstrates, once again, that she has a special vision of the world.[26]

Vincent Canby in the *NewYork Times* echoed this: 'The wonder of *An Angel at My Table* is that so much of it plays as if it had sprung from the imagination of the same young woman who made *Sweetie*.'[27] The *Village Voice* correspondent concurred: 'The painful, beautiful *An Angel at My Table*, now being released as a film isn't nearly as skewed as *Sweetie*, but it's recognizably a Campion work . . . another triumphant chapter in Campion's ongoing *A Girl's Own Story*.'[28]

Given the stretch in connecting *Sweetie* to *Angel* on the basis of stylistic similarities, perhaps what is going on here for critics is something less about whether there is a consistency of signature between these two films and more about Campion's ability to repeatedly fulfil expectations about authorial influence. That Campion is consistently *seen to be trying* her hand is just as, if not more, important than the specific continuity of her penmanship. This perceived inclination for making evident the director's presence in her films might at one level run counter to the

familiar auteurist belief that great directors unconsciously and effortlessly articulate their selves through a sequence of texts. Reviewing
Holy Smoke, for example, Stanley Kaffmann notes as a problem, the
'stertorous doing' in Campion's filmmaking.[29] In her early career, in
1986 Campion herself declares: 'It's better if you aren't trying so hard
– things you really badly want often go wrong; I find it's best to take
it easy.'[30] But only a few years later, she counter-suggests that, for her,
there is a substantial amount of preparation required in making a film,
drawing particular attention to the exertion entailed in her filmmaking:

> I think what goes wrong is that people don't realize how hard it is to do
> good work. That may sound awfully school maamish of me, but you can't
> just turn up on the day and call yourself a director. The homework is
> horrendous and you have to be prepared to compete with world
> standards.[31]

In emphasizing the arduous nature of her work, Campion conforms to
the cultural commonplace that success will only be achieved through
hard effort and professionalism. It is the effort of ability, premised on
the idea that auteurism is something that is done, often with difficulty,
that particularly informs the next auteurist mode typically associated
with Jane Campion and perpetuated in media commentary about her.

## THE AUTEUR OF UNCOMPROMISING ARTISTIC VISION

This understanding of Campion's agency emphasizes her inventive film
style as the source of her 'signature' but it also hinges on the idea that
the evident formal innovations of her films represent and substantiate
the filmmaker's power (over the image), that her signature indicates
not just her unique presence but describes her potency as a director.
It's no surprise that Campion's MySpace fan page is titled 'Strange and
strong', from a line in The Piano: 'I am frightened of my will. Of what
it might do, it is so strange and strong.'[32] The contemporary auteur
needs to be able to assert the perception of control ('strong') while the

commercial reality of the industry presents her as a distinctive brand name ('strange'). The auteur in this sense is someone who gets things done, which raises the possibility that the post-auteur is not so much something you 'are' as something you can 'do' (in the same way that tourists can 'do' Paris or executives 'do' lunch). Ways of 'doing auteur' might include, but are not defined solely by: styles of filmmaking (as we have already discussed, through signature effects and so on); practices of filmmaking (emphasizing the various ways in which the filmmaker controls the specificity of their work environment); and modes of authorship (in which the depth and breadth of a filmmaker's creative agency is measured in terms of their ability to consistently realize a personal vision, for example).

From the outset Campion was portrayed in the media as unbending in the pursuit of her artistic ambition. The original press kit for her tele-feature *Two Friends* (1986) quoted her:

> A lot of people compromise their vision for the box office. I'm not prepared to do that. You have to remain firm about what you think is a good idea, and make it work. In this case we could have found ourselves pressured to do things, but we ignored the negative, and finally had no restrictions on doing what we wanted.

Here Campion posits the 'box office' as the nemesis of artistic freedom. By the time she came to make *Sweetie* she was less sure about this opposition, instead couching the dimensions of her own success in terms of her ability to predict public preference, to be ahead of the audience rather than oblivious to it: 'I'm hoping to be a hit and anticipate public taste . . . I think it's part of what you have to do. There's no point in making what people wanted to see ten years ago.'[33] By the time she was promoting *Angel* she was even clearer about the benefits that flow from aiming for box office: 'I have nothing against the idea of having a comfortable budget at my disposition to make my films with and I believe that the system doesn't necessarily erase your personality.'[34]

It is easy to see these statements as evidence of a personal shift on Campion's part, a sign of an inevitable 'maturing' of her approach to her creativity and her attitude towards the commercial film industry. But it is just as likely that these positional and pragmatic shifts over the commercialization of her filmmaking have just as much to do with the significant changes that were occurring across the film industry, specifically in the way in which Hollywood itself was approaching the question of independent cinema and authorship. The rise of independent distributors in the US such as Miramax after the film industry shakedown of the 1980s and the subsequent emergence of the 'indie blockbuster'; the widespread development of 'specialty divisions' in most major studios and their sourcing of film projects from overseas all benefited Campion at different stages of her career (and which are discussed in more detail in chapter three).[35]

Several critics have, over the years, also noted the question of authorship and its relationship to commerce in Campion's work. Some critics, for example, have proposed that access to higher budgets has been to the detriment of Campion's creative integrity. So, despite previously confessing to being a 'passionate fan' of Campion's cinema and defending her against a premature critical backlash after the release of The Piano, Jonathon Rosenbaum declares of the progression of her films from Sweetie to Portrait that: '[T]he more money director Jane Campion has to spend, the more of her formidable talent she wastes.'[36] Or, from an explicitly retrospective vantage, as Variety's Todd McCarthy would have it, Campion's decision to make a genre film with In the Cut, represents an understandably failed attempt to redress past box office performances:

> While it's clear what attracted Campion to this material, there is also more than a whiff of her desire to make an overtly 'commercial' film after the flops of her two most recent pictures . . . It's doubtful fans of The Piano will embrace In the Cut but Campion's sensibility here remains too defiantly non-mainstream to win over the masses.[37]

For both Rosenbaum and McCarthy, Campion's success as an authentic auteur is somehow compromised by her choice of commercial projects or large budgets. For Rosenbaum, it is not Campion's advancement as an artist that is the heart of the problem, it is the progression of her finances that has spoiled her standing as an auteur. For McCarthy, the failed commercialization of Campion's cinema has served to further emphasize her 'self' as an essentially non-mainstream filmmaker.

So, even accounting for her later attraction to large budgets or commercial projects, the theme of Campion's unflinching commitment to her artistic vision resonates in media accounts of her career. In a notorious interview with British TV talkshow host Michael Parkinson, actor Meg Ryan, speaking about her role in In the Cut, was quick to point out her own sense of personal deficiency in the face of Campion's more salient virtues: 'I wasn't ready for Jane Campion, the director. Jane is a very strong-minded and uncompromising artist who has a profound interest in investigation.'[38] Kate Winslet, remembering her work on Holy Smoke speaks similarly:

> Jane is a really extraordinary woman . . . She's very determined and if I were to compare her with any director I've worked with, I would say she's probably most like James Cameron. Purely because she will absolutely go for what she wants.[39]

The frequent descriptions of Campion's tenacity slot nicely alongside the traditional auteurist emphasis on the auteur's contrariness (often characterized in terms of their difficulties within the Hollywood studio system for example). But Campion – unlike classical auteurs – simply cannot be constructed as working in opposition or reaction or resistance to cultural or industrial powerbrokers (remembering that there is no studio system per se in Australia or New Zealand). Whereas Campion's early success strongly suggests her ability to work well within cultural and financial systems what instead proliferate are discourses of personal prickliness and rebellion; her self-professed status as outcast in film school, her repeatedly pronounced reputation as a 'difficult woman'. That she was taken up very early in her career by feminist writers and critics also assists in creating an air of contradiction about her – the lone woman in a male-dominated industry. The matter of Campion's gender is then another source of media fascination (see Figure 1.3).

For the most part, the media play on the question of Campion's gender as a tired story about filmmaking that doesn't really bear repeating, except, perhaps, in this one instance. So in her fabulously titled article, 'What if she'd been a boy?', Anne Demy-Geroe writes: 'There's an inevitability about viewing women's achievements in gender terms. But when it's Jane Campion such positioning gains new meaning.'[40] Or from Wendy Ide:

> There's a school of thought that argues that the gender of a film-maker shouldn't be an issue. One can either direct movies or one can't, and all the debate about the dearth of successful female film-makers serves only to create a 'women's cinema' ghetto. But then you see a film like Jane

FIGURE 1.3 Difficult woman: Ruth Barron (Kate Winslet) in *Holy Smoke*
Miramax/The Kobal Collection/Jenkins, Gerald

> Campion's *In the Cut* . . . which revels in its female perspective, and it is
> abundantly clear that the film was made by a gifted, intuitive director, and
> that the director was, without doubt, a woman.[41]

For Ide, Campion's In the Cut is not only obviously directed by a woman but it is helmed by her with an air of rebellion: 'It's an indication of the *defiantly* female touch that it is the social element, rather than the suspense, that takes precedence.'[42] By way of contrast, Lizzie Franke introduces an interview with Campion by pointing out the way in which her achievements are often diminished by media headlines focused on her gender. Asking 'what's female got to do with it' Franke identifies media platitudes such as 'Campion is the world's most [insert superlative] female director' as back-handed compliments at best.

But, in relation to the issue of her pursuit of creative control, Campion's gender becomes a conceptual quagmire for some media commentators. In a fascinating, and one presumes deliberately provocative article, Stephanie Bunbury begins by noting Campion's unconventional fashion sense and yet her popularity with the fashion press during the promotion of In the Cut: 'She looked fantastic. Even the fashion gurus thought so. And they acknowledged that it was because she had found a look that absolutely suited the person she is. Campion has never been one to fit the mould.' Bunbury then directly segues to a discussion of Campion's style as a director that is supported by a series of quotations from the film's cast proposing a type of gender mutability on her part. So Meg Ryan again: 'I loved being around Jane every day. I loved it. She's so forthright and ballsy and just so for real! She has redefined what being an artist means to me.' Taking the adjective 'ballsy' in its most physiological sense, Bunbury then recounts John Malkovitch who apparently said he liked working with Campion on Portrait because she enjoyed an argument and 'she doesn't do "girl's stuff"', to which Campion archly replies: 'That's because he did all the girl's stuff.' Still, Bunbury persists in further drawing the connection between Campion's on-set manner and a type of masculinity, moving on to Mark Ruffalo: 'I never saw anyone have such a handle on manhood as this woman, you know?'[43] There are a lot of assumptions being made, mostly through association, in this passage of reportage. Through a sequence of quotations, Bunbury implicitly indicates that Campion's ability to realize her artistic vision is, at least in part, produced by her facility with what is assumed to be the 'masculine' operations of the film set and therefore that her artistic 'control' is not a feature of her femininity, for instance. And, unlike the apparent authenticity of Campion's couture, Bunbury's article suggests that, in terms of gender, Campion's subjectivity is not fixed but is provisional and performative in nature, but that this is also 'real' in the context of the film set.

In contradistinction, Kevin Bacon, speaking of the same film, but in a different media outlet, rejects the idea that there is something significant to be said about Campion's working method in relation to her sexuality: 'It was fun working with Jane. It's funny, but I never think to myself that I'm working with a woman director or not.'[44] Kate Winslet spoke similarly about her time on *Holy Smoke*: 'In terms of working with a female rather than a male director, there were very few differences other than Jane always wanted to borrow my lipstick, girly things like that.'[45] In their own way, these quotations suggest, to the extent one can assume that film sets are masculinized work places, that Campion's real success has been to elide her difference in this environment. In these quotes, Campion's gender is characterized as a matter of positionality rather than performance. For Bacon and Winslet, Campion is not noticeably unlike male directors. It is not that she is successfully performing 'like a man' on the film set, but that she is not conspicuously positioned as a woman that seems important.

Campion herself has, over the years, and in a multitude of media, adopted many different positions, including ambivalence, in relation to the argument that women directors work differently or that there is an identifiable 'women's sensibility' that can be deduced from what appears on-screen:

I'm not really sure what they mean by that. It would be interesting to work out if there was such a thing. I think we're talking about sensitivity in general and I don't think that is only the territory of women. But I'm sure gender is a part of that.[46]

On this occasion, speaking about In the Cut, Campion is quick to draw a distinction between categories of gender and sexual identity, aligning a trait such as 'sensitivity' with the social category 'femininity' rather than the category 'women' for example. In this manoeuvre, Campion proposes femininity as a heuristic category – a means by which we might investigate the variability and contingency of conventional understandings of sexual difference. Unsurprisingly, these exploratory opportunities are rarely taken up in Campion's media interviews even when she periodically attempts to prompt them. The vast majority of media articles unabashedly link Campion's uncompromising pursuit of an artistic vision to her gender (as the exemplary 'woman director' making films for and about women) or on many occasions, linking it to the more stridently political ascription, 'feminist director'.

Campion herself has reiterated in interviews her belief that with one exception, the overtly feminist short film, After Hours (1984), she has had 'total' control over her films. Interestingly, she describes herself as internally conflicted in several directions over this project: 'My motive for making it was compromised. There was a conflict between myself, the project and my artistic conscience.'[47] Campion, who regularly describes herself as an obsessive compulsive on set, has reflected on how her need for control is instrumental to her sense of self: 'What is part of me is a certain sense of the absolute and the desire to control things. I've always had trouble understanding the separation between myself and the world; the mystery of sexuality, of hatred, of passion, has always been a problem.'[48] She goes on to suggest that ultimately it is herself that she needs to direct, something achieved through meditation which she says: '[H]elps me to control myself. I'm also more aware of my real feelings. Often one does things out of sheer excitement, when really it doesn't fit one's real self.'[49] In referring to her 'real' self, Campion seems to suggest an underlying sense of her self as an essentialist identity but her earlier comment implies there is no easy alignment between this self and her 'artistic conscience' or that this self has an unimpeded motivating influence over her actions. So despite her belief that she possesses a 'real' self, Campion presents her identity as comprising multiple and layered selves interconnected but not always cohesively united.

The pointed connection Campion makes between her professional aspirations and personal attributes recurs throughout many interviews and appears right from the outset in her thinking about her own role in the cinema:

> The privilege I have at the moment [1990] is to pursue the kind of ideas that wouldn't happen in America . . . I think it's important to broaden the scope of the cinema appetite. If you go and do the American thing, you are not really exploring your own freedom.[50]

Campion creates cascading conceptual links, implicitly likening anti-Hollywood sentiment with artistic freedom, which in turn is linked with her own personal development. Maintaining the idea that her filmmaking is principally motivated by the pursuit of personal freedom, Campion later recasts her attitude to Hollywood or genre cinema. When an interviewer suggests to her that many people may be surprised to find Campion's name on In the Cut, she replies: 'I think people will just get a fresh view of a genre movie, and there's a freedom in genre I never expected to enjoy.'[51] In these terms, an actual career might seem like an accidental side-effect in the pursuit of pleasure or freedom:

> I seem to have been able to make a career out of doing what I feel like doing, so why not keep doing it? What's corrupting is wanting to be more important. You want to be more arty – you get your identity from that. Or you get your identity out of making more money. I get my pleasure, which is far more important to me, out of trying to follow my instincts.[52]

This would seem to be the obverse of Campion's self-professed predilection to complete creative control. Rather than trying to regulate the conditions under which a career is conducted, Campion is suggesting in these statements that it is only in following one's instincts that one can remain uncorrupted, that the really important aspects of both personal and professional motivation are intrinsically elusive, out of her control. More recently she has expanded on this idea:

> The thing I've learned from the filmmaking I've done, and life in general, is I really don't think you know a lot about what's going on as it's going down, but maybe if you're really lucky, and really calm you can learn about 65–70% of what's happening. That's pretty good. But if you're getting uptight and you're getting anxious, you can think you know what's going on and be 90% wrong.[53]

Unlike the precepts of traditional auteurism, which would have the personal preceding the film text, such that the author's personality and personal life neatly informs the cinema they create, Campion intimates that the personal and professional exist in an unpredictable relationship, on occasion in conflict, that they are, now and again, reciprocal or even intangibly related. At other times, Campion has intimated how the specific coincidence of momentous personal and professional events (the death of her son and winning at Cannes) held a 'lesson' for her about the nature of control itself: 'The irony of Jasper dying at the moment of winning the Palm d'Or is that you learn that what you want is not always under your control.'[54]

The issue of creative control, and its relation to perceptions of the auteur's authenticity, is most delicately played out in media coverage of the US classification of In the Cut. In order to avoid an NC-17 rating (which bans under-18s from viewing the film in cinemas), Campion agreed to make a series of cuts to the film, not necessarily because the film was intended for a younger audience but because many US cinemas are contractually obliged not to show these movies and many media outlets will automatically refuse advertising for films with this rating. For the most part, Campion presented herself as the very model of corporate cooperation, even managing to turn her allegiance to the film's distributors into a defiance of sorts:

> I think their censorship board is fine. They loved our movie and they were begging us to make an example of ourselves as being a responsible adult-themed film that could change the way that America treats those films, but we'd already made an agreement with the distributor that we would cut a version of the film that they could advertise and I didn't mind that.[55]

More broadly, however, Campion has spoken of the way in which distributor expectations about the intended audience for In the Cut influenced her creative decision making, for example altering the way in which she approached the ending of the film which differed from the ending of the book on which it was based: 'Frannie lives or the movie dies. So you have to find a way for her to survive and still keep it bare.'[56] But for Campion, this narrative malleability is not just about bowing to commercial pressure, it is about the nature of the translation from one media to another, about the possibilities and limitations afforded by the cinema: 'It was pretty much undoable the way it was originally.'[57]

Campion's rethinking of the relationship between a filmmaker's personal life and professional aspirations invite consideration of a further theme in the media's approach auteurism in which both the films and the personal life of the director coalesce to produce revelatory explanation of each other. So when a critic declares to her that Holy Smoke follows a theme developed in all Campion's films, 'of female wilfulness gone awry and the punitive consequences that can arise', Campion plays it both ways, as something undetermined and yet possibly present: 'People are always saying this, but it's not something I analyse . . . I'm a wilful person and so that's something I experience in the world and explore.'[58]

Across various interviews, Campion has confessed her own aware-ness of a type of obstinacy and defiance in her self-presentation and she attributes these traits different meanings at different times. While making *Portrait of a Lady*, she recognized that film sets establish their own environments of authority with explicit communication conventions: 'I like the bluntness because I'm the queen of scene and everybody is interested in what you have to think and say.' But Campion also acknowledges the specificity of her situation: 'That's not normal.'[59] In other interviews, Campion stresses that she had to make strategic choices in certain situations: 'I had to be very obstinate to impose my views.'[60] Another time Campion describes how her rebelliousness is out of her control: 'It's not enough to be nice . . . All I ever wanted was to be liked and accepted by everybody else, but I always seemed to swing back into a rebellious attitude – being a bit obnoxious.'[61]

What underlies some of these media observations of Campion's potent artistic vision is the underlying idea that it is at least her self, if not her success, that is unbroken and continuous. This confidence in the constancy of creative identity and endeavour, in the idea that films act a form of self-realization for the auteur, is further reiterated in the following mode of auteurism practised by various media commentaries on Campion.

## THE 'SIGNATURE SELF': THE AUTEUR IN THE FILM

Popular auteurist writing frequently proposes an easy alliance between the personal and the filmic, which rests on the idea that films 'speak' on the director's behalf, that they alone provide a link between her self and the world, giving viewers automatic access to her identity. This belief is underscored by industry practices that would erase the act of making a film, replacing it instead with a seamless identification. So before *The Piano*, even in her early short films, Campion's credit was always coupled with the terms, 'Directed by' or 'Written and directed by'. The idea of a 'Jane Campion film' where the director and the movie seem to merge materializes with the credits for *The Piano*. Other industry practices also allude to the literal 'presence' of the auteur in the film text, such as those occasions in which directors cast themselves in cameos, although this ritual takes place in both classic and post-auterist filmmaking including the work of luminaries such as Hitchcock, Scorcese and Tarantino. In this spirit, Jane Campion makes an uncredited appearance as a waitress in In the Cut, dancing with the man who will later be revealed as the mystery murderer (see Figures 1.4 and 1.5). In these images, the director alternates between glancing reassuringly at the film's heroine and looking straight down the barrel of the camera towards her audience.

In auteur interviews, the credence that the filmmaker's life is illuminated by, and/or reflected in, her films is most commonly manifest in questions about the director's take on her lead characters and Jane Campion has had more than her fair share of these media moments. There is a wonderful piece on *Holy Smoke* in which she almost toys with the interviewer as she methodically over-identifies with every character in the film:

> At first I thought I was Ruth, the younger woman, and I still do. Real love seems psychotic most of the time. I haven't been very success-ful at it myself! I feel myself as Yvonne, too – the complete ditz, who gets manipulated all the time, falls in love, is just a romantic idiot

FIGURE 1.4 Jane Campion dances with danger in *In the Cut*
Frameshot

FIGURE 1.5 Jane Campion looks back at the camera in *In the Cut*
Frameshot

who fantasises sex and love all day long. Then I realized that I am the older man. PJ is such an uptight guy. He uses breath freshener and wears ironed jeans.[62]

This is possibly not just a light-hearted swipe on Campion's part. What she is taking issue with here are some of the ways in which the media typically understand identification (and therefore identity) in the cinema. Instead of presenting her identification with the characters of *Holy Smoke* as an essentialist exercise (reducing the act of identification to a single axis of identity based on her gender for example), Campion reveals ambivalent, multiple and partial identifications that are themselves associated with desires or scenarios rather than identities per se. So, in identifying with both Yvonne and PJ for example, Campion acknowledges that differences can exist between but also within identities; that belonging to a particular identity does not necessarily determine which characters an audience member or filmmaker should identify with; and that there are many different ways of experiencing a supposedly singular identity position such as femininity. Sallie Munt's work on the 'multivalent self' in which 'the ground of the self shifts and recombines with the intervention and chafing of other selves, which sculpt a new self based on inter-subjectivity' goes some way to describing Campion's point here.[63]

Nevertheless, the uncomplicated collapsing of the director into her film text is a constant theme in the media interviews Campion has conducted on almost every one of her films. On Sweetie: 'It was inspired by people and events I know. I always work that way. I then have more authority over my writing and even if I later move away from these experiences, I still have a basis I can come back to.'[64] On Janet Frame and An Angel at My Table: 'It's the story of her life but it could have been my life.'[65] On The Piano: 'The Piano, like A Girl's Own Story is my territory – things I know about, that nobody else could easily get access to.'[66] On Portrait of a Lady: 'I am Isabel and I think every woman on this film thinks the same thing – that her story touches us all.'[67] And, for In the Cut: 'Could I be Frannie? I don't know if I could, really. But as an artist I'm attracted to subjects I feel I have to grow into. I had a reluctance and a willingness – which I guess is Frannie.' Despite Campion's disinclination to identify with aspects of In the Cut, the reporter effortlessly skips along to definitively state: 'The filmmaker identified strongly with this character who studies violent and sexual slang, yet uses her intellect as a shield.'[68] In other interviews, Campion reiterates the idea that it was not necessarily the conflicted persona of Frannie per se that she initially identified with but rather the film project as a whole: 'Like an actor takes on a role, I took on and grew into In the Cut, making it finally very me, more me than even I knew.'[69]

Reading her interviews, it would appear that Campion's discomfort in explicitly admitting a personal identification with Frannie has everything to do with that character's complicated calibre as a figure of film noir and the prescriptions that the generic places around characterizations of women, as variations of the vamp or victim, for example. Before In the Cut, Campion explained her attraction to films with central female characters as a type of identification on her part:

> I like to be able to project myself into the parts and being a woman I like to therefore have heroines. We don't have many, you know? So I feel like it's my job. Not a crusade – just a natural thing to want to do.[70]

Genre films like In the Cut would appear to dent the 'naturalness' of the fit between Campion and her heroines.

Media emphasis on the close identification of directors with their lead characters is typically presented in terms of an overemphasis on 'sameness' and self-recognition rather than this identification being understood as a process that might also encompass evident differences and incongruities. This exaggeration of the assimilation of director and film causes many commentators to draw startling conclusions about Campion herself. One reporter, for example, waiting for Campion to arrive for her interview, muses on the unrecognizability of Campion herself, 'a sleek woman with low-slung pigtails and a tailored skirt'. She ventures: 'I guess I'd envisioned someone a bit more ostentatious.' Why? Because Campion doesn't look to her like any of the women in her 'extreme portraits of femininity'. She elaborates: 'After all, Campion embroiders her movies with eerie motifs of abduction, entrapment and rapture, and peoples them with wilful heroines who face dire circumstances.' When she explains this to her, Campion counters in a faintly mocking tone: 'And yet my own persona is so sunny. It's ridiculous, isn't it?'[71]

But if I appear to be presenting Campion as in any way consistent on the idea of her biographical presence in her films then I am doing her a disservice. From scepticism ('I don't know to what extent An Angel at My Table is about me. I'm a bit like an actor who chooses her projects and likes to do different things');[72] to outright rejection ('I don't think that I project my fantasies on my characters and in any case I don't know who I am. We are everything we do'), Campion has also tried to distance herself from the idea that her films provide insight into her personal lives, partly because from her perspective 'the personal' is so very difficult to distil (let alone its relationship to her films).[73]

The media, by the same token, are adept at bio-spotting, keeping one eye open for those prized moments in which the director's personal experiences or predilections might appear on screen. So it's not surprising that Campion's sudden news that she had a half-sister, a discovery that occurred when she was in pre-production for In the Cut, is celebrated as sole cause for her on-screen addition of Frannie's half-sister Pauline, who does not appear in the original novel and who is sacrificed by Campion in place of Frannie (despite what this might suggest about Campion's feelings to her new sibling).[74] Or that the tenor of the relationship between Ruth and PJ in *Holy Smoke* is based on a short romance Campion once had with a guy with cystic fibrosis – a topic also picked up in her short story 'Big shell', in which a woman's disastrous one-night stand with a wheelchair-bound man is told in first person.[75] Or that her mother's treatment for depression was an influence on her during the making of *An Angel at My Table*.[76]

A variation on this theme were the comments made by film critic Michael Medved in which he used events in Campion's personal life to undermine the legitimacy of two critic's awards given to *The Piano* in the lead up to the Oscars. Medved suggested Campion's cause had been somehow unfairly aided by sympathy over the death of her son, Jasper:

> Contrary to popular belief, critics are people – and we do have emotions. This sad tale most certainly created an additional wave of sympathy and support for Campion.[77]

Representative critics responded by openly chastizing Medved for airing the director's 'very private grief in public' and accusing him of being 'solely interested in self-promotion'.[78] In their rejoinder to Medved, these critics turn the tables describing how it is Medved's 'self' which is revealed in his writing, rather than the filmmaker's career advancement that is 'explained' by events in her personal life.

It may be, however, that the media's fascination with those moments in which there appears to be a coalescence between events in Campion's life and those that appear in her films is not necessarily part of a larger commentary on the cinema (i.e. it is not an attempt to establish a causal relationship between filmmakers and their films) but instead represents an opportunity for the media to emphasize and capitalize on Campion's celebrity credentials. There is certainly additional kudos attached to those particular flashpoints when a public figure's personal life is seen to meld into their work, therefore attributing them a type of raw 'truthfulness' not often associated with the performative media. At these moments audiences and fans are encouraged to believe that glimpses of a celebrity's 'real' self might be discerned.

In *The Film Director as Superstar*, a book of interviews with independent American directors published in the early 1970s, Joseph Gelmis establishes what he calls 'the first authentic film generation', a group of filmmakers defined by their personal investment in their films and which is the defining feature of their status as celebrity auteurs. The title of his book comes from its opening quotation in which Roman Polanski declares: 'To me the director is always a superstar. The best films are best because of nobody but the director.'[79] Gelmis continues, asserting the celebrity credentials of his interview subjects by further quoting Bernardo Bertolucci: 'I am making always just one film . . . It's one film even if it has many titles or many chapters . . . If we take out the title of the film and "The end" and put the films all together, we will have the figure of one man, of an auteur, the life of an auteur, transferred in many characters naturally.'[80] In Gelmis's somewhat circular account, great directors are solely responsible for the production of great film texts and exemplary film texts provide retrospective evidence or proof of their personal primacy.

In his analysis of auteurs as stars, Timothy Corrigan distinguishes the contemporary star–auteur from earlier versions of celebrity auteurism such as the one offered by Gelmis which identify textual distinction as the source of the autuer's celebrity. This earlier version of the auteur's celebrity is particularly well captured by Gelmis who describes how Hollywood, 'which in its decline has become a euphemism for banks, backlots full of TV series and overseas production – is so desperate to find ways to please fickle audiences, it is willing to give the director the kind of control and money to make personal films'.[81] For Gelmis, the explicit point of the director's celebrity is to address a deficit in film production, i.e. to make films (texts) which in turn address a problem with cinema audiences, i.e. that they are not consistent and can only be 'turned' by experiences of authentic authorship. Corrigan, however, describes how 'auteurs have become increasingly situated along an extratextual path in which their commercial status as auteurs is their chief function as auteurs'.[82] In other words, the relationship between auteurs and their texts comes in many forms – they may be loose from one another, their relationship reversed or subject to persistent renewal. This is a phenomenon that Richard Dyer had already noted in relation to the conventions of the Hollywood star system as a method of organizing actors:

> [T]he star is also a phenomenon of the cinema (which as a business could make money from stars in additional ways to having them make films e.g. in advertising, the fan industry, personal appearances) and of general social meanings, and the instances of stars whose films may actually be less important than other aspects of their career.[83]

So when Michael Chion says 'There is nothing more common than an auteur. Auteur films (which create their auteur) are rarer stuff', he proposes the film text as one among many voices in the criss-cross conversation that circles around the figure of the auteur.[84] Or when William D. Routt says:

> My own analyses nowadays almost always place 'the film' where the name of the director used to be placed. It seems more accurate to place the weight of authority on the present text rather than on an absent, past, generator. The author is the identity we can do without.

In so saying, he signals a surrogate or proxy relationship between film and filmmaker, which, unlike Timothy Corrigan, retains the film text at the expense of the author.[85] And when Jane Campion says 'it's just a medium. People define it each time they make a film' she suggests an unpredictable relationship of constant reinvention between filmmaker and film. Campion's self-perception here is of the film director as someone engaged in a constant process of 'becoming-author' – each film a new opportunity to think through or enact her agency. In this way, Campion challenges the value of too much generalization and points to the idea of filmmaking as a form of self-renewal.

## THE AUTEUR AS NOVEL SELF

Campion's suggestion that each film newly defines it relationship to an author makes more sense if the context of the Australian film industry is taken into account. Realizing productions in the Australian film industry (including productions by Australian filmmakers working on the international stage) is almost always a peripatetic process – and therefore so is the possibility for agency within the industry. It is not surprising to hear an Australasian filmmaker speak about filmmaking as a constant form of self-invention when so many Australian films stutter fitfully into life, sustained by a precariously fragile alliance of private and public equity and with no guarantee of future projects on the horizon. You can also understand why, in this environment of uncertainty, a filmmaker like Jane Campion frequently summons up in interviews her apparent ambivalence towards filmmaking (culminating, of course, in her temporary withdrawal from feature filmmaking), an ambivalence that seems to contradict the conventional belief that auteurs are impassioned cineastes and filmmakers who live and breathe only to realize their films:

> I'm in a very lucky position with film-making because I'm not that ambitious. It never really worries me if I make another film or not. Once I'm on something, I'm as persistent and driven as the next person to make it as strong and as good as possible, but if the financing got pulled out I'd just go, 'Oh, well . . . there are a lot more important things in life'.[86]

Campion reiterates this ambivalence at different points in her career. Most recently she has generalized even further, suggesting that: 'I'm not the same person I was. I'm not as driven.'[87]

When prompted by one reviewer, in light of her plans to take a break from filmmaking, to consider 'a more home-based occupation such as writing', Campion expresses reservations about even this pursuit, describing to the interviewer her broader disaffection with the promotional aspects of any creative industry:

> I have no plans to write. I have no ambitions at all. You think about writing a book and then you realise you'd have to publicise it. It seems like no matter what you do, it always ends up back in a room like this.[88]

But at other times, she has publicly floated other possible career options for herself. In an interview with Lynden Barber, for example, she talks about becoming a therapist and writing novels.[89]

Campion's love of reading novels is another persistent theme in media profiles, a topic she seems happy to dwell on:

> I love novels. I get more enjoyment out of novels than I do out of cinema now. I used to love cinema more but now I think that too many films are too cheap, and they're kind of censored by an expectation of a stupid audience. They're not the challenge or the excitement that you can get in books.[90]

It has been noted that, across the history of her media interviews, Campion is more likely to refer to literary sources than cinematic ones when discussing her influences.[91] And the idea that she is attracted to wild romantic extremes is often attributed to her interest in nineteenth-century literature by reviewers and commentators. Ken Gelder has noted the way in which even The Piano, which was not explicitly based on a literary source, was nevertheless perceived to be 'literary', and certainly more 'literary' than the novelization itself, which was released a year later. For example, in one interview with Campion, a journalist remarks on how the screenplay benefited from a long gestation: 'Spare, direct and elegant, rich with resonances, it reads like a novel, revealing Campion as nearly a gifted writer as she is a filmmaker.'[92]

In drawing attention to her love of books, Campion presents herself as a filmmaker, an author, who is also a reader. This is further underlined by her attraction to literary adaptations such as *An Angel at My Table*, *Portrait of a Lady* and *In the Cut* but going as far back as *Two Friends*, which is based on a Helen Garner short story (see Figure 1.6).

Garner has spoken about Campion's apparent ease in interpreting a written work for the screen:

> I was surprised at how Jane could take an idea of mine and take a different slant on it, and yet understand exactly what I was on about. She'd find a richness I didn't know was there . . . I love the way she has done it. There are a lot of laughs but ultimately it's full of pain.[93]

Garner's comments are designed to safeguard the integrity of Campion's status as an auteur, emphasizing her capacities as an active and interventionist interpreter, rather than as someone who is derivative, a slave to their sources. Over the years, views such as Garner's have been

FIGURE 1.6 **Kelly (Kris Bidenko) and Louise (Emma Coles) in** *Two Friends*
Courtesy ABC Library Sales

echoed by others and by Campion herself. For example, speaking about the significant changes that were made to the shape of Susanna Moore's novel In the Cut, Campion assured one interviewer that 'Susanna [with whom she wrote the script] was happy for me to change it' and defended the film's integrity in observing the spirit of the book: 'It's still very dark – it's noir, which is something you're not supposed to cheer up too much.'[94] Still, Campion proffers several reasons for making the changes, one of which entails acknowledging the way her own personality differs from Moore's:

> I didn't want it to end like the book and we would never have found financing to do it that way. While Susanna and I really love each other, we're different people. I'm an optimist and a survivor; I'm interested in redemption and survival, but she's kind of a sadder person, more fatalistic, and I think more inclined towards female self-sacrifice than I am.[95]

Although identifying Campion's interpretive contributions as evidence of her unique authorship, media coverage of Campion's adaptations and collaborations also frequently calls on the text's other originators for approval. Martin Grove has described this, not only as a typical media moment, but a crucial reason that film industries turn to source novels:

> Just the fact that a novel is being turned into a movie sets in motion a chain of media coverage that invariably centers on how the book will have to be changed to become a movie, how its author feels about Hollywood making those changes, who will or won't or should or shouldn't be cast in the film and how the author really feels deep down about those particular actors.[96]

One of the most notable instances of this practice occurs when Laura Jones, screenwriter on Portrait, hopes that Henry James himself would be 'turning [in his grave] with pleasure' at Campion's vision of his book.[97] A similar fantasy, in this case of posthumous disapproval, occurred when some observers sought to link *The Piano* to an uncredited source, Jane Mander's novel *The Story of a New Zealand River*:

> It is rumored that Jane Mander, who died in 1949, disliked the movies. Still, her great-niece speculates angrily on her behalf: 'If Aunt Jane had been alive today, she would have kneecapped Jane Campion.'[98]

Of course, for auteurists of a fundamentalist bent, Campion's latterly interventions are like a red rag to a bull. Writing in *The New York Times*, Jesse Green doesn't mince words in his assessment of Campion's filmed version of Henry James's novel, *Portrait of a Lady*:

> [C]alling this Nicole Kidman vehicle an adaptation is like saying that Hitler adapted Poland; what Ms. Campion has done in her 'Portrait' is to steal parts of James's plot, make the fascinating Isabel Archer a weepy bore, substitute a blurry, inconsequential vision for the original's shocking clarity – all this and call it homage.[99]

It is easy to guess that Green is mostly indisposed to film adaptations, after all, the title of his article 'That was no "lady": pilfering literature', is a dead giveaway. And it doesn't get any nicer. He accuses 'plot poor directors' of searching for inspiration on the bookshelves and using what we assume must therefore be 'plot-rich books' as a shortcut to the assertion of their own authorship credentials:

> [I]t seems inevitable that the most passionate novels will always be turned into the coldest, most inarticulate films, not only because people love cheese, but because the desire to make legends out of ourselves will always outweigh the love for legends that already exist.[100]

For Green, the principal point of film adaptations is self-aggrandizement; to erase the traces of prior authorship while at the same time annexing the source material. Stanley Kaufman, a vehement Campion critic, would seem to concur when he damns her with faint praise in his review of *Holy Smoke*:

> Jane Campion's career takes on a shape. Before her latest film, she made four features. The two that were based on books were appealing. *Angel at My Table* treated Janet Frame's autobiography with compassion and vigor; *The Portrait of Lady* gave Henry James some lively, if presumptuous, advice about the novel he ought to have written. But the two Campion films made from original scripts were disappointments.[101]

Kaufman strongly suggests that the integrity of Campion's 'originality' is open to question; her work at its best when it is derived from somewhere else (other than her self). For other critics, this same observation is the basis for praise. Lee Marshall, reviewing *Portrait of a Lady* for *The Independent* declares: 'This is a film which renders the debate about faithfulness to the source text irrelevant. Jane Campion has not adapted Henry James's novel; she has digested it.'[102]

Several commentators have described how the high footing given to literary sources in Campion's films and media appearances is based on a need to prove herself a director of bookish credibility, to increase her stocks as an auteur of serious intent.[103] However it is also possible to see how Campion's literary references (and influential collaborations with screenwriter Laura Jones, for instance, or the advisory role given to the British poet laureate, Andrew Motion, on the *Bright Star* screenplay) also allude to a divestiture of personal authority in which the author is instead one interpreter in a chain of interpretations and in which the film is a link with no origin not even in an author. This dispersal of any notion of 'pure' authorship is further accentuated by Campion's credits as an interpreter of her own work, on more than one occasion translating them back onto the page in novelizations of *The Piano* (co-authored with Kate Pullinger and commissioned in the wake of the film's success) and *Holy Smoke* (with her sister Anna Campion and released in advance of the movie). Campion, by the same token, has countered this potential assignation of her talents as an 'adapteur', preserving her role as a reader from her role as a filmmaker with comments like this: 'I'm not the kind of director who reads a book and sees scenes or shots. I just read the book like everybody else.'[104]

Dana Polan has noted the ways in which novelizations function, alongside other tie-ins (like Michael Nyman's highly successful soundtrack to The Piano, for example), to extend the appeal of the film into new markets.[105] But despite their longstanding role in the film industry, there is very little media coverage of these works of a filmmaker's alternative authorship. So with few exceptions, there have been very few reviews of Campion's other forms of authorship: the novels and novelizations, short stories, journalism. The media, it seems, prefer to locate their authors in one media type and not across several. One notable media interview, with Campion's co-author Kate Pullinger, does provide quite a lot of detail about the process of preparing The Piano: A Novel, claiming that Pullinger was treated by Campion as 'more like a scriptwriter than a novelist', in other words, that she was subject to strict directions and timelines and that she was not personally afforded the status befitting an 'auteur'.[106] Pullinger adds to the idea that Campion's involvement was distant: 'Jane had right of approval, and in the end she did contribute a lot – all by fax from Australia.' In this instance, it is the filmmaker, understood as the author of the source material, whose approval is (contractually) required in developing the adaptation. But the reviewer/interviewer makes it plain that, in their opinion, Pullinger is the 'authentic' novelist in the relationship and that the novel's specific literary failings are most likely to be Campion's (an assertion that Pullinger is careful to avoid). However, in criticizing the book's literary merits (and Campion's literary talents) the interviewer does also admit to the limitations of the novelization genre itself:

> I was struck by how untrue the adage is, that television and film leave no room for the imagination, unlike novels . . . The novelistion of The Piano attributes motives and parental influences to the characters which I wish I'd not been told. It dots 'Is' and crosses 'Ts' and cancels out the impressions with which you left the screen.[107]

Anne Demy-Geroe, in one of the rare reviews of the novel of *Holy Smoke*, noting that it was released prior to the film, observes that it shares some space with *The Piano* (the film, not the novelization) in terms of bare plot points. She describes the book of *Holy Smoke* as 'extremely visual' and wonders how its use of overlapping subjective voices would be developed in the film. Demy-Geroe's review of the book of *Holy Smoke* is written as if the book is simply a precursor to the 'main event', the later release of the film, reiterating Campion's primacy as an author of films and not novels which is perhaps also why Demy-Geroe's interest in the book's dual perspectives does not extend to the question of its own co-authorship and Anna Campion rates only a passing mention.

The presentation of Campion's multiple and collaborative authorships by the media proposes a series of complexities to how we understand her as an auteur. On the one hand, she is the figure that functions to connect various media, her name the 'glue' that unites disparate textual occasions into one long event of authorship. Here we rely on a conception of the author that is still founded on the idea of a continuity of self – that despite the ups and downs of her career, despite the various expressive formats, underneath it all she is still the same Jane Campion. On the other hand, in working across a range of media, in exploring different creative methods and expressive genres we can also view Campion's self as multivalent and post-auteurist in nature, her authorship characterized by processes of periodic self-renewal and formed from various experiences of inter-subjectivity (both with others but also in encounters with previous and current versions of her 'self'). The next mode of auteurism popularized by the media in relation to Campion is particularly concerned with one specific type of creative collaboration that has overshadowed commentary about her.

## THE ACTOR'S DIRECTOR

One of the most consistent and predominant themes in reportage about Campion is the idea that she is an 'actor's director' (see Figure 1.7).

While Campion has spoken at length on her approach to directing actors, it is the remarkable flattery returned by actors themselves that is notable. The list of actors eager to go on the record singing her praises adds weight to the idea that Campion is an auteur with a particular skill in directing actors. This is further emphasized in 'making of' documentaries such as *Portrait: Jane Campion and the Portrait of a Lady* (Long and Ellis 1996) and *The Audition* (1990), a short film directed by her sister Anna featuring Campion as she auditions her mother Edith for a role in *Angel*. That her mother was once a high-profile stage actor and her father an eminent theatre director in New Zealand adds layers of credence to these stories. There is an inordinate amount of interest in media interviews with Campion on the psychology of dealing with actors, which is understood as both a technical skill in plotting motivation and blocking scenes as well as a 'people' skill – in bringing out the best in performances in those who appear in her films.[108]

Sam Neill, reflecting on his working relationship with Campion on *The Piano*, describes her capacity to be both caring and uncompromising:

FIGURE 1.7 Jane Campion directs Meg Ryan and Mark Ruffalo in *In the Cut*
Screen Gems/Pathé/The Kobal Collection/Bridges, James

Jane works in an unusually intimate way with people. When you're an actor, you're always putting yourself in other people's hands anyway, and she repays the gesture many times over. Jane's interested in complexity, not reductiveness, and she's very sure of what she's doing. If you have an opinion contrary to hers, she listens with the greatest care and consideration, then does what she had in mind all along.[109]

Genevieve Lemon (*Sweetie* and *The Piano*) describes a different process but is equally approving:

She digs deep when she's working with an actor, and that can be pretty confronting. She's always saying, 'Strip, strip, give me less acting', and you try to give her exactly what she wants because her instincts are so sound. Most of the time with a director you think, 'Stop! What's going on here? Where am I going?' But you trust Jane absolutely.[110]

The idea of 'stripping' is in part about producing a kind of naked authenticity from the actors and operates both metaphorically and literally in consideration of the many infamous nude scenes in Campion's films. According to one newspaper report, Jane Campion agreed to direct an explicit sex scene in *In the Cut* without clothes on, in order to make the actors more comfortable (an offer which was not taken up by them).[111] For the media, this event can also be read as reiterating Campion's willingness to present herself as an unimpeded, completely transparent auteur, evoking not just a trust with the actors but with the audience as well.

Trust is also an important element in Kerry Fox's time with Campion on *An Angel at My Table*:

I think she's a very rare and precious director. She would do anything within her – considerable – power to get the best performance. She believes all actors will give a good performance if she allows them to. She was always allowing the actors to do that, by giving us a sense of trust. Jane gave me the ability to believe in my own working methods, absolutely.[112]

But probably the most vehemently defensive actor associated with Campion is Harvey Keitel, who declares in both certain and poetic terms that: 'Jane Campion is a goddess, and it is difficult for a mere mortal to talk about a goddess. I fear being struck by lightening bolts . . .What's unusual about her has to do with ethereal things. She is at play, like a warm breeze.'[113] Keitel refers here to another theme in the presentation of auteurs – that they operate on a universal (transnational) scale above the sort of petty concerns that might occupy 'mere mortals'; that they are in a sense, celestial. Kenneth Turan of the *Los Angeles Times* notes Campion's dual abilities – to be both a star maker as well as being a star herself: '[T]hough Campion is inevitably no less than the co-star of her movies, she also can, as she did with Holly Hunter in *The Piano*, coax the performance of a lifetime out of actors.'[114]

In referring to Campion as an actor's director, the media make a distinction between this aspect of her auteurism and previous associations made between directors and stars which informs much classical auteurist criticism. The work of Victor Perkins, Jim Kitses and John Baxter has at different times developed the idea that a 'fit' between a particular star's image and an auteur's directorial pattern contributes further meaning to their *oeuvre*. Possibly Jane Campion's repeat association with the prosaic masculinity of Harvey Keitel in both *The Piano* and *Holy Smoke* could be construed in this way and certainly this relationship has produced copious media commentary, both favourable and negative. But it is Campion's casting of new lead actors from film to film that distinguishes her from this idea. Instead, her successful professional relationships with a succession of actors suggests to media commentators that this is a distinctive feature of her own auteur abilities, emphasizing her capacity to inspire her 'personal' vision in a multitude of others, and to satisfy both expectations for continuity (strong lead performances) and the demand for originality (new actors for each project) in the auteur's practice.

## TERTIARY CIRCULATION

Much of the media discussion of Campion presented in this chapter constitutes what is known in the promotion of film stars as 'secondary circulation' – the way in which, in this case, the auteur, participates in media other than that which she has produced, such as TV chat shows, newspaper and magazine interviews and so on. But Campion has also been treated, especially in Australia and New Zealand, to a form of 'tertiary circulation' in which the media report on how the media are reporting on Campion. Media navel gazing can be found in reviews of Campion's movies as well as festival reports and interviews. It is truly remarkable just how many media reviews and interviews about Campion begin with a reference to a previous media report or alternative critical position.

In many media accounts, Campion's films, and sometimes her career, are a cynosure around which a variety of interpretive stances are distinguished. Prominent Australian critic David Stratton spends much of his review of In the Cut trying to unravel what other critics thought of the film (that it is a radical departure from the period romantic entanglements of The Piano and Portrait; or that Campion is attempting to go mainstream, making a genre thriller about a serial killer to reap box office rewards):

> Some of the negative critical reaction I've read thus far about In the Cut has been mystifying to me; it's certainly a confronting film, and few films have been as intense and electrifying as this. I think it's Campion's masterpiece.[115]

While film critics will often point to previous reviews of a film as a way of defining their own position within a critical context (a form of 'paper tiger' criticism), in the case of Jane Campion it would seem that many critics have, over the years, felt compelled directly to address Campion's own position in a critical context, for example as a figure who has been subject to a substantial amount of negative criticism since The Piano. A lengthy 'review of the reviews' for In the Cut took the release of the film as an opportunity to address Campion's attitudes to negative appraisal of her work. The uncredited journalist asserts that Campion's 'high-profile supporters blamed such criticism on ignorance and the tall-poppy syndrome'. Instead, they find that Campion's responses to reviews of her work have given her a reputation as a 'filmmaker who can't take criticism'. Campion, contrariwise, is quoted at length describing her vision of ideal film criticism, one that draws reference to the flowering of auteurist writing:

> When the critical community have taken responsibility to elevate cinema, like when Truffaut was writing about film in France, they really changed cinema, really elevated the craft and the art, because they encouraged and rewarded filmmakers for doing this interesting work. We've got amazing people here who can make our country a better home for independent filmmaking, than say, America is. Everyone's work can be discussed, and I accept that. I never feel above criticism, I always feel there's a lot to criticize in my work.[116]

Entertainment journalist, Sue Williams, has also contributed to the idea that Campion cannot take criticism and opens her article on the critical response to Holy Smoke by reporting on an encounter with Campion in which the filmmaker rebukes her for writing about the lukewarm response to the film. Later, during a formal interview Campion continued to challenge Williams:

> Actually I've had some of the best reaction I've ever had to a movie. That's been from film critics who've been excited because they've said it's, for them, one of my best movies . . . It's a very provocative piece and I think I'm aiming at myself, so not everybody's going to understand it the same way. But I'm speaking for myself, just as I think and, you know, truly feel. That is the challenge for film-makers when they are working in that manner because very often it's absolutely impossible not to have people who don't understand what you are going to do. You're going to take the risk of newspapers saying it was a big flop or there was divided opinion.

But that's not how it exists. The challenge is to get your film to your audience who are looking to see films that challenge them and excite them and they find fun. So, there you have it.[117]

Williams reduces Campion's lengthy explanation to a pithy summary: Campion believes her film is a success and 'Anyone who feels differently simply doesn't understand the movie.' It would, instead, also be possible to see Campion as expressing something of the difficulty of balancing standardized expectations (in this case, expressed as the production and distribution of films made in the name of an author; 'to get *your* films to *your* audience') with the simultaneous expectation of novelty (defining her audience as one that is 'looking to see films that challenge and excite them'). Campion reiterated this difficulty in another interview:

There's always going to be resistance to new ideas. I know I'm not Picasso but if you took 200 people into Picasso's new show, 150 of them would wander out and say "What was that? It sucks." If that's what ruled the world, we'd never have any new work.[118]

But all is not lost. Predictably, Williams concludes her article by recovering Campion as an uncompromising auteur:

It's in Campion's nature, in any case, never to shy away from controversy . . . Whatever the reaction to her work, however much criticism she may end up forced to bear, no-one could ever criticise her for not being bold and brave in her choice of movies.

Similarly, Lee Marshall recuperates Campion's propensity for controversy by invoking her auteurist 'single mindedness' which he says has not just one but two spin-offs:

First it means that her films give rise to some great arguments. Dinner parties have turned ugly over Campion . . . The second consequence of

> Campion's obsessive harping on the same themes is this: she is one of
> the very few modern directors whose films make us curious about the
> mind behind them.[119]

Campion, by way of contrast, has on many occasions tried to dissuade
interviewers from the idea that it is something about her own personality that gives rise to all this reaction. Fiona Morrow, interviewing
her about In the Cut begins with a typical reference to her capacity to
inspire controversy: 'The film, like most of Campion's work, has
divided the critics at festivals where it has shown. And, as usual, it's a
love it or loathe it deal. Campion doesn't peddle indifference.' Campion
quickly responds with: 'I don't know why I inspire such strong
reactions. I don't walk around as a person creating such a furore – and
you'd think that might be what's going on.'[120] In another interview,
she places the onus for divisiveness back onto critics and audiences
themselves reminding the journalist that 'people are reactive to strong
work.'[121]

The net effect of all this reviewing of reviewers is to establish
Campion as a figure who inspires passionate and often polarized
debate, a description enhanced by newspaper headlines such as: 'If it's
Campion, think again: Holy Smoke, the latest in director's provocative
film treatises, twists romance and religion' or 'Erotic thriller has censors
watching the director's cuts: Jane Campion's latest film has divided the
critics'.[122] It's part of a broad redefinition of auteurs, away from the idea
that their films enter the canon because there is general agreement of
their quality among connoisseurs (critics, industry figures, academics
and so on), to the idea that it is their notoriety that counts. Filmmakers,
like Campion, whose work generates the greatest heat, who chew up
the most column centimetres, are the new auteurs. A filmmaker's
enduring status is no longer measured by the specific qualities of their
films per se but the intensity and diversity of interpretation they
produce.

## CONCLUSION

Historicizing the figure of the auteur is not just about presenting a history of her reception (good and/or bad). It is also about the history of the construction and continuous reconstruction of the author herself, a conception of agency in which the filmmaker also participates, typically through media interviews, promotional opportunities, infotainment outlets (such as commentary tracks on DVDs or celebrity documentary profiles).

Auteurist observers of the film industry's relationship to the media are often suspicious of what they perceive to be an essentially parasitic relationship in which the media, especially television, 'freeloads' off an original, authentic source – the cinema – represented by the figure of the director. Industry commentator, Neal Gabler, takes this a step further, describing an ever growing culture of 'knowingness' among film audiences in which their apparently increasing level of interest in film celebrities (including directors) is seen as inversely proportional to their interest in the films themselves:

> In this culture, the intrinsic value of a movie, or of most conventional entertainments, has diminished. Their job now is essentially to provide stars for *People*, *Us*, 'Entertainment tonight' and the supermarket tabloids, which exhibit the new 'movies' – the stars' life sagas . . . There may have been a time when these stories generated publicity for the movies. Now, however, the movies are more likely to generate publicity for the stories, which have a life, and an entertainment value, of their own.[123]

Although Gabler provides no evidence to support his assumption that celebrity promotion is at the cost of movies themselves his observation that the image of stars and other movie personnel are equally vital to media sales is important and is suggestive of their instrumental role as 'transmediators'. Indeed, from an industry vantage there are significant benefits for film studios and their publicists to work with media outlets, deliberately providing free publicity about stars to maintain their currency for audiences and to promote specific films. The way in which the promoters of the film *Borat* (Charles, 2006) were able to successfully use the video-sharing website YouTube to generate advance publicity or 'web buzz' of that film's release is a good working example of the reciprocal, intertwining relationship between the media, including new media, and the movies. High-profile film directors such as Jane Campion, also provide a crucial link within and between these industries, connecting various types of media promotion (their endorsement activities moving seamlessly between electronic and print-based media for example) as well as playing a major role in mediating various film industry configurations (art, independent, national and commercial industries), as the next chapter explores.

## NOTES

1 Janet Malcolm, *The Journalist and the Murderer*, London: Granta, 2004, p. 32.

2 Fiona Morrow, 'Jane Campion: the director's cut', *The Independent*, 17 October, 2003, http://www.independent.co.uk/arts-entertainment/film-and-tv/features/jane-campion-the-directors-cut-583580.html?service=Print.

3 Janet Staiger, 'Authorship approaches', in David A. Gerstner and Janet Staiger (eds), *Authorship and Film*, New York: Routledge, 2003, pp. 49–52.

4 Judith Lewis, 'Wholly Jane', *LA Weekly*, 19 January, 2000, http://www.laweekly.com/ink/09/film-lewis.shtml. Here Campion echoes Janet Malcolm's observations of what happens in media encounters: 'One would think that extreme wariness and caution would be the order of the day, but in fact childish trust and impetuosity are far more common' (Malcolm, p. 32).

5 Lewis, 'Wholly Jane'.

6 Virginia Wright Wexman (ed.), *Jane Campion: Interviews*, Jackson: University Press of Mississippi, 1999, p. 14.

7 Michael Budd, 'Authorship as commodity: the art cinema and *The Cabinet of Dr Caligari*', *Wide Angle* 6, no. 1, 1984, p.16.

8 Budd, 'Authorship as commodity: the art cinema and *The Cabinet of Dr Caligari*', p. 19.

9    For a detailed account of German media accounts of Jane Campion's films, see Stan Jones, 'Ecstasies in the mossy land: New Zealand film in Germany', in Deb Verhoeven (ed.) *Twin Peaks: Australian and New Zealand Feature Films*, Melbourne: Damned Publishing, 1999, pp. 151–70.

10   Phillip Adams, 'The subtlety of the subtext', *The Weekend Australian Magazine*, 18 January 1986, p. 11.

11   Freda Freiberg, 'The bizarre in the banal: notes on the films of Jane Campion', in Annette Blonski, Barbara Creed and Freda Freiberg (eds), *Don't Shoot Darling: Women's Independent Film Making in Australia*, Richmond, VIC: Greenhouse, 1987, p. 328.

12   In The Bulletin, 2 January 1988, cited in Meredith Quinn and Andrew L. Urban (eds), *Edge of the Known World: The Australian Film Television and Radio School. Impressions of the First 25 Years*, Sydney: AFTRS, 1998, p. 136.

13   See the editors' 'Introductory notes' on textual analysis, in Blonski, Creed and Freiberg (eds), *Don't Shoot Darling*, p. 279.

14   Thomas Elsaesser, 'Putting on a Show: The European art movie', *Sight and Sound*, vol. 4, no. 4, April 1994, pp. 22–7.

15   Adrian Martin, 'Losing the way: the decline of Jane Campion', *Landfall*, vol. 200, no. 2, 2000, p. 101.

16   Adrian Martin, 'Master or myth?' *The Age – A3*, 13 November, 2003, p. 6.

17   Todd McCarthy, '*In the cut*', *Variety*, 15 September 2003, vol. 392, no. 5, p. 24.

18   Lynden Barber 'Angel with an eccentric eye', *Sydney Morning Herald*, 8 September 1990, p. 75.

19   Mark Chalon Smith, 'A disturbing but uplifting *Angel at My Table*', *Los Angeles Times (Part F)*, 7 May 1992, p. 2.

20   Jonathan Rosenbaum to Jim Jarmusch in Jonathan Rosenbaum, *Dead Man*, London: British Film Institute, 2000, p. 84.

21   Katherine Tulich, 'The big screen', *Sydney Morning Herald*, 20 September 1990, p. 31.

22   Jane Campion speaking on the director's soundtrack, *An Angel at My Table: Criterion Collection DVD* (1990).

23   Gary Maddox, 'For film-maker Campion, it's a wrap – for now', *Sydney Morning Herald*, 7 November 2003, p. 3.

24   Campion interviewed by Steve Weinstein, 'Critics: now she's a Sweetie', *San Francisco Examiner-Chronicle*, 23 June 1991, p. 28.

25   Weinstein, 'Critics: now she's a Sweetie', p. 28.

26   David Stratton, '*An Angel at My Table*' (Review), *Variety*, 20 June 1990, p. 32.

27   Vincent Canby, 'In the end literature conquers all', *New York Times*, 4 October 1990, p. C26.

28   Georgina Brown, 'Down under and dirty', *Village Voice*, 21 May 1991, p. 58.

29   Stanley Kaffman, 'A passion in the desert', *The New Republic*, 7 February, 2000, p. 26.

30   Andrew Urban, 'The contradictions of Jane Campion, Cannes winner', *The Australian*, 21 May 1986, republished in Wexman, p. 15.

31   Hunter Cordaiy, 'Jane Campion interviewed by Hunter Cordaiy', *Cinema Papers*, no. 81, 1990, p. 36.

32   Jane Campion, *The Piano*, New York: Hyperion, 1993, p. 115.

33   Wexman, *Jane Campion: Interviews*, p. 36.

34   Wexman, *Jane Campion: Interviews*, p. 85.

35   For an elaboration, see Alisa Perren, 'Sex, lies and marketing: Miramax and the development of the quality indie blockbuster', *Film Quarterly*, vol. 55, no. 2, Winter 2001/2002, pp. 30–39.

36   Jonathan Rosenbaum, 'Sexual discourse (The Piano)', originally published in *Chicago Reader*, 10 December 1993, reprinted in Jonathan Rosenbaum, *Movies as Politics*, Berkeley: University of California Press, 1997, pp. 140–44 and 'The Portrait of a Lady', *Chicago Reader*, http://onfilm.chicagoreader.com/movies/capsules/14935_portrait_of_a_lady.

37   McCarthy, 'In the cut', p. 24.

38   Parkinson, BBC One, aired on Saturday 25 October at 10.25 pm.

39   Stephen Applebaum, 'Great expectations: Kate Winslet on *Holy Smoke*, gurus and peeing in public', *Empire Online*, 30 March, 2000, www.empireonline.com/interviews/interview.asp?IID=136.

40   Anne Demy-Geroe, 'What if she'd been a boy?', *Courier Mail*, 10 July, 1999, p. 9.

41   Wendy Ide, 'In the cut', *Times Online*, 24 October 24 2003, http://entertainment.timesonline.co.uk/tol/arts_and_entertainment/article100 3925.ece?print=yes&randnum=1212030127568.

42   Wendy Ide, '*In the cut*'.

43   Stephanie Bunbury, 'Cutting in on Campion', *The Sunday Age* (Agenda), 16 November, p. 18.

44   Walter Chaw, 'Kevin Bacon is very visible these days', *Film Freak Central*, http://filmfreakcentral.net/notes/kbaconinterview.htm.

45   Kate Winslet in 'Great expectations: Kate Winslet on *Holy Smoke*, gurus and peeing in public', *Empire Online*, 30 March, 2000, www.empireonline. com/interviews/interview.asp?IID=136.

46   Libby Brooks, 'Let's talk about sex', *The Guardian*, 10 October 2003, p. 8.

47   Michel Ciment, 'Jane Campion and *Positif*', Part II in Raffaele Caputo and Geoff Burton (eds), *Second Take, Australian Film-makers Talk*, St Leonards, NSW: Allen & Unwin, 1999, p. 52.

48   Ciment, 'Jane Campion and *Positif*', p. 79.

49   Ciment, 'Jane Campion and *Positif*', p. 60.

50   Tulich, 'The big screen', p. 31.

51   Anthony Quinn, 'Lady Jane's bloody reign', *Sydney Morning Herald* (47 hours), 25 October 2003, p. 1.

52   Mary Cantwell, 'Jane Campion's lunatic women', *New York Times*, 19 September 1993, p. 51.

53   David Konow, 'Rough cut: Jane Campion and Susanna Moore on *In the Cut*', *Creative Screenwriting*, vol. 10, no. 5, 2003, p. 72.

54   Lizzie Franke, 'Jane Campion is called the best female director in the world. What's female got to do with it?', *The Guardian*, 21 February 1997, p. 4.

55   Claire Sutherland, 'Jane Campion considered directing her latest film naked', *Herald Sun*, 13 November 2003, p. 5.

56   Quinn, 'Lady Jane's bloody reign', p. 8.

57   Quinn, 'Lady Jane's bloody reign', p. 1.

58   Mick Brown, 'Where there's smoke', *Courier Mail Weekend Arts*, 11 September 1999, p. 11.

59   Jane Campion in *Portrait: Jane Campion and the Portrait of a Lady* (Long and Ellis, 1996).

60   Dana Polan, *Jane Campion*, London: British Film Institute, 2001, p. 85.

61   Angie Errigo, 'Jane Campion: Antipodean director', *Empire*, no. 53, 1993, p. 63.

62   Howard Feinstein, 'The Jane mutiny', *Guardian Unlimited*, 2 April 1999, http://film.guardian.co.uk/Feature_Story/Guardian/0,,39226,00.html #article_continue.

63 Sallie Munt, *Heroic Desire: Lesbian Identity and Cultural Space*, New York: New York University Press, 1998, p. 2.

64 Ciment, 'Jane Campion and *Positif*', pp. 54–6, on *Sweetie*.

65 Cordaiy, 'Jane Campion interviewed by Hunter Cordaiy', p. 34.

66 Cantwell, 'Jane Campion's lunatic women', p. 51.

67 *Portrait: Jane Campion and the Portrait of a Lady* (Long and Ellis, 1996).

68 Joy Press, 'Making the cut', *Village Voice*, 21 October 2003.

69 Jane Campion, 'Directors speak: *In the Cut*', *InsideFilm*, no. 60, November 2003, p. 15.

70 Lewis, 'Wholly Jane', *LA Weekly*, 19 January 2000, http://www.laweekly.com/ink/09/film-lewis.shtml.

71 Press, 'Making the cut'.

72 Ciment, 'Jane Campion and *Positif*', p. 67.

73 Ciment, 'Jane Campion and *Positif*', p. 79.

74 Konow, 'Rough cut, Jane Campion and Susanne Moore on *In the Cut*', p. 72.

75 Jane Campion, 'Big shell', *Rolling Stone*, no. 426, 1988, pp. 74–6.

76 Jane Campion, 'In search of Janet Frame', *Guardian*, 19 January 2008. Available at http://books.guardian.co.uk/print/0,,332118204–999 30,00.html.

77 Michael Medved writing in the *New York Post* and quoted in John Evan Frook, '*Piano* defenders blast Medved', *Chicago Sun-Times*, 18 December 1993, Section 2, p. 24.

78 John Evan Frook, '*Piano* defenders blast Medved', *Chicago Sun-Times*, 18 December 1993, Section 2, p. 24.

79 Joseph Gelmis, *The Film Director as Superstar*, Harmondsworth: Pelican, 1974, p. 13. Gerald Mast, concluding his *A Short History of the Movies*, also notes that the American director has become one of the film's stars and finds, as a result, an explanation for a decreasing influence of movie actors on the greenlighting of projects: Gerald Mast, *A Short History of the Movies*, Indianapolis: Bobbs-Merrill, 1981, p. 424.

80 Gelmis, *The Film Director as Superstar*, p. 16.

81 Gelmis, *The Film Director as Superstar*, p. 14.

82 Timothy Corrigan, *A Cinema without Walls: Movies and Culture after Vietnam*, New Brunswick: Rutgers University Press, 1991, p. 105.

83   Richard Dyer, *Stars*, London: BFI Publishing, p. 70

84   Michel Chion, *David Lynch* (trans. Robert Julian), London: British Film Institute, 1995, p. 94.

85   William D. Routt, 'Lois Weber, or the exigency of writing', *Screening the Past*, no. 12, 2001, http://www.latrobe.edu.au/www/screeningthepast/firstrelease/fr0301/wr1fr12a.html.

86   Brown, 'Where there's smoke', p. 11.

87   See Joan Dupont, 'The Cannes festival: Jane Campion, on drought and isolation', *International Herald Tribune*, 31 May 2006, http://www.iht.com/articles/2006/05/26/news/dupont.php.

88   Morrow, 'Jane Campion: the director's cut'.

89   Wexman, Jane Campion: Interviews, p. 61.

90   Cordaiy, 'Jane Campion interviewed by Hunter Cordaiy', p. 35.

91   David Callahan, 'Review of Jane Campion: interviews', *Journal of Popular Film and Television*, vol. 31, no. 4, p. 188; and Gail Jones, *The Piano*, Sydney: Currency Press, 2007, p. 10.

92   Kim Langley, 'Dark talent', *Vogue Australia*, April 1993, p. 140.

93   Philippa Hawker, 'A tale of friendships . . . a few little surprises', *The Age Green Guide*, 24 April 1986, p. 9.

94   Quinn, 'Lady Jane's bloody reign', p. 1.

95   Helen Barlow, 'A cut above', *The Age* (EG), 7 November 2003, p. 3.

96   Martin A. Grove, 'Novel reading decline not good for Hollywood', *Hollywood Reporter*, 4 August 2004, hollywoodreporter.com.

97   Jones, L. *'The Portrait of a Lady': The Screenplay based on the Novel by Henry James*, London: Penguin, 1996, p. x.

98   Hillary Frey, 'The purloined piano?', *Lingua Franca*, vol. 10, no. 6, September 2000. http://linguafranca.mirror.theinfo.org/print/0009/field-piano.html.

99   Jesse Green 'That was no "lady": pilfering literature', *New York Times*, 11 May 1997, http://query.nytimes.com/gst/fullpage.html?res=9C0CE7DE1130F932A25756C0A961958260&sec=&spon=&pagewanted=print.

100  Green, 'That was no "lady": pilfering literature'.

101  Kaufman, 'A passion in the desert', p. 26.

102  Lee Marshall, 'What Jane Campion did next', *The Independent*, 22 September 1996.

103  Ellen Cheshire, *Jane Campion: The Pocket Essential Guide*, London: Harpenden, 2000, p. 52.

104  *Portrait: Jane Campion and the Portrait of a Lady* (Long and Ellis, 1996).

105  Polan, *Jane Campion*, p. 161

106  Michele Field, 'The *Piano* becomes an industry', *The Canberra Times*, 30 April 1994, p. C8.

107  Field, 'The *Piano* becomes an industry', p. C8. Similarly, scholar and writer Gail Jones describes the book as 'dull, tonally flat and without the enigma of muteness and patrimony that lends inquisitiveness pleasure to a viewing of the film'. Paradoxically, the book's revelations draw attention to the 'virtuosity of the film', in particular to its 'reliance on the rhetoric of the image, rather than explanation, and the centrality of the soundtrack in constructing an idiosyncratic emotional dimension'. Gail Jones, *The Piano*, Sydney: Currency Press, 2007, p. 11.

108  A very detailed on article on Jane Campion's method of directing actors (including her 'top ten tips') is Sheila Johnston, 'Peter Weir/Jane Campion: directors cut to the chase', *The Independent*, 9 July 2004, pp. 2–4.

109  Cantwell, 'Jane Campion's lunatic women', p. 51.

110  Cantwell, 'Jane Campion's lunatic women', p. 51.

111  Sutherland, 'Jane Campion considered directing her latest film naked', p. 5.

112  *An Angel at My Table*, Sharmill Distributors (press kit).

113  Keitel in Cantwell, 'Jane Campion's lunatic women', p. 51.

114  Kenneth Turan, 'The Portrait of a Lady: Campion paints bold "portrait"', *Los Angeles Times*, 24 December 1996, http://www.calendarlive.com/movies/reviews/cl-movie961224–2,0,4433274.story.

115  David Stratton, 'Campion cuts to the heart and soul', *Weekend Australian – Review*, 15 November 2003, p. 18.

116  No author or title, *Canberra Times*, 15 November 2003, p. 6.

117  Sue Williams, 'An unholy mess: Jane Campion is fighting against the poor reception to her new movie', *Sun-Herald*, 12 September 1999, p. 11.

118  Gary Maddox, 'Campion fired up at "career crisis" jibes', *Sydney Morning Herald*, 10 September 1999, p. 2.

119  Lee Marshall, 'Mystery Jane', *Independent on Sunday*, 9 February 1997, p. 4.

120  Morrow, 'Jane Campion: the director's cut'.

121   No author or title, *Canberra Times*, 15 November, 2003, p. 6.

122   Eric Harrison, 'If it's Campion, think again: *Holy Smoke* the latest in director's provocative film treatises, twists romance and religion', *LA Times*, 3 December 1999, p. F2. Christina Cremen, 'Erotic thriller has censors watching the director's cuts: Jane Campion's latest film has divided the critics', *The Australian*, 11 September 2003, p. 11.

123   Neal Gabler, 'The Oscars: Hollywood's fade to black', *Los Angeles Times* (Part M), 25 February 2007, p. 1.

# 2

---

# REALIZING JANE CAMPION

## The industry, politics and economics
## of contemporary auteurism

> She was in neither a state of innocence nor a state of grace . . . She was
> like a piano in a country where everyone has had their hands cut off.
>
> Angela Carter[1]

Jane Campion's father, Richard, visiting the set of *Holy Smoke*, recounts
a conversation he once had with his daughter when she was 5 years
old:

> I was doing the parental thing about what she might want to do later on.
> She looked up at me with those big blue eyes and her golden hair and
> said, 'Dad, I am my own self!' And that's been the basic thing in her work.
> Her first film *Peel*, was about a father telling his son to get out of the car
> and pick up an orange peel. That's what *Holy Smoke* is about: all in the
> family lean on this girl, but she finds her own way.[2]

In this one brief anecdote, Richard Campion reiterates many of the
ways in which (even embryonic) auteurs are imagined; as preordained,
prone to expressive repetition, on a singular course and, above all else,
completely self-possessed and resistant to external (parental) influence;

influences that for an adult auteur are more likely to take the form of a perceived political, economic and industrial paternalism.

The persistent image of the auteur as someone unsullied by, or at loggerheads with, the concerns of industry or economics is increasingly difficult to sustain in the contemporary moment (if it ever could be sustained). As Justin Wyatt suggests 'economics influences every step in the life cycle of film'.[3] Wyatt is not simply referring to the distribution of films in the marketplace, 'but also at the level of the individual filmmaker, textually through style and collective works, and even in the construction of the author as a social subject'.[4] A detailed examination of Jane Campion's career would seem to support this observation.

In Campion's case, there have been any number of industry influences on the course of her career: the availability of subsidized film training in Australia; government-supported short film funding and distribution; policy initiatives designed to support first-time feature directors; political attention to the rates of participation of women in the film industry; the growth of the global film festival circuit; changes in the financing and distribution of international art films (the rise of CIBY 2000 and Miramax as well as Canal Plus); the development of an institutionalized, studio-supported 'indie' circuit in the US (such as Disney's acquisition of Miramax, which occurred just prior to the release of The Piano and which coincided with other big studios opening their own specialized offshoots, like Sony Pictures Classics and New Line Cinemas, Fine Line Pictures), to name but a few.

Taking film industry politics and economics into our consideration of a director's career does not necessarily suggest that the auteur's agency has been paralysed, that they are the puppets of unseen hands or that they are operating under the false belief of their own independence. What it does enable is a revised set of questions to be proposed. Rather than worrying about what role economics plays in the establishment of the filmmaker as an auteur, we might conversely wonder what precisely constitutes the 'independence' of the auteur as an element distinct from the rest of the cinema business. For directors like Campion, who find themselves working within and between national film industries, we might also ask: Are there discernible 'Australian' or 'New Zealand' modes of production that can be analysed in terms of how the director's 'authority' or agency is specifically established and practised in those industries? How might these intersect with global film financing and distribution systems to mobilize new authorial practices and discourses and new conceptions of 'national' film industries?

## THE GEOPOLITICS OF JANE CAMPION

For David Bordwell and Steve Neale, the post-war development of (European) national 'art' cinemas as an industrial alternative to mainstream Hollywood was instrumental in establishing both the auteur's institutional and textual value.[5] Neale observes that the auteur's principle role was as a 'brand name', 'a means of labelling and selling a film and of orienting expectations and channelling meaning and pleasure in the absence of generic boundaries and categories.'[6] In other words, auteurism is a mechanism for categorizing otherwise highly differentiated film texts, a feat achieved through recognition of a series of textual strategies deployed by the auteur and identified by Bordwell as a heightened sense of realism, stylistic signatures, the loosening of cause and effect in the narrative and ambiguity. This emphasis on the taxonomic role of the auteur stresses their systemic, cohering function, at the same signalling the value of textual ambiguity and formal distinctiveness. This version of the auteur, however, diminishes the contributions of filmmakers whose corpus is less organizationally coherent.

As a classificatory system, auteurism is historically linked by Neale to national cinema but, as the case of Jane Campion shows, auteurism is also subject to processes of globalization. The frequent expectation for international distribution and co-financing and for the translatability of globalized art films also expands the spaces occupied by the auteur. As Catherine Grant asks: '[H]ow might auteurism continue to adapt itself to the processes of "globalisation", namely the apparent "deterritorialisation" of some forms of cultural production and the elaboration of new transnational systems of distribution with their accompanying fragmentation of mass markets and the targeting of particular audience segments?'[7] More specifically, we might ask how the establishment of Campion's credentials as an auteur contributed to the production and distribution of The Piano, for example, as a contemporary globalized 'popular art film' or to In the Cut as a 'specialized genre film'. And, conversely, how the political–industrial context of Campion's cinema has become realized and dramatized as part of the fabric of her auteurism. How has the global success of The Piano or the dismal financial performance of Holy Smoke, for instance, altered and marked out the terms by which Campion's own 'currency' is evaluated?

So, rather than establishing film industry politics and economics as the setting or background for auteurist practice, we might also consider how they contribute to and shed light on the ways in which the auteur is understood and measured. Earlier sections of this book have already discussed how discourses of consumption have negatively marked assessments of Campion's auteurism for some critics (both in terms of her approach to inter-textuality and in the idea that she is prone to 'inappropriate' acts of self-consumption rather than 'pure' production). And, more broadly, in the previous chapter, we looked at the media's presentation of Campion as an antagonist, in which various interviewers politicized her, underlining an element of protest prevalent in the auteur's image.

I want to make the case that the various geopolitical dimensions attributed to Jane Campion's auteurism would seem to occupy two broad spaces that frame the auteur's agency and which at various times overlap and operate with changeable degrees of intensity and complexity at different points in her career. These spaces describe the scope of Campion's contemporary authorship as both supplementary to and as exceeding the solitary orbit of the traditional auteur. The filmmaker is drawn into and emerges from these epistemic spaces, working as an 'auteur' within an ambit that is, in a sense, a loose elaboration of (but should not be confused with) the territorial terms of trade that organize the movement of films around the globe. So, instead of understanding the auteur as an isolate figure, related to broader cultural categories simply by virtue of aspects of their personal biography, such as birthplace in the case of the auteur's noted role in national cinema, it is possible to identify at least two other spaces in Campion's auteurism:

1. The 'endemic auteur' in which Campion's value is measured by her ability to realize cultural policy objectives but which also recognizes that her political or national 'originality', her ability to be claimed as 'home-grown' is subject to ambivalence since Campion is a New Zealander resident in Australia and has been the recipient of subsidized support from both governments (as well as other co-producing countries). With this in mind then, it is possible to see how the establishment of the categories 'Australasian' or 'Antipodean' filmmaker have been important to the way Campion is understood.[8] And here, too, her success in realizing projects through co-production agreements that operate on the plane of reciprocal political–cultural partnerships. Hence also the reliance on legal definitions of Campion's authorship at various times, as the matter of contracted expectations rather than the belief that the national origin of the author herself is explanation enough. This is the space of what we might call an international Australian or New Zealand cinema.

2. The 'dispersible auteur' in which Campion's 'globality' and 'nomadism' is emphasized. This is especially evident in the presentation of Campion's success in the European and US industries as a 'bankable outsider'. We can also see it in the way her auteurism acquires value in ancillary terms, revealing a supplementary impulse at the heart of the auteurist project and conceptualizing the auteur as an infinitely 'value-adding' proposition rather than proposing the individual artist as someone who is already and essentially universal in any prior sense. It might also incorporate the various ways in

which Campion's auteurism can itself 'cross over', appealing to and accommodating different, previously counter-posed approaches to the auteur. This is the space of the post-national auteur.

Both these descriptions of the auteur emphasize her movement through multiple geopolitical locations. The auteur does not occupy unattached terrain – she travels between texts, audiences, and institutions through spaces, networks and structures. These spaces offer an alternative way of thinking about the conceptual and professional possibilities of contemporary filmmaking by shifting politics, economics and industry from the position of background clutter to part of the text of the auteur herself. Furthermore, they explicitly understand the auteur as occupying multiple locations distinguished by differences in scale rather than the pure originating position of traditional auteurism. The endemic auteur is defined and evaluated in terms of contiguous locations (with emphasis on her origins, on 'where she's coming from' as a complex place made up of multiple sites). The dispersible auteur is in constant movement toward destinations never fully achieved (with emphasis on 'where she's going' as an uncertain calculation). In Campion's case, we can see the endemic operating when her authorship is legitimized by, or criticized for, her proximity to certain subjects or themes. In response to assertions about her 'female sensibility' and feminist politics, Campion has made rejoinders that emphasize the endemic; in which there is no unmediated causal relationship between her politics and her gender but where she recognizes that there are conceptual contiguities between them. The dispersible is apparent when her directorial prowess is argued in terms of her ability to work outside her comfort zone in a range of locations and genres or alternatively when she is corrected for being too (emotionally) distant. For example Campion confesses:

> For me New Zealand has all the complexity of home about it, whereas Australia has all of the possibilities of a brave new world. And I think I've flourished in Australia as an artist or filmmaker because of that. So I'm

very grateful for the Australian government for spending so much money on me . . . it was a great opportunity. In New Zealand there are also good opportunities but somehow it's frozen there by virtue of the smallness of the place. Everybody knows who you were. To my mind it doesn't have the same sense of new potential that Australia has. I feel this way because I grew up there. New Zealand has an attitude of keeping people in their place.[9]

She proposes on this occasion the value of the dispersible; that her auteurism is benefited by the 'potential' of the Australian film industry; and that it is stifled by the confined but complex social world of a New Zealand 'home' in which she does not reside. Similarly, in an earlier discussion of the endemic nature of the origins of *An Angel at My Table*, she simultaneously focuses on the global breadth of the film's concerns and appeal:

I hope people find it just part of humanity. Its origins are obviously New Zealand. It's Australian as much as I consider myself Australian; my home is Sydney. I think it's a human story and they belong to the whole world.[10]

Here Campion describes her expressivity as originating in endemic (culturally regional) terms, but she argues a global explanation for the destination of the film ('the whole world'). More broadly than these examples, in revealing the spaces of the auteur to be attached, rather than unattached, to be fundamentally *social* rather than solitary, we can begin to contemplate the auteur in ethical terms; as constantly engaged in negotiating issues of reciprocity, affinity, collaboration, belongingness and identity rather than simply seeing her as personally driven by the prospect of position, profit or political gain.

Much of the trans-Tasman rivalry over Campion's achievements (see Figure 0.2) is really about the value of retaining the idea of the 'originary' national auteur for cultural politics. In both Australia and New Zealand, this is most pronounced in the belief that the government-subsidized film industry's primary purpose is 'to tell our own stories'. The difficulty of sustaining the 'purity' of correspondences in these rationales – between birthplace, citizenship and representation – ensure that the Australian and New Zealand national cinemas are constantly engaged in a process of 'domesticating' contradiction and paradox.[11] Campion's auteurism, by way of contrast, particularly in terms of its national dimensions, is largely about the disavowal of the idea of 'chaste', unblemished origins in both her cinema and her practice as an auteur. The 'problem of origins' that is evident in competitive nationalist appreciations of Campion's auteurism opens her work to the possibilities of mediation. This can involve the recognition of the international dimensions of Australian or New Zealand cinema, the inter-textuality of Campion's sources or it might in turn suggest that Campion herself can draw political meaning to her self and to the terms of her rhetoricity as an auteur and not just to identifying her place in either the national or the global film industry.

On more than one occasion Jane Campion has assured interviewers she knows very little about, and has very little interest in the netherworld of film industry organization or politics. Despite these disclaimers, Campion has made numerous personal interventions into the political arena, putting pen to paper on several industry issues as well as social or community causes. In these instances, there would appear to be a mutual benefit in Campion's involvement. There is value in the recognizability of Campion's name and equally her involvement in these causes reinforces many precepts of her auteurism such as the idea that she acts from a position of uncompromising and passionate belief for example. More broadly, one of the effects of this activity is to underscore perceptions of Campion, in Australia at least, as an outspoken social and political agent such as when in December 2003, Campion took a high-profile stance against the Iraq war, headlining articles in which she exhorted Australians to attend peace rallies.[12] Or, for instance, her successful battle to maintain women-only bathing at a community swimming pool in 1995. In support of this cause, Campion was imputed, but not actually quoted, as saying that the archetypal Australian male was a 'lecherous creep who preyed on women sunbathers'.[13] Responses from outraged (mostly male) correspondents appeared in the media throughout the following weeks describing Campion herself as an archetypal example of contemporary feminism. Geoff Muirden, secretary of the Australian Civil Liberties Union, wrote:

> The news that feminist film director Jane Campion and others have won a fight to continue a bar on men at a public swimming pool is only another instance of the sexual discrimination practiced in Australia under the auspices of feminism.[14]

Under a photo of Campion titled 'Lechers go home: Jane Campion wants women-only pools', another correspondent noted:

> Once again the feminist movement has used rash generalizations to grab headlines . . . Australia in the 90s has two standards, one for the minority groups who are pandered to by the Government and the media, and one for the rest of us who only want a fair go at work and on the social issues that affect us all.[15]

Campion's feminism is understood as tied to observations of 'headline grabbing' (underlined one imagines by her celebrity) and 'narrowness' (underlined by the government support for her films and her focus on a single issue cause rather than 'social issues that affect us all'). The association of Campion with a separatist form of feminism persists despite her own misgivings about this political ascription, already confessing in the context of her filmmaking: 'I have to admit I no longer know what this means or expresses . . . This whole discussion is too limited. I am interested in life as a whole. Even if my representation of female characters has a feminist structure, this is nevertheless only one aspect of my approach.'[16] Instead, Campion argues for an understanding of her politics that goes beyond the screen and that her representational politics is multiple in nature.

The upshot of Campion's activism is to plainly paint her as a public figure, an auteur with a social as well as an artistic conscience. Her political pursuits fully position her, as an auteur, in the social world and not just as the outcome of a set of film texts. The extent to which Campion's public profile is seen to exceed and in turn affect her role as a filmmaker is evident in an item of newspaper correspondence titled 'Just as brutish' which compares *The Piano* with the Lorena Bobbit scandal (in which a woman severed her husband's penis) and concludes that feminism is responsible for both in 'showing us just how little time it took for women to become just as nasty and brutish and self-serving and violent as the men they condemn'.[17]

Campion's political candour, her participation in public campaigns also extends to the film industry and specifically to the role of the film director within it. In the course of her career, Campion has actively engaged in two explicit debates about 'authorship' and originality. The first, which directly concerns Campion herself, involves media and scholarly speculation about the relationship of Jane Mander's 1920 novel, *The Story of a New Zealand River* to Campion's film *The Piano*. The second more broadly involves Campion's support for a repositioning of the director in the legislative frameworks of the Australian film industry.

## STORIES OF A NEW ZEALAND PIANO

Some years after its release, a debate erupted over *The Piano* that was, curiously, almost entirely restricted to media located in New Zealand and the capital of Australia, Canberra. The debate centred on the difference between legal/industrial and prosaic definitions of provenance and attribution. Was *The Piano* 'based on' or 'inspired by' a book? The reason the debate became so heated is in large part because of what some saw as the implications for Campion's best original screenplay Oscar. If *The Piano* were 'based' on a book, then, they argued, it would be technically ineligible for this award (See Figure 2.1).[18]

The issue reached its apotheosis after the *Oxford Companion to Australian Film* published an entry on *The Piano*, which, controversially, included two scriptwriting listings, one crediting Campion, the other identifying the film as 'based on the novel *The Story of a New Zealand River* by Jane Mander; uncredited'. In the same year, 1999, Jane Mander's novel came out of copyright and was republished with the following sentence on the back cover: 'This is the most celebrated of Jane Mander's six novels and is believed by many to be the source of Jane Campion's film *The Piano*.'

FIGURE 2.1
**Oscar winner 1994**
Photo by Fotos
International/Getty
Images

The debate intensified with journalists and academics weighing in. Claims about *The Piano's* alternative origins were made on the basis of a checklist of similarities in broad plot points (a woman, her daughter, a piano, two men) with little or no account given to significant discrepancies especially in emotional tone. These similarities were in turn focused on the opening sections of the book only. All the emphasis on openings and 'origins' distracts from due consideration of the divergences in narrative conclusions and therefore underestimates the intervening work done by interpretation in mediating flows of intertextuality for instance. Instead, the debate echoes a key way in which national cinemas such as the Australian cinema formally measure their output. When the citizenship of the key creative team is not 'enough' then the film text itself is assessed for what are called 'on-screen indicators', the nationally identifiable aspects of the plot and setting. Campion's critics adopt a methodology that relies on the idea that there are tangible textual measures of creative 'originality' in the same way national film industries try and measure geopolitical 'originality' (and the way some auteurists reach for evidence of the filmmaker's signature) as the product of a crude accumulation of conspicuous textual objects.

Chief among Campion's critics was the crusading *Canberra Times* journalist, Robert Macklin:

> In my opinion, it is impossible to resist the view that consciously or otherwise, Jane Campion incorporated so many elements of the book that it could properly be described as published source material for *The Piano*. Accordingly, the film in my opinion is based on the book.[19]

In New Zealand, where Mander's novel was relatively well known, Campion was similarly questioned but she also received her most staunch support there, in which her foundational role in the New Zealand film industry was stressed:

> We should believe her and not allow her to become another victim of New Zealand's penchant for chopping the stems of its tall poppies . . .

> Campion has done much to alert the world to the possibilities of filmmaking in this country. *The Piano* is New Zealand's most acclaimed film and credited with kickstarting our now flourishing film industry.[20]

In the logic of this defence, Campion's 'originality' in relation to the New Zealand national cinema should not be questioned and therefore neither should the more specific originality of her script. Certainly *The Piano* initiated a wave of international interest in New Zealand cinema. Less than one year after its Oscars win the head of marketing at the New Zealand Film Commission, Lindsay Shelton, noted that *The Piano* showed how 'someone from New Zealand could make a huge amount of money in the United States'.[21] He then observes that Miramax's subsequent acquisition of New Zealand titles *Desperate Remedies* and *Heavenly Creatures* had caused other distributors to think that if they didn't do something: 'Miramax was going to take over everything.'[22] So other films became sought after property: *Once Were Warriors*, for example, promptly snapped up by New Line.

However, *The Piano's* relationship to the New Zealand film industry was slightly more complicated and not simply because of the cultural convolution of its financing (described by its own producers as a 'French-financed, New Zealand-based, Australian production of a New Zealand story'). For a short time, prior to *The Piano's* production, there existed another project directly based on Mander's novel. This proposed film, *The River*, had received some script assistance funding from the New Zealand government. Quite some time earlier, in 1985, its producers John Maynard (who later worked with Campion on *Sweetie* and *An Angel at My Table*) and Brigid Iken (*An Angel at My Table*) had offered it to Campion who declined on the basis that she was already working on *The Piano Lesson*, which eventually became *The Piano*, and which she says in correspondence with them was also inspired by Mander's book: 'The first thing I ended up working on was *The Piano Lesson*, my inspiration from Jane Mander's melodrama and you will see there is precious little of the original, but the inspiration was still there.'[23] Campion's letter then politely rejects their offer and asks if they might not instead be interested in her scenario which she is thinking of setting in Tasmania. Eventually, only the one project prevailed and Campion paid a small amount of money to the Mander estate as compensation for the redlighting of *The River*. This payment is the result of the relative size and progress of the two projects and the capacity of either national cinema to support more than one period drama at any given time. For her critics the compensation paid to the Mander estate firmly indicates that Campion 'owed' her authorship to the novelist. [24] At best it could be argued that it is an admission of the similarities of the two prospective films (rather than the similarity of *The Piano* to Mander's novel).

Ultimately, Campion herself wrote a letter to Wellington's *Dominion* in which she defended herself against what she described as 'imputations which were defamatory to me, including the accusation that I copied someone else's work, that I may be forced to relinquish my Oscar and that I am involved in a scandal'. [25] As far as Campion is concerned: 'The debate about the copying of Jane Mander's book hits a reef when it comes up against fact and copyright law. I am distressed that uninformed speculation continues in the press.' In contrast, Campion summarizes the legal view of the matter in a series of bullet points:

- Our client's (Jane Campion) script is an original work.
- Our client was aware of Jane Mander's book.
- Any issues concerning the book were dealt with years ago, prior to the production of the film and as part of the ordinary process of reviewing and confirming copyright chain of title prior to the financing of the film.
- As part of this process, nine years ago, the book, the final screenplay, story outlines and other materials were subject to a comprehensive expert legal opinion by Queen's Counsel who concluded very clearly that there was no foundation for any suggestion of copyright infringement and that any similarities were superficial.

- Importantly, the legal agent of the owner of copyright in the Mander book confirmed in writing that it had no claims of any kind in connection with the book or our client's screenplay or film.[26]

Campion notes that some small good may have come out of the discussion in that Jane Mander and her book will be known to a greater New Zealand public, who may be encouraged to read it (and one presumes therefore to establish its difference from her film).

The feature of Campion's detailed response that is the most interesting is that it was published in a New Zealand media outlet when her complaints are made against two Australian publications – *The Canberra Times* and the *Oxford Companion to Australian Film*. And that in her defence, Campion directly appeals to a kind of cultural nationalism, pointing out that there has been an implicit slur against New Zealand in the debate:

I put a great deal of creative effort over many years into this work, as did many fine creative people. The awards that the film has received are a credit to us all as well as to New Zealand. The continuing uninformed speculation undermines the efforts of everyone involved.[27]

What Campion seems to be aiming for in this description of *The Piano* is a sense of multiple authorship and collective cultural ownership rather than the idea that there can only be one authoritative source and that the benefits, the 'credits' can only flow in one direction, back to that singular source, the filmmaker. Academic Diane Hoeveler's reading of the controversy, however, presents Campion not only as self-vested, profiting personally at the expense of others, but as someone who then covers up her tracks through textual deception:

After reading *The River* and the biography of Jane Mander, one is tempted to see Campion's Ada as a symbol of the muted, buried New Zealand woman artist herself. And yet ironically she has been silenced by

> another woman, and one who has repeatedly depicted herself as a marginalized New Zealander. Whereas Campion was more than willing to resurrect the reputation of Janet Frame in her earlier film *An Angel at My Table*, she would appear now to be confident enough to cannibalize the work of one of her dead and long-forgotten New Zealand sisters.[28]

For Hoeveler, Campion disavows both the national and the textual origins of *The Piano* through her duplicitous depiction of Ada. And once again it is Campion's inappropriate consumption – this time a domestic act of cannibalization – that condemns her.

One notable feature of this debate over the provenance of *The Piano* is the evident difference between industrial–legal understandings of authorship and popular and scholarly expectations of the auteur. And yet common to both Campion and her critics is the question of Campion's relationship *as an author* to the geopolitics of originality in New Zealand, a question that is addressed in terms of the social capacities of the auteur. Both are concerned to evaluate her authorship on the extent or success of the sociality of her self. Has Campion been a good 'sister' (Hoeveler); has she been a good compatriot (Hoeveler and Campion)? With these questions we can begin to see how any discussion of the multiple spaces of the auteur is necessarily also a discussion of the ethical dimensions of contemporary auteurism.

## TELLING AUSTRALIAN STORIES

The second arena in which Campion has published her views on the industrial definition of authorship occurred at the very end of the 1990s as the Australian government first contemplated moral rights and then digital retransmission legislation for the film industry. In a letter published in various Australian newspapers, a number of high-profile filmmakers, headed by Campion, proclaimed:

> At a time when Australian films are being celebrated on the international stage, the very writers who created these works are being denied the right

of authorship under the Federal Government's proposed moral rights legislation.[29]

As the letter writers describe it, the government has misunderstood the role of the writer in the processes of film production, which they explain: 'The screenplay is the film on page; the blueprint everyone involved in the production uses to make the film.' They recognize 'the collaborative nature of filmmaking' but suggest that acknowledging 'the creator of the blueprint would seem a matter of fundamental justice'. They emphasize the globality of their concerns; not only are they acting beyond their own interest (since many of them are not screenwriters per se) but:

> Sixty-seven countries around the world have moral rights legislation. In every one of them, the screenwriter is recognized – along with the director – as author of a film. Australia is the only country proposing to take authorship away from screenwriters and give it to producers.[30]

The unwritten history of Australian film policy is the one that examines the way in which 'the producer' becomes the originary moment around which various 'ancillary' industry positions and key political moments collect. Instead, Campion and her companion letter writers 'call on the Attorney General to recognize the critical role played by our nation's storytellers'.[31] Here they explicitly link authorship to acts of cultural enunciation, hitching their argument to the foundational rationale for post-1970s Australian national cinema, 'to tell our own stories'. Like so many entries in Australian film industry policy debates, this letter reiterates the idea that the Australian cinema, above all else, should be engaged in the search for the lost original Australian voice. Their letter is a reminder that attributions of authorship, with their claims of creativity and originality, are not the property of specific industrial roles or even personalities but are culturally and politically contingent.

Less than 2 years later, another letter addressed to the prime minister and signed by Campion and a number of high-profile Australian directors (Peter Weir, Baz Luhrmann, Gillian Armstrong and so on) noted another omission. This time the government's failure is not its misunderstanding of the filmmaking process but of film history. The letter complains about a proposed scheme in which cable television companies would pay royalty fees to producers, writers and composers – but not to directors: 'Only a historical anomaly prevents a director being recognized as the "author" of a film', the letter says. 'This legislative oversight . . . was created [in] the late '60s, hardly a watershed in Australian cinema, and one in which there was little understanding of the director's . . . control over the making of a film.'[32]

The letter writers seek to recuperate the director as auteur, a controlling figure, rather than 'director for hire' or *metteur en scène* and in making this distinction they draw attention to the legislation's connection between creative authorship and ongoing financial recoupement. The director, they seem to say, is present in every iteration of a film, not just on set. In arguing for directors to receive ancillary royalties, they are also arguing for a notion of the director as a 'commercial' entity, as someone who is invested in the film at manifold levels. This represents a shift in habitual thinking about Australian cinema identity which from the 1970s onwards has been built around acts of production with an emphasis on understanding the industry as a summary of things, fixed objects, trophies of past achievements rather than an evolving and changing set of relations that also reach forwards. It also categorically welds the idea of the auteur to a set of commercial expectations, a shift that was emerging as a significant trend in the broader culture of the global film industries.

These shifts in how the auteur has been understood by the Australian film industry have much to do with that industry's perception of the various geopolitical spaces of the auteur. For example, as expectations for a more commercial role for the auteur are elaborated, and bearing in mind that very few Australian films will make money from domestic audiences alone, then there is an concomitant expectation of a necessary 'translatability' of the Australian auteur and her films. In this sense, Campion shares with other notable Australian directors such as Gillian Armstrong, Philip Noyce, Baz Luhrmann and George Milller an emphasis on creative collaboration; versatility across genres/budgets and financing; success on international scene and loyalty to local industry. And although Campion's fortunes have surpassed the national industry configuration from which she emerged, she has recently been recipient of an Australian government subsidy for the British–Australian co-production *Bright Star*.

Although I am broadly making a case for Campion's various auteurisms as operating outside an instrumentalist approach to the career of the auteur, there are several key 'beat changes' apparent in Campion's industrial history that signal both changed industry configurations and changed understandings of her agency in which the personal, endemic and the dispersible spaces of the auteur coalesce in new formations. To the extent that these moments signal transformed historical circumstances, they are not strictly sequential since they share many common characteristics and events. This next section will examine Campion's career in terms of three of these key moments: Campion as the aspirational Antipodean; Campion as the bankable outsider; and Campion as the upstart auteur.

## THE COMPLICATED CULTURAL POLITICS OF JANE CAMPION

Campion's celebrated initiation in the Australian film industry, through her enrolment at the national film school AFTS, runs parallel to the idea that the national film industry itself is somehow an apprentice cinema, supported by government on the basis that it is perpetually 'in development'. This is, in turn, reflected in the idea that filmmakers in Australia can pursue expressive outlets that are not always obviously purposeful in terms of their career as feature film directors, returning at different times to short films or television, for example.

In a very early interview, Campion testified to the importance of short films in non-career terms, insisting that she was 'adamant that one shouldn't see short films as a training ground for features . . . short films are often maligned. They are a distinct art form in themselves'.[33] Campion's recent return to the short form with *The Water Diary* (2006) and *The Lady Bug* (2007) suggests her interest in short filmmaking has exceeded her career as a feature director. It also invites us to consider how her career, her cultivation of an auteurist self, can be characterized as scalable and non-progressive. *The Water Diary*, for example, is part of a global collaborative effort of eight filmmakers developed in partnership with the United Nations Development Program (UNDP). Campion was commissioned by the UN to make a film on contemporary environmental challenges:

> Dealing with environmental sustainability was very interesting. What we came down to very quickly was that without water, there is no life. Then it was a matter of, how do you do this without being preachy or too overtly political? How do you do it in a very gentle, consciousness-raising way – through a story? I decided to use the device of a child keeping a diary on how the drought affects her family, neighbours, animals and her own life.[34]

Campion's reasons for using a child as a central character were not simply about her desire to minimize the pedagogic tone typical of many worthy documentaries. As she explains it, she had a personal motivation for involving her daughter Alice in the production, particularly remembering that this film was produced in 2006 interrupting Campion's self-imposed, extended sabbatical:

> I wrote the script for Alice, knowing her strengths. I used her best friends too because I know these children and they trust me. I wanted to share my work with Alice because she has to bear the brunt of my work, and it meant a lot to her.[35]

And certainly it has been a trait of Campion's short filmmaking practice to use these productions as an opportunity to work with friends and those closest to her.

This UN commissioned production also represents an opportunity for Campion to join a lengthening list of screen stars who also want to be regarded as social activists. Celebrities such as Angelina Jolie, Brad Pitt, Mia Farrow, Sir Bob Geldoff or Bono have used their star wattage to throw light on humanitarian work and global political causes. Working on a short film such as *The Water Diary*, which does not appear to have any direct instrumental value in the unfolding of a film director's career, constitutes the auteurist equivalent of a charitable act, which, in turn, has ancillary value for the director's image as a 'celebrity diplomat'. But Campion's first short films also played a direct role in her early career success, setting out the overlapping dimensions of the personal, endemic and dispersible aspects of her auteurism and that characterize her later triumphs.

Campion's early achievement with her short films was facilitated by a particularly vibrant short film exhibition and distribution environment in Australia during the 1980s. Short film festivals and competitions abounded and successful shorts were given theatrical releases in support of features or as part of short film packages in their own right. Awards and prizes for short filmmakers were numerous, annually given by the Sydney and Melbourne film festivals, the St Kilda Film Festival and the Australian Film Institute. The Australian TV programme *Eat Carpet* devoted exclusively to the art of the short film began on SBS television in 1988. By the mid-1990s it was estimated that some 200 short films were made in Australia each year (and this is prior to the wide availability of digital home editing systems).

As they were produced when Campion was a student, her short films belonged to the AFTS but a distribution deal with an independent distributor meant that the film *Peel* enjoyed more exposure than many other AFTS student films. Later, after experiencing success co-distributing *An Angel at My Table*, Australian distributor Andrew Pike took on a package Campion's short films. According to Pike,

Campion's short films were an easy proposition especially in the education market:

> We never had to do much marketing – the short films really sold themselves. Theatrically, the films were always supports to features (either our own or releases from other distributors), and so didn't attract much attention from the media. On video, in the educational market, we relied on direct mail and (later) our catalogue on the internet.[36]

Although attempts to release the films on home video never really amounted to much, sales (16mm and video) to schools, universities, technical colleges and public libraries boomed. Campion's short films also found favour overseas, particularly in Japan where they were shown theatrically and non-theatrically with considerable success (see Figure 2.2).

FIGURE 2.2 **Short cut to success:** *A Girl's Own Story*
Courtesy of Women Make Movies, www.wmm.com

The profile of Campion's short films can't be underestimated and their visibility lent itself to other forms of recognition. In a national survey to determine Australia's top 100 films, published to coincide with Australia's centenary of cinema in the mid-1990s, Campion's *Passionless Moments* was listed at 142, the highest result for a short film. In 1994, after *The Piano*, her earlier works were memorialized when a selection of short films by a new generation of Australian women was selected for screening in Vienna under the working title, 'The daughters of Jane Campion' (it was later changed to the marginally more subtle 'Girls' own stories').

But Campion's success as a short filmmaker does not entirely explain her rocket-like rise to feature film auteurdom. To understand her swift promotion requires some awareness of the particular features of the Australian film industry – especially as they stood in the 1980s. At the time Jane Campion entered film school, the Australian film industry was undergoing a period of massive cultural and economic upheaval from which, some argue, it has never fully recovered. Having initiated government subsidies for film production in the mid-1970s, policy-makers became increasingly frustrated by the limited amount of private investment in the industry. In 1981 the government legislated generous tax deductions for film investors known as 10BA after the section of the Taxation Act which outlined them.[37] The result was almost instantaneous and the profligate production activity that ensued, around 335 feature films were made in Australia in the 1980s, created unprecedented opportunities for local filmmakers with even a modest degree of experience.[38] There was a discernible swagger in the industry which could also be detected, albeit not always with triumphant results, on the screen.

The government's 10BA policies also had the effect of widening the perceived gap between the forces of culture and commerce in the industry, as investors, accountants and lawyers were granted the kind of influence previously held by cultural arbiters charged with spending the 'soft money' of government funds in the national interest. As 10BA was wound back in the late 1980s, this division between measuring the industry's success in either cultural or commercial terms was institutionally divided between two government funding agencies, the Australian Film Commission (AFC), responsible for industry 'development', and the Film Finance Corporation (AFFC), responsible for bringing bankable projects to fruition. Once film investment was returned to the public service after 10BA, the government's private investment policy shifted to one of encouraging international investment in Australian-located productions. Happily this coincided with a long period in which the Australian dollar was low in comparison to the US dollar encouraging many large-scale international film projects to Australia (e.g. *The Matrix, Babe, Moulin Rouge*).

Campion's early features such as *Sweetie* emerged during this period of transition and the film shares elements of the cultural expectation for a national screen vision and the swagger that comes from finding 'cash on the table'. Influential Australian critic, Sandra Hall, describes *Sweetie* as a 'landmark film' linking it directly to its industry context. *Sweetie* was: '[A] sign of what was to come once we'd seen the last of the big-spending 80's. They hadn't been good for the industry, bringing a concentration of the art of the deal at the expense of the films themselves. Yet the brashness and confidence they typified soon began to appear on the screen.'[39] For Hall, *Sweetie* is an intermediary document, the well formed result of an exemplary marriage between on-screen conviction and cautious cultural policy. When the industry took pause from the renegade energy of 10BA, it also stopped to give consideration to those that might have been shrouded in the dust kicked up by the stampede of production.

So, in 1984, just as Jane Campion graduated from film school, the film industry began lobbying for funds for emerging and creative filmmakers prepared to work with low budgets. This resulted in the establishment of the 'No Frills Fund' 'for people wishing to make highly creative, ingenious, unorthodox, innovative works in any gauge or format'. The fund also supported more straightforward work from 'promising beginners'. Although Campion did not receive funds from this source, it was quite clear that the Australian film policymakers in the early to mid-1980s were particularly concerned to support emerging talent in one way or another (see Figure 2.3).

Campion did receive support from the Australian Film Commission (AFC) early in her career, collecting grants to attend international festivals as well as development funding for *Sweetie* and *The Piano*. The AFC's policy in relation to filmmaker support was influenced by its director of film development (1989–92), Peter Sainsbury, a strong believer in the value of advancing the director's vision and who advocated for investing in talented filmmakers (rather than making decisions based on producer-led criteria).[40] Sainsbury's approach was supported by a shift in the organization of film funding that favoured a strategy of limiting the expenditure of funds within highly defined parameters. So rather than dispersing funds as widely as possible, Sainsbury took the option of following a few select filmmakers, mostly writer–directors from script stage through to marketing. These were fighting words for the time – unlike Hollywood, the Australian film industry was not easily able to sustain big personal films. Having said that, Sainsbury's emphasis on filmmakers did mean that agency chiefs

FIGURE 2.3 **Cannes 1989: Jane Campion, Genevieve Lemon and Karen Colston**
AFP/Getty Images

and government ministers anxious to avoid culpability in the event of a film's failure could blame the author instead (and yet at the same time take credit for a system of what appeared to be personalized art patronage). History suggests this was an exceptional moment in time. Government agencies in Australia now favour dealing with producers. But in the late 1980s the writer–director ruled and the industry rested on their success and supported and produced 'auteurs'. By the early 90s a new generation of 'names' were being lauded by the funding agencies: Baz Luhrmann, Tracey Moffatt, P. J. Hogan, Jocelyn Moorhouse, Geoffrey Wright, Stephan Elliott.

## WOMEN AND THE AUSTRALIAN FILM INDUSTRY

The other area of policy activity in the early to late 1980s was the introduction of affirmative action for women's participation in the film industry. In November 1983 a joint report issued by the AFTS and the Australian Film Commission's Women's Film Fund (1976–88) exposed some startling statistics. Between 1974 and 1982 only one woman, Gillian Armstrong with My Brilliant Career, had made a feature film (compared to 81 men); only 16 women had worked as screenwriters (compared to 132 men) and only 15 women had produced films (compared to 87 men).[41] In 1984 a second feature film directed by a woman, Sophie Turkiewicz's Silver City, was released.[42] In addressing the inequitable representation of women in the production industry the Women's Film Fund established a Women's Film Unit, initially as a Commonwealth Employment Programme (CEP) project with 12 months' funding and then later based at Film Australia. One of the filmmakers employed in this programme noted its emphasis on producing auteurs as well as films: 'There is definitely a feeling among certain women that the ultimate achievement would be to be a female Peter Weir.'[43] Writing about this period of feminist intervention in the Australian film industries, Anna Grieve suggests that as the 1980s wore on, the Women's Film Fund became increasingly dependent on the media production of auteurs, 'especially those who could provide media coverage for the Women's Film Fund with a festival award'.[44] It is no surprise, then, that Jane Campion was one of the first filmmakers chosen to work in the Women's Film Unit. Her films were already winning awards, and she herself had already made several public statements about her personal commitment to making films of relevance to women. Her outgoing statement in the notes accompanying her graduate film screening made this perfectly clear:

> 'On leaving the school, I want to work for Kennedy-Miller (when they start making "girls" films). Until then I'll continue working on my own projects and helping others who share a similar commitment'.[45]

Accompanying these interventions at the production end of the industry were a series of events designed to capture and develop an audience for films by and about women. The Women's Film Fund for example supported the employment of a feminist film distribution worker at the Sydney Filmmakers Co-op. Women's film screenings flourished, for example Film Fatale (1987–9) and various incarnations of professional associations such as Women in Film and TV (WIFT) were established.

The idea that audiences might be more receptive to films directed by women through these activities could have given filmmakers such as Campion a certain amount of confidence to pursue their projects. Reflecting at a much later date on the controversial Cannes screening of Sweetie, however, Campion describes an international audience that was less attuned to films directed by women:

> For us it was shattering . . . We had no idea what we were doing or how conservative that world is really . . . Now I do think, and its something you are always very careful about commenting on, that there is a lot of aggression towards women expressing themselves.[46]

Although Campion was already a seasoned festival presenter, her experience of the Cannes reception of Sweetie (in which some audience members audibly jeered the film) ranks as a watershed moment in redefining her approach to the industry, her method of marketing of her films through festivals and her aspirations on the international stage. By the time she came to presenting *The Piano* at Cannes, Campion had transformed her earlier experience of being the cultural 'outsider' into a bankable asset.

## THE BANKABLE OUTSIDER: AUTEURISM AND ART CINEMA CROSSOVER IN THE 1990S

It is easy to underestimate the extent to which, in a very short period of time after the release of *The Piano*, Campion became the personification of the 'international national' auteur in the Australian film industry. Her former collaborators, Gerard Lee and John Maynard, opened the film *All Men are Liars* (1995) with a deliberate reference to *The Piano*. In the film, a country rock star sells his wife's piano for a small amount of money. After it is taken away by removalists, the piano is accidentally smashed, precipitating a crisis in the marriage. According to Maynard: 'We're great friends with Jane and there's nothing personal in it, but I suppose it is taking the piss out of auteur filmmaking.'[47] Lee goes a bit further, complaining about how Campion's success has left his own collaborations with her invisible: 'I suppose the media has only enough space for one female director and there's an attachment to the idea of the single vision that comes from deep within the soul . . . It didn't sit comfortably with me, though I think Jane's pretty attached to the idea of originality and the singleminded vision.'[48] Maynard claims that French auteur theory 'has riddled Australian cinema for years' Lee adding: 'It's stronger here than in France.' If these comments tell us anything, it is that contemporary Australian auteurs live with the legacy of auteurism itself. Campion, for example, studied auteurism at AFTS where she wrote essays on auteurs such as Fellini. But, in Australia, filmmakers also live with the legacy of *The Piano* and Campion's filmmaking has left an indelible mark on the industry, fundamentally changing expectations for the national cinema, shifting them from beyond the focused cultural values of the originating auteur, beyond the regional resonances of the Antipodean endemic to the post-national promise of the dispersible.

In producer Jan Chapman's recital of the production history of The Piano, there is an evident change in register in how she traces the development of its multiple auteurist spaces:

> We took trips to deserted beaches in New Zealand while we re-drafted the screenplay, assisted with development money from the Australian Film Commission and the New South Wales Film & Television Office, and finally had a presentation package of the script and some inspirational photographic material of romantic Victorian women, Rousseau paintings, Maori mokos and depictions of New Zealand leisure activities like the women hanging their heads through a sheet as part of a Bluebeard play. We sent this to selected companies who we deemed suitable to finance us . . . Of course by the time we arrived our presentation boxes and photographic material had been discarded, and the scripts had been photocopied and distributed everywhere, and we were being advised that there were A, B and C lists of actors who would get us the finance . . . This financing provided us with the creative freedom to cast as we wanted to, and although we did decide to avail ourselves of the experience of some American actors, Holly Hunter and Harvey Keitel were never the ones mentioned by our would-be financiers as reliable box office material.[49]

In this distilled account, Chapman tells a story that moves from a picture of the traditional auteur (solitary inspiration on deserted beaches); to endemic inter-textuality (merging French painters and Maori mokos); to rampant dispersal, creative freedom and untram-melled commercial expectation.

Certainly, in industry terms, The Piano catapulted Campion from the art house to the multiplex. It stands as one of the most successful crossover art films earning more than $100m US at the box office (and with several DVD releases still counting), a defining 'artbuster'. As such it is also viewed as a 'tent pole' release for the Australian national film industry, the national industry blockbuster which excused less success-ful industry decisions.

But to see *The Piano* in purely cultural–nationalist terms would diminish the role played by events occurring well outside the Australian and New Zealand film industries. In 1990 ailing French construction industry and media mogul Francis Bouygues launched a film production company called CIBY 2000. Under his directorship, CIBY 2000 began signing some of the most recognizable auteurs in Europe including Wim Wenders, Pedro Almodovar and Bernardo Bertolucci. On the recommendation of Cannes spotter and Campion supporter, Pierre Rissient, he signed her too. *The Piano* was only the eighth film to be financed by the company. Bouygues lived long enough to see his investment in *The Piano* realized in a Palm d'Or.

*The Piano*'s profit line was further helped by the legion promotional efforts of its US distributor Miramax, which sealed the deal with CIBY 2000 while its closest competitors were looking the other way (to the forthcoming Sundance Festival in Utah not to Paris). Even the story of its acquisition by Miramax added to the narrative of expectation and preconception around the film. Despite being told they would have to wait like everyone else for the Cannes screening, Miramax's relentless Harvey Weinstein went straight to the newly appointed manager of CIBY 2000 who agreed to show him the film a fortnight before the festival, giving Weinstein 48 hours to make an offer for the US distribution rights and thereby inadvertently causing a serious rift with just about every other acquisition outfit in the US. And all this before even one public or trade screening of the film.

*The Piano* acquisition was significant given that Miramax was, at that time, being much more selective about its purchases. In 1992, the year prior to *The Piano*, Miramax released 19 films, down to just 15 in 1993. For some industry commentators, the film's French financing was crucial to its success in Cannes. Campion puts its success down to the calculated media campaign:

> The French financing lead to nasty rumours. Would *The Piano* have won in Cannes if it hadn't have been made with francs? 'They paid a lot of money in order to get the Palme d'Or, and I think they should have got it',

Campion says, deadly serious. Then, again with the laugh: 'Campion exposes fraud in Cannes!' In fact, Campion explains how the press screening for *The Piano* and interviews she did about it was what got people excited. Indeed, she feared the pre-Cannes hype may have prompted judges to react against the vibe, as happened a few years before when Spike Lee's *Do the Right Thing* was snubbed.[50]

Nevertheless, after their Academy Awards triumph, The Piano's producer Jan Chapman took out a full-page advertisement in *Variety* in the form of a letter signed by Chapman, Campion, Holly Hunter and Anna Paquin thanking their financiers and gifting them credit for their perceptive and foundational vision: 'Without the exceptional vision of CIBY 2000 The Piano could not have been made.'[51]

## FILM FESTIVALS AND THE TOPOGRAPHIES OF CONTEMPORARY AUTEURISM

It is possible to see Campion's triumph at Cannes for The Piano as the culmination of her many years of success on the festival circuit which necessitates a deft ability to play to a combination of local motivations, endemic cultural politics and post-national dispersibility. Several commentators have tried to capture these complicated dynamics at work in contemporary film festivals. B. Ruby Rich has spoken of the need to understand festivals as both expressions of the political and as battlegrounds of ideology: 'No film festivals are truly non-political. Politics is their birthright, in their blood.'[52] Thomas Elaseasser also refers to the corporeal qualities of film festivals in describing their role in the new topographies of cinema. Contemporary film festival networks, he says, are characterized by 'capillary action and osmosis through the various layers'.[53] Whereas Rich is concerned to show the pedigree of festivals in local, national and regional political systems, Elsaesser wants to also emphasize the indeterminacy of their relations:

Taken together and in sequence, festivals form a cluster of consecutive international venues, to which films, directors, producers, promoters and

> press, in varying degrees of density and intensity, migrate, like flocks of birds or a shoal of fish. And not unlike these natural swarm phenomena . . . the manner in which information travels, signals are exchanged, opinion hardens and consensus is reached at these festivals appears at once thrillingly unpredictable and yet follow highly programmed protocols.[54]

The selection of festivals for Campion's later films has obviously been a matter of some detailed determination. *Portrait*, for example, was pulled at the last minute from the prestigious opening night of the London film festival, one presumes after its less than ideal reception at the earlier Venice film festival. *In the Cut*, by way of contrast, premièred at the Toronto film festival. Toronto, which takes place in early September, marks the beginning of the promotional campaign for the following year's Oscars, held in March, a decision that seemed calculated to capitalize on buzz around Meg Ryan's performance. Anticipation was high enough to sell out the film's festival session and organisers were forced to schedule an additional screening for the press (although in the end Ryan did not receive a nomination).

It is also possible to argue that the festival circuit has been crucial for Campion, not just as a premiere form of circulation or for assigning value through selection and prizes but for attracting influential supporters and financiers for the instigation of new films. For example, the Cannes festival scout (and later production broker) Pierre Rissient has been an enormously important figure for Campion. Not only did he recommend the then untested short filmmaker to Cannes, later also advocating for *Sweetie*; not only did he broker the funding for *The Piano* but he also brought the French studio Pathé to *In the Cut* after the previously announced co-financiers Universal and Miramax withdrew from the project. Unsurprisingly, Rissient is also a significant figure in the early history of French auteurist theory and practice, especially in his role as a founder of the influential Cinema MacMahon. In 1993 prior to Campion's win at Cannes he summarized his feelings about her prospects: 'She's the future', he summed up. 'Jane must be included in the most important new generation of film-makers worldwide. Her new film, *The Piano*, is a great film.'[55] Similarly, Campion credits her Italian distributor Roberto Cicutto with 'saving' *An Angel at My Table*, attributing him responsibility for the series becoming a film and for the film being at the Venice film festival where it won the Silver Lion.

Although she has premièred several films at Venice, and returned there as a juror for its 75th anniversary, Campion's fortunes seem indelibly tied to the Cannes Film festival, described by Benjamin Craig as the 'King of Festivals . . . one of the largest media events on the planet.'[56] Thomas Elsaesser more specifically argues that Cannes played a crucial role in establishing the auteur as the 'gold standard of European festivals'.[57] In consideration of both these descriptions, it is possible to see how Cannes is especially distinguished for its role in the production of the celebrity auteur.

In 2007, an important year for Cannes, Campion was selected as a contributor to a portfolio movie featuring Cannes-approved auteurs and she also featured on the 60th anniversary poster promoting the festival (Figure 2.4). The poster depicts a selection of world cinema 'celebrities' (with almost as many directors as actors). Directors Jane Campion, Souleymane Cisse, Wong Kar Wai, Pedro Almodovar and actors Gerard Depardieu, Penelope Cruz, Juliette Binoche, Bruce Willis, Samuel L. Jackson are all depicted jumping in the air in a homage to American photographer Philippe Halsman who is quoted (a little inaccurately) on the Cannes website: 'When you ask a celebrity to "jump", his attention is essentially concentrated on his jump, the mask of posture falls and reveals his true personality.'[58] The quote reiterates the idea that witnessing the true self of the celebrity auteur lies at the heart of our interest in them. The poster was digitally compiled after hundreds of artists at the previous 2006 festival were invited to spring into the air between their film's photo call and their press conference, in other words, while they were between performative media appointments. Described by the Cannes festival as 'an ecstasy of the pleasure of acting and creation', the image restates the celebrity credentials of film directors, exploiting their image with the same enthusiasm that film promoters reserve for star actors alone. And yet this is also the most traditional of images of the auteur. With their feet clear of the ground, the poster collectively suspends auteurs and actors alike against a blank background. Poised momentarily at the point before their descent back

FIGURE 2.4 Cannes 2007: Jane Campion and other leaping luminaries
AFIRC

to earth and devoid of context or support, they occupy the weightless, celestial space of solitary achievement.

## PLAYING THE PIANO

The story of *The Piano*'s remarkable success lies in part with its performance at the Cannes film festival but it is also a story of American entrepreneurial enterprise. Miramax was one of the leading participants in the independent film revolution of the 1990s. The company was extraordinarily successful in this period in financing or distributing films that made more than $100m and was highly successful at securing Oscar nominations. For example, Miramax had considerable success in previous years with moving specialized films into the mainstream (such as *The Crying Game* and *Shakespeare in Love*). In early 1993, just before *The Piano*'s Cannes screening, Miramax was acquired by Disney (which reserved final say on what was distributed) but was otherwise run independently of Disney's other companies by the Weinstein brothers until 2005. The extra 'muscle' provided by Disney benefited *The Piano*'s reach.

What distinguished Miramax from other emergent independent studios in this period was the amount of attention they gave to marketing technique, building up hype for titles by screening pre-release films or extracts of them to journalists in private screenings, conducting pre-release test screenings to general audiences, creating excitement out of festival screenings and investing in lavish marketing campaigns. For Miramax, marketing was an activity like any other production. They were renowned for spending big to support anticipated hits and being equally quick to pull the plug on anticipated failures (an approach which distinguished them from larger studios with larger more complex internal politics). This strategy of calculated risk aversion underpinned Miramax's portfolio approach to film financing, using the big hits to subsidise their production slate while minimizing the impact of suspected loss makers by cutting out early. Justin Wyatt has noted that Miramax's aggressive approach to marketing art house films represented a volatile moment for art cinema, high-lighting the disparity between independent companies with ties to larger conglomerates and those without such support.[59] Indeed the success of mini-majors like Miramax inspired some major studios to establish art house subsidiaries or 'speciality divisions' such as Fox Searchlight Pictures, Warner Independent Pictures, Paramount Classics and Focus Features.

Campion herself was not immune to Miramax's hard-line account-ing, the studio abandoning In the Cut prior to production. As Campion tells it:

> Us girls – Laurie [Parker], Nic [Kidman] and myself – had this fabulous idea. We were trying to be like moguls. We thought that we could finance the entire film out of foreign pre-sales and that we would keep the USA for ourselves. We had started up a deal with another company but then Harvey Weinstein, who I had done Holy Smoke with, came into the picture. I said that I thought it could be a thriller like Seven or something. I think that was a really big mistake, because then he became attached to the idea. When I said those words he seemed to light up. I have to take responsibility for that – I wanted to get the price up![60]

Several years later, on presenting the completed script to Weinstein, Campion says 'he had a very dark response to the efforts we made'.

Intensive marketing for The Piano began in the lead-up to its première at Cannes, right through its various theatricals seasons and reached its heights in the lead-up to the Oscars. Throughout these campaigns, the promotion of The Piano was marked by a heavy emphasis on the personal investment of key cast and crew in the production and their experience of working with Campion herself. A lush 60-page colour booklet produced for Cannes film festival, made to look leatherbound and literary and printed on expensive parchment, included glorious production stills and extensive production notes with biographies of the main personnel such as Campion and producer Chapman; stars Keitel, Hunter, Neill and Paquin; and crew from the cinematographer to the editor (including a 'biography' of the financiers CIBY 2000). Each biography pointedly begins by identifying the birthplace of the person in question, cumulatively emphasizing the dispersed nature of the participants.

This booklet itself opens with a story of the film's genesis as one preceding all Campion's other features – promising that this is the real beginning of her cinema. It then turns to Campion's own beginnings: 'Although living and working in Sydney, Campion's imagination was drawn back to the colonial past of her birth country, New Zealand.' The booklet's approach to the question of Campion's personal origins casts new light on the place of originality in her authorship. As Hillel Schwarz describes it: 'Originality is not the urge to be different from others, to produce the brand new; it is to grasp (in the etymological sense) the original, the roots of both ourselves and things.'[61] Along these lines, Campion observes:

> I think that it's a strange heritage that I have as a pakeha New Zealander, and I wanted to be in a position to touch or explore that. In contrast to the original people in New Zealand, the Maori people who have such an attachment to history, we seem to have no history, or at least not the same tradition. This makes you start to ask 'Well who are my ancestors?' My ancestors are English colonisers – the people who came out like Ada and Stewart and Baines.

Campion is presented as a migrant in a history of migration and constant movement, pointing out that, in an Antipodean context, even her own endemic movement is always already global. The temporal, spatial and social displacement Campion describes is represented in the concluding image of the booklet – a lonely piano on a sea-swept beach, a despondent picture of pure, unmediated instrumentality.

This same media kit was directly mailed to Academy members in the lead-up to the awards and was used as the basis for the pre-Oscars advertising campaign for which Miramax itself won a Hollywood marketing award. Miramax's promotion of the film was relentless. At times up to seven advertisements a day in appeared in the trade press: *Daily Variety*, *Hollywood Reporter* and *Screen International*. Harvey Weinstein himself claimed credit for the campaign explaining how: 'We tried something different this year, letting the people involved in the film have a voice.'[62] At first, the campaign began with single- and double-page ads listing the film's array of awards and Golden Globe nominations with quotes from film critics (*Rolling Stone* and *The New York Times*). It then concludes: '135 critics agree *The Piano* is one of the year's ten best'. These early ads emphasize the film's critical kudos, focusing on what other people have thought of the film and presenting their opinions to readers, 'For your consideration' (see Figure 2.5). This advertising series then gave way in the immediate pre-Oscars period to the 'Voices of the nominees' campaign, with multiple pages (sometimes seven or eight) in every magazine. Congratulatory in tone, these ads featured the nominated cast and crew flattering each other and, particularly, Campion.

The campaign's stress on the enunciative seemed specifically geared to recognizing and generating positive word of mouth, a factor crucial to the success of Miramax's platform release strategy. So at the beginning of February 1994 *The Piano* could be found playing on 500 screens in the US. A week later, after the nominations announcement, it was playing on 600. To coincide with the awards ceremony, this leapt to 1000 screens. Weinstein anticipated increased revenues simply from the film's good performance in the nominations based on his experience the previous year when the Miramax nominee *Crying Game* took a $25m jump after the nominations announcement. Previously, the Academy Awards were considered by industry players as the crowning moment that came after a long theatrical run. After Miramax's innovative use of the awards as a launching pad for increased box office revenues for *The Piano*, there has been a noticeable shift in how distributors release films in the US.

But it was not just *The Piano* that was being promoted. From the outset, Campion acknowledged, albeit inadvertently, that these campaigns reflected on the circulation of her self:

| BEST PICTURE | BEST DIRECTOR | BEST ACTOR | BEST ACTRESS | BEST SUPPORTING ACTOR |
|---|---|---|---|---|
| **JAN CHAPMAN,** PRODUCER | **JANE CAMPION** | **HARVEY KEITEL** | **HOLLY HUNTER** | **SAM NEILL** |

| BEST SUPPORTING ACTRESS | BEST ORIGINAL SCREENPLAY | BEST ART DIRECTION | BEST CINEMATOGRAPHY | BEST SOUND EFFECTS EDITING |
|---|---|---|---|---|
| **ANNA PAQUIN** | **JANE CAMPION** | **ANDREW McALPINE** | **STUART DRYBURGH** | **LEE SMITH** |

| BEST COSTUME DESIGN | BEST EDITING | BEST SOUND | BEST MUSICAL SCORE | BEST MAKE-UP |
|---|---|---|---|---|
| **JANET PATTERSON** | **VERONIKA JENET** | **GETHIN CREAGH**<br>**MARTIN OSWIN**<br>**TONY JOHNSON** | **MICHAEL NYMAN** | **NORIKO WATANABE** |

## 6 GOLDEN GLOBE NOMINATIONS – Best Picture (Drama)

| Best Director | Best Actress | Best Supporting Actress | Best Screenplay | Best Original Score |
|---|---|---|---|---|
| JANE CAMPION | HOLLY HUNTER | ANNA PAQUIN | JANE CAMPION | MICHAEL NYMAN |

## BEST PICTURE

Cannes Film Festival • The Australian Film Institute

**BEST DIRECTOR**
Jane Campion
New York Film Critics' Circle
Los Angeles Film Critics Association
The Australian Film Institute

**BEST ACTRESS**
Holly Hunter
New York Film Critics' Circle
National Society of Film Critics
Los Angeles Film Critics Association
Boston Society of Film Critics
National Board of Review
Cannes Film Festival
The Australian Film Institute

**BEST ACTOR**
Harvey Keitel
Boston Film Festival Audience Award
The Australian Film Institute

**BEST CINEMATOGRAPHY**
Stuart Dryburgh
Los Angeles Film Critics Association (Tie)
The Australian Film Institute

**BEST SCREENPLAY**
Jane Campion
New York Film Critics' Circle
National Society of Film Critics
Los Angeles Film Critics Association
The Australian Film Institute

**BEST SUPPORTING ACTRESS**
Anna Paquin
Los Angeles Film Critics Association (Tie)

**BEST SCORE**
Michael Nyman
The Australian Film Institute

*"'The Piano' is a Jane Campion triumph-unmissable, unforgettable entertainment. Her visionary brilliance holds you in its grip from the first frame."*
–Peter Travers, ROLLING STONE

*"Harvey Keitel gives the performance of his career. Holly Hunter, Sam Neill and Anna Paquin are extraordinary. Unlike anything most of us have seen before. Prepare for something very special."*
–Vincent Canby, THE NEW YORK TIMES

### 135 CRITICS AGREE
"'The Piano' Is One Of The Year's Ten Best."

## the Piano

**MIRAMAX**   CIBY 2000

FIGURE 2.5 One hundred and thirty-five critics agree: Hollywood trade press campaign for *The Piano* in the lead-up to the Oscars

I'm not really trying to sell myself. I'm trying to let people know that the film's on and a little about what it's about. I'm not selling myself. I don't need to sell myself. I've got work. There's not a lot of interest for me personally in doing profiles. I really don't want to be famous.[63]

But despite her qualms, Campion was subject to an explicit endorsement campaign in the trade press (Figure 2.6). A pensive, uncomfortable looking Campion literally rests on an iconic scene from The Piano, which is framed by awards laurels. Jane Campion, the advertisement tells us, is to be lauded, above all else (professionalism, energy and enthusiasm) for her passion.

Well before the Oscars campaign was launched, Campion expressed her own prescient concern for the possible impact of media overexposure on her filmmaking:

It's the way these things work. There is a public perception of someone having had enough attention or too much attention, and a sense that the public has to help them by putting them in their place! That's the truth and I think it's wise to watch the amount of exposure you get.[64]

Certainly what is extraordinary about the promotion of The Piano is the way in which its niche marketing campaign, intended exclusively for the members of the film industry such as Academy voters, became itself the subject of mainstream, daily media commentary. David J. Fox for example, writing in the LA Times and syndicated through other media outlets, noted the sheer volume of Piano ads appearing in the trade press, which, he claims, 'raised eyebrows for veteran Oscars observers'[65] (see Figures 2.7 and 2.8). He estimates the campaign to have cost some $750,000 and quotes Weinstein's response: 'Our ads are black and white. They don't cost as much . . . I'm glad the campaign has been so effective that it seems like we're spending more than we did.' Fox suggests the campaign is unusual in its emphasis on the achievements of women which he says is risky given that women's membership of Academy is only about 15 to 20 percent. Weinstein's response claims

FIGURE 2.6 Passion above everything else: Hollywood trade press promotion for Jane Campion in the lead-up to the Oscars
AFIRC

## THE VOICES OF THE NOMINEES

*T*his year the independently financed, independently distributed motion picture 'The Piano' has impacted cinema throughout the world. The film recently received eight Academy Award° nominations, seven of which honored the creative achievements of women.

Jane Campion is only the second woman in the 66-year history of the Academy Awards° to be nominated as Best Director. She began writing 'The Piano' nearly a decade ago and made the film for a limited budget of only 8 million dollars.

This year Miramax Films and CIBY 2000, breaking with tradition, hope to offer insight into the long, challenging journey from original idea, to one of the world's most honored films by listening to those who were so instrumental in shaping the film's ultimate success...

## the Piano

MIRAMAX   CIBY 2000

FIGURE 2.7 Voices of the nominees: Hollywood trade press campaign for *The Piano* in the lead-up to the Oscars

FIGURE 2.8 Voices of the nominees: Hollywood trade press campaign for *The Piano* in the lead-up to the Oscars

a different motivation, granted that seven of the eight *Piano* nominees were women: 'It's clearly a women's achievement . . . Basically we're just trying to say, hey, we're here. That the race isn't over.'

Weinstein's stated intention, to draw awareness to the continued presence of *The Piano*, succeeded perhaps all too well. In the month prior to the Oscars, an article nominating 'Seven reasons not to like *The Piano* was published in the *New York Magazine*. *Newsweek* reported on rising irritation in Hollywood to the campaign William Grimes in the *New York Times*, in an article titled 'After a first wave of raves, *The Piano* slips into a trough,' speculated at length about the fluctuating currents of reaction to *The Piano*.[66] The article quotes industry figures who postulate a double-wave theory of audience response to publicity overkill: great word of mouth raises unrealistic expectations and produces disappointment among audiences, which, in turn, drives expectations downwards again causing the next wave of theatre audiences to be pleasantly surprised. Fox finds not just the saturation advertising but several other factors at work in the reaction against the film including: love exhaustion (people are over loving it); that critical viewers previously silenced by the seemingly universal enthusiasm for the film could now find the courage to dissent; the discovery that your private pleasure in the film is publicly shared and so it loses its lustre. What is especially notable about these articles on *The Piano*'s trade campaign is that they describe a backlash against Campion's cinema well before to the box office disappointments of *Portrait* and *Holy Smoke*. In fact, they suggest that disappointment in Campion's 'performance' originates in her unexpected commercial success rather than her later commercial 'failures'.

The overwhelming advertising used in the trade press was not taken up in daily newspaper campaigns such as the one promoting the Australian theatrical release. *The Piano* proved to be extraordinarily successful in Australia, outlasting *Jurassic Park* on cinema screens. Instead, the Australian press advertisements for the theatrical season aimed at two different market segments (see Figures 2.9 and 2.10). One advertisement is clearly designed to attract a crossover audience,

FIGURE 2.9 Praised and acclaimed: Australian press advertisement for *The Piano*
AFIRC

exhorting viewers to 'See the most highly acclaimed and praised film of the year' (Figure 2.9). In this advertisement prominent position is given to the film's Academy Award nominations and less to the fact that the film had won both best film and best actress at Cannes. A very large space, however, is given to a series of enthusiastic, exclamatory quotes from Vincent Canby's *New York Times* review: '*The Piano* is so good, so moving, so original!'; 'One of the most enchanting and erotic love stories to be seen on the screen in years'; 'Exhilarating!'; 'Breathtaking!' With these American endorsements, readers are pressed to take a punt on going to the film as a measured economic and personal investment. In framing consumption of *The Piano* as a 'low-risk' activity based on the recommendation of others, the ad addresses mainstream audiences as socially pliant yet self-preserving subjects.

Another series of simultaneously used theatre advertisements is more obviously aimed at art house viewers (Figure 2.10) and quotes Australian film reviewer Evan Williams, emphasizing his comparatively considered observations: 'masterpiece', 'richly imagined', 'enriching and beautiful'. Implicit in these distinctive campaigns is the belief that some segments of the Australian mainstream audience will be motivated to see the film on the basis of its success in America, but art house audiences will be more interested to hear the opinion of a familiar, broadsheet newspaper reviewer extolling the canonical aspects of the film and inviting them to undertake a personally elevating experience. In framing film consumption as an experience this ad addresses art house audiences specifically as individually responsible, empowered and self-caring subjects.

*The Piano*'s Australian campaign is unusual in that it deviates from the ordinary association of mainstream audiences with enhanced cinematic 'experiences' such as those produced by special effects and so on. As Janet Harbord puts it: 'Mainstream film culture elides the experience of everyday life with the corporeal experience of the senses, imbricating the aestheticised world of the film with everyday life. In contrast the arthouse and the art gallery remain focussed on the image of the text.'[67] Art, for Harbord, remains a specialized domain, divorced from

FIGURE 2.10
Enriching and beautiful:
Australian press
advertisement for
*The Piano*
AFIRC

everyday life and individualized at the level of the aesthetic. And yet, there is, in The Piano's theatrical campaign and as we shall see in the next chapter, in the experiences of some audiences, an appreciation of the corporeal experience of the image at work.

If nothing else, these advertisements also show us the way in which distributors and exhibitors were approaching the audience as a series of multiple niches, each requiring a specific set of marketing strategies. The extensive promotional activity unleashed for The Piano, becomes one or more in a series of multiple productions, each advertisement targeted at a specifically imagined audience. In this way the campaign reflects on the film text as well, suggesting it as hermeneutically open to multiple audiences.

The Piano's promotion continued for some time after the lengthy theatrical and awards seasons had concluded. Nowadays it is an industry truism that many films can realize the majority of their profits through ancillary sales. Screening at a cinema is in many instances a 'loss leader', an extra promotional step on the way to the main game – DVD sales. This was not the case in the early 90s when DVD was still a fledgling technology. The Piano was, however, was an early example of a highly successful media crossover with breakout ancillary sales in both books (script and novelization), sell-through videos and later DVDs. Even Variety was moved to admiration: 'Though published film scripts aren't traditionally strong sellers, Disney's Hyperion book arm has been moved to print more copies of The Piano after going through its initial print run of 47,500 copies.'[68] Miramax carefully planned to release Campion's novelization in conjunction with the Academy Awards ceremony. Some 12 months after its theatrical release in Australia The Piano was launched as a sell-through video, 'destined to become a great classic with timeless appeal'.[69] Purchasers could choose from several packages: a standalone video, a video bundled with a book or a video combined with a CD of the movie soundtrack. Here, the purpose of the marketing strategy is to assemble the audience around specific but related products rather than to assemble specific audiences around the film text itself. In addition, customers at an exclusive department store who bought *The Piano* or one of *The Piano* packs entered a competition to win a grand piano. Through this somewhat literal tie-in, consumers were offered the opportunity to experience the film's story of the domestication of a piano for themselves (and without the requisite removal of a digit). In this way the film also inveigles its way into 'everyday' life, as an object of cultural appreciation and aspiration, one lifestyle choice among many.

More importantly, *The Piano* becomes inter-textually related to itself, to its other ancillary iterations. In these circumstances, the 'auteur' can be seen as both a cohering or mediating factor in the marketing of the film within a proliferating range of related products and promotional materials and as a type of hypertext, linked in, but also linking off, to alternative avenues and narratives of consumption.

## AFTER THE DELUGE: THE UPSTART AUTEUR

And then just as quickly as she was floated, she sank. Prevalent industry opinion has Campion's career achieving its apotheosis with *The Piano* before sliding away one film at a time in relatively quick succession. Soon after the release of *Portrait of a Lady*, Campion's follow-up to *The Piano*, her status as an auteur was deemed to be in crisis. By the time *Holy Smoke* hit the screens, it was her entire career that was supposed to be on the skids on the basis of poor projected box office. Crucial to this period of Campion's career was the belief that her value as an auteur was, in large part, a matter of crunching the numbers (see Table 2.1). But changes to the relationship between the media and the industry were also at play. At the time of the media's criticism of *Portrait* for example, some media commentators focused in on the idea that Campion was not 'playing the game', failing to attend the parties and press calls because she didn't think her films had received the requisite level of positive appraisal:

> The reason Campion so determinedly spurned the limelight at her
> glittering bash seems to be simply because not everyone loved her film.

And if there's one thing she cannot bear, it's for her eccentric, dark visions, so painfully delivered, not to be treated with the tenderness and respect she believes they deserve. It was Campion's party and – hey! – she could sulk if she wanted to.[70]

In this highly personalized article, journalist Sue Williams claims Campion has a difficult relationship with the press and that this has had almost as much affect on assessments of her performance as her films. Williams censures Campion, reminding her that the media are as much a part of the industry as the production of films. And they are also more than this. It is no longer just about recognizing the media as a crucial component of the promotion process. What clearly emerges at this time is a new form of media expertise attached to the film industry, an expertise in the cinema that challenges the connoisseurship of film critics, providing, instead, a form of film commentary based on claims to a proficiency in economic prediction.

Campion's response to the predictions about her career demise, that

TABLE 2.1 Box office figures for Campion films

| Film and year | US | Aust. | UK | Other | Budget |
|---|---|---|---|---|---|
| In the Cut (2003) | $4.8 m | $1.2 m | $1.8 m | $2.0 m | $12 m |
| Holy Smoke (1999) | $1.8 m | $ 0.9 m | $0.5 m | $0.4 m | $10.6 m |
| The Portrait of a Lady (1996) | $3.7 m | $1.4 m | $1.1 m | $1.5 m | $28 m |
| The Piano (1993)** | $40.2 m | $7.6 m | $7.2 m | $37.4 m | $7 m |
| An Angel at My Table (1990) | $1.1 m | $1.5 m | $0.7 m | $0.8 m | $1.2 m |
| Sweetie (1989) | $0.9 m | $0.2 m | $0.2 m | NA | $1.0 m |

*All figures in USD based on those provided by Variety, Box Office Mojo, Screen International, Australian Film Commission. 'Other' does not include French box office and is indicative rather than total. Currency conversions calculated using historical rates.

**According to The Piano's producer, by the beginning of September 1994 all global territories had realized $US140 million. French box office alone accounted for US$40m less than a year after its release.

occurred in the lead up to the screening of *Portrait* at the Venice film festival, suggest she is well aware of the importance of economic arguments in assessments of her performance as a director:

> You choose a novel like *Portrait* and you aren't trying to win a popularity prize; it isn't middle-of-the-road cinema. I know I can't please everyone but I hope to please some people immensely . . . I can afford to make a failure . . . maybe even two or three now. It wouldn't really matter.[71]

Campion defends the idea of her audience as being located in one (or perhaps more than one) market segment, but it seems to her critics that once you have 'crossed over' to the mainstream it is not so easy to cross back and cast yourself adrift in a different stream. There remains in criticism of Campion's performance, the vestigial suggestion of a mainstream versus niche opposition – rather than the industrially accepted idea of the audience as comprising a multitude of segments.

Her next film fared no better. Campion noted an almost gleeful attitude on the part of the Australian media baying for her downfall after *Holy Smoke*:

> We've had the most amazing reviews from Britain I've ever had. I'm in shock. What's great about this film is that it is on the edge. But those Australians are making it very hard for these sorts of films to survive. They don't give them a chance to survive. They don't even give them a chance to take breath.[72]

Campion couches her criticism in geopolitical terms, finding a problem in the relationship between the Australian national media and her cinema. It is the Australian media specifically that are unable to support the development and survival of internationally financed, national output. In this way, Campion retrieves the possibility of an Australian cinema understood as comprising diverse audiences from the homogenizing commercial expectations that have otherwise become associated with her auteurism. If the media are to claim an industry role, then, as far as Campion is concerned, they can also be held accountable (see Figure 2.11).

For the most part, Campion, however, was providing positive spin. On the Venice film festival screening of *Holy Smoke*: 'I would definitely not describe it as a failure. I have been at failure screenings, I've had them myself.' Instead, she asserted that from her experience, directors making films that are challenging to Hollywood fare know that having an audience with different opinion is 'exciting rather than a disaster'.[73] Campion was also in Venice to line up finance for her next film, *In the Cut*: 'We want people who've got the same guts as we have in taking it on and will give us all the freedoms we want to have.' From her perspective, finding this sort of financial backing is hard because they didn't want to disappoint anybody: 'I don't know how guys do business but girls are always worried about everyone's feelings.'[74]

FIGURE 2.11 **Critical desert: Ruth Barron (Kate Winslet) in** *Holy Smoke*
Miramax/ The Kobal Collection/Jenkins, Gerald

What is most interesting about this account of Campion's Venice screening is the pivotal role of the commercial in evaluating her work. What once might have been relevant only to the trade press such as *Variety* or *Hollywood Reporter* also consumes the popular press in their accounting of Campion's value. The première of *Holy Smoke* was greeted in Australian newspapers with alarmist headlines such as 'Campion comes a cropper', 'No sweet tidings for lady of the piano' and 'Holy smoke, Campion faces a commercial death in Venice'. One press report declared this to be the biggest crisis of Campion's career:

> Anxious film company reps polled the industry heavyweights as they left the screening of *Holy Smoke* early yesterday at the prestige Venice film festival and seemed alarmed by some responses.
>
> 'I can't believe Jane Campion made this movie', said an Italian TV journalist, who described herself as a Campion fan.
>
> 'It was not her style at all. Very disappointing.'[75]

Here, again, we have journalists quoting other journalists as the new cinema 'experts'. Campion responded vigorously to predictions of her post-*Holy Smoke* demise in a series of media articles: "That's just a complete fantasy . . . Without blowing my own horn, that is so far from the truth I can't even comment on it. It's too embarrassing. Like, what, I'm not going to get another job?'[76]

The following report on the first screenings of *Holy Smoke* is especially interesting in the way it hangs onto Campion's auteur status as an uncompromising artist as well as defending her against criticisms that she has departed too far from her signature style but yet still predicts the film's failure with audiences:

> 'It doesn't seem to quite know what it wants to be', says Derek Malcolm, former critic of the London *Guardian*. *Time Out*'s Tom Charity agreed: 'There are about three different films in there and, in the end, none of them work.' Part of the problem is in the film's refusal to conform to expectations. After the triumph of *The Piano* (awarded the Palme d'Or in

Cannes in 1993), and the subsequent critical and commercial failure of *The Portrait of a Lady*, Campion clearly wanted to make a different kind of film – looser, less studied, more contemporary. As a result, many viewers have declared *Holy Smoke* is almost unrecognisable as 'a Jane Campion film'. But in fact, with its moments of deadpan humour and dysfunctional, slightly surreal view of family life, the director returns to the territory of her first feature, *Sweetie* (1989). The film will most likely prove a box-office disappointment, even with the star power of Winslet and the Miramax marketing machine.[77]

The reviewer notes that the film does not conform to audience anticipation quoting critics who say that Campion has overplayed the expectation for novelty in *Holy Smoke*, creating instead a work that is not even recognizable in terms of her own signature inclination for innovation. He then asserts his own critical credentials by pointing out that there are similarities between *Holy Smoke* and Campion's earlier film *Sweetie*, although these assurances do not really redress the criticism that the film is unrecognizable as a Campion film, since *Sweetie* is not widely known to non-specialist audiences. However this strategy, of stressing the similarities between *Holy Smoke* and Campion's previous films appeared in other reviews:

The film looks great, thanks to the elegance of cinematographer Dion Beebe's lighting, but to me it plays like a compendium of all Campion's films so far. It has a mesmerising opening that plunges into the story with an intimacy reminiscent of the first scene of *The Portrait of a Lady*. It also has some of the emotional intensity of *The Piano*. But the *Sweetie*-like touches expended on Ruth's family, who belong to the tribe we think of as Australian comic-grotesque, makes for such a wildly disparate range of styles and moods that the film comes dangerously close to falling apart.[78]

For Derek Malcolm in the *Guardian*, it is actually the film's failure that is what links it to Campion's previous work, describing it as a 'film of some ambition which stumbles curiously as Campion's films invariably do'.[79]

What is most notable is that these are not reviews of a film in theatrical distribution but accounts of a festival screening that bears on the reputation of the auteur as well as the potential for the film's box office success and the filmmaker's future prospects as they pursue market interest in financing their next film. Not everyone was predicting doom and gloom. Many traditional critics focused their assessments on the merits of the film itself. *The Australian*'s David Stratton is typical of supportive reviews:

> It's understandable, I think, that Campion's work should be provocative. Personally, I think it's a marvelous film and, indeed, you could argue that the film's success can be determined by the arguments it provokes . . . It's an original, exciting, funny, painful and immensely invigorating film, and certainly one of the best screened in the Venice competition.[80]

And some reviewers thought the film had commercial appeal. *The Evening Standard* decided, erroneously as it transpired: 'Holy Smoke is going to be a huge popular hit . . . It is Jane Campion's most accessible box office mix.'[81] *The Hollywood Reporter* also believed the film would 'deliver some strong numbers, particularly in the upscale urban markets', but warned: '[T]he movie clearly lacks the breakthrough commercial acceptance of Campion's third feature, *The Piano*, so expectations should be appropriately gauged.'[82]

The vast majority of mainstream media reviewers writing about the Venice screening of *Holy Smoke* picked up on trade press and industry expectations, taking on the idea that Campion's 'bankability' was at risk. What emerges is a new type of film journalism in the mainstream press, charcterised by an inclination to measuring the commercial value of the auteur, a development also present in new online approaches to valuing contemporary auteurs. For example, assessments of Campion's industrial pull are reflected in other forms of film industry appraisal such as the Hollywood Stock Exchange (www.hsx.com) which has measured market expectation of Hollywood films and stars since the late 1990s. As the HSX would have it, Campion's stocks slipped and then spiralled on a downward trend after November 2001, plateauing just before the release of In the Cut. Sites such as the HSX are, by their nature, highly speculative but there is no reason to think that, in these prescient times for auteurs, the information aggregated by the exchange will prove significantly worse than the guesswork of journalists, critics, audiences or than the best informed participants in the market.

## CONCLUSION

This chapter has, as part of its discussion of economics and industry in Jane Campion's auteurism, noted the increasing role that the culture and industries of consumption play in generating, regulating and evaluating techniques of self-conduct for both the auteur and the consumer. Advertising, marketing, reportage and criticism, the proliferation of content itself but also the multiplication of modes of purchase are all part of a social project that distinguishes the contemporary auteur's sense of self from previous ones. That being said it is not the purpose of this chapter to imply that auteurs are purely 'rational' agents in the theoretical sense provided by classical economics; in which auteurs would be expected to only behave in instrumental ways that are designed to maximize their self-interest, although that remains one current of interpretation of some auteurist behaviour. For example, Jane Campion's decision to take time out from feature filmmaking could be viewed as anti-rational behaviour; the deliberate removal of her author name from circulation not to her best economic or industrial advantage. Or it could be seen as a necessary and fruitful moment of personal self-regeneration having the effect of heightening anticipation in her subsequent work. Neither does this book suggest, like classical auteurism, that auteurs can essentially be understood as primarily psychological beings, mobilized by unconscious, anti-rational desires and forces, although again this remains an avid way of understanding the auteur from both within and without the industry. If the auteur is not external to social, economic and political life but imbricated within it, if she does not just produce films but also knowledges of the self then what happens when we re-conceptualize the individual author as a social self?

What this book does want to introduce to the discussion of the auteur as a social self is the way in which the dimension of ethics might also contribute to our understanding of their behaviour; to begin to think about the problems they encounter as ethical problems, tied up in ideas about reciprocity, mutuality, cooperation, belongingness and identity. And to understand the auteur as capable of producing reflection both in the sense of their own capacity for self-reflection but also as participants in broader cultural knowledges about the capacities of existence. If we can get beyond the idea of the auteur as industrially instrumental, as ultimately directed to achieving certain specific personal or social goals, then we can imagine them instead in terms of spontaneity, improvization, drifts and evasions – as occasionally unproductive and contradictory in a way that applies to our understanding of auteurism itself and not just to certain auteurs as a characteristic feature of their filmmaking. The next chapter also examines the stakes of the 'rational' for the evaluation of Campion's cinema, but this time as a feature of a particular authorizing audience rather than the auteur herself.

## NOTES

1    Angela Carter, *Black Venus's Tale*, London: Next Editions, 1980, p. 11.

2    Howard Feinstein, 'The Jane mutiny', *Guardian*, 2 April 1999, p. 4.

3    Justin Wyatt, 'Economic constraints/economic opportunities: Robert Altman as auteur', *The Velvet Light Trap*, no. 38, 1996, p. 52.

4    Wyatt, 'Economic constraints/economic opportunities: Robert Altman as auteur', p. 52.

5    David Bordwell, 'Art cinema as a mode of film practice', *Film Criticism*, vol. 4, no. 1, 1979, pp. 56–64; and Steve Neale, 'Art cinema as institution', *Screen*, vol. 22, no. 1, 1981, pp. 11–39.

6    Steve Neale, 'Art cinema as institution', p. 36.

7    Catherine Grant, 'www.auteur.com?', *Screen*, vol. 41, no. 1, Spring 2000, p. 101.

8    See Tom O'Regan, *Australian National Cinema*, New York: Routledge, 1996, p.72 for an account of Campion's role in the growing convergence and integration of the New Zealand and Australian film industries in the 1990s, which O'Regan wonders might undergird an Australasian identity.

9    Mani Petgar, 'Getting under the skin: an interview with Jane Campion', *Film International*, vol. 1, no. 1, Winter 1993, p. 6.

10   Hunter Cordaiy, 'Jane Campion interviewed by Hunter Cordaiy', *Cinema Papers*, no. 81, 1990, p. 36.

11   See Verhoeven, *Sheep and the Australian Cinema*, Melbourne: Melbourne University Press, 2006, for a lengthy discussion of the 'problem of origins' in Australian national cinema.

12   'Australians urged to attend weekend peace protests', *AP Worldstream*, 2 December 2003.

13   'Campion gives men the flick from pool', *Herald Sun*, 20 January 1995, p. 3.

14   'Letter to the editor', *Herald Sun*, 26 January 1995, p. 14.

15   Rohan Gow, 'Letter to the editor', *Herald Sun*, 31 January 1995, p. 14.

16   Virginia Wright Wexman (ed.), *Jane Campion: Interviews*, Jackson: University Press of Mississippi, 1999, p. 87.

17   Michael J. Lines, 'Letter to the editor', *The Australian*, 31 March 1994, p. 10.

18   See Hillary Frey, 'The purloined piano?', *Lingua Franca*, vol. 10, no. 6, September 2000, http://linguafranca.mirror.theinfo.org/print/0009/field-piano.html.

19   Robert Macklin, 'Oscar doubt over Campion's *Piano*', *Canberra Times*, 25 March 2000, p. 1.

20   'A wrong note for Campion's piano', *Waikato Times*, 28 March 2000, p. 6.

21   Phil Wakefield, 'New respect for Kiwi creations', *Hollywood Reporter*, 6 December 1994, p. 11.

22   Wakefield, 'New respect for Kiwi creations', p. 11.

23   In Robert Macklin, 'Campion's award-winning screenplay "inspired" by novel', *Canberra Times*, 8 April 2000, p. 1.

24   Robert Macklin, '"Chain-of-title steps taken" for film', *Canberra Times*, 1 April 2000, p. 3.

25   'Campion puts her case', *The Dominion*, 8 April 2000, p. 31.

26   'Campion puts her case', p. 31.

27 'Campion puts her case', p. 31.

28 Diane L. Hoeveler, 'Silence, sex and feminism: an examination of The Piano's unacknowledged sources', *Literature/Film Quarterly*, vol. 26, no. 2, 1998, pp. 109–16.

29 'Film plan cheats writers', *Herald-Sun*, 18 August 1997, p. 22.

30 'Film plan cheats writers', p. 22.

31 'Film plan cheats writers', p. 22.

32 'Letter to the editor: "denied right of authorship"', *The Australian*, 20 August 1997, p. 12. See also Lauren Martin, 'Howard's way: the director's cut', *Sydney Morning Herald*, 28 June 1999, p. 5.

33 Campion in Margaret Smith, 'Australian short film' *Media Information Australia*, no. 300, August 1984, p. 60.

34 United Nationals Development Program, 'Lights camera action: the millennium goals make their debut at Cannes', *Practices Priorities Programs*, 15 May 2006, http://content.undp.org/go/newsroom/2006/may/MDG-cannes-20060516.en;jsessionid=af8LBi1WoL_6?categoryID=349516&lang=en.

35 Joan Dupont, 'The Cannes festival: Jane Campion, on drought and isolation', *International Herald Tribune*, 31 May 2006, http://www.iht.com/articles/2006/05/26/news/dupont.php.

36 Interview with the author, 24 September 2006.

37 The incentives provided for a 150% deduction on capital expenditure on the production of an Australian film. From 1988 this was progressively scaled back to 133% then 120% and finally 100%. Section 10B of the Tax Act was also amended to provide for a 50% deduction on profits arising from an investment in a film production. This was also scaled back to 33%, 20% and finally 0%.

38 By 1982 there was around $120m AUD in the industry rising to more than $180m AUD pa by the late 1980s. Government subsidies for training, development, production and marketing remained static at around $25m AUD per year.

39 Sandra Hall, 'Peter Pan country', *Sydney Morning Herald* (Spectrum), 16 December 2000, p. 1

40 Jeremy Eccles, 'Finding a path through the movie maze', *The Herald*, Monday magazine, 19 June 1989, p. 7.

41 Penny Ryan, Margaret Eliot and Gil Appleton, *Women in Australian Film Production*, North Sydney: Women's Film Fund & Australian Film and Television School, 1983, pp. 26–34.

42 Interestingly, Turkiewicz is seldom written about as an 'auteur' – her film describes the migrant experience in Australia and is usually relegated to the 'social problem' category, which is apparently anathema to the aesthetic undercurrent of auteurist practice.

43 Anonymous Women's Film Unit film worker quoted in Annette Blonski, Barbara Creed and Freda Freiberg (eds), *Don't Shoot Darling: Women's Independent Film Making in Australia*, Richmond VIC: Greenhouse, 1987, p. 166.

44 Anna Grieve, *Don't Shoot Darling*, p. 80.

45 Jane Campion, 'Program notes', *A Screening of Selected Graduate Film and Video Productions*, Chauvel Cinema, Wednesday 11 and Thursday 12 April 1984, Sydney: AFTS, p. 7. Kennedy Miller was the producer of the successful *Mad Max* movies released in 1979, 1981 and 1985.

46 Commentary track for *Sweetie* (Criterion).

47 Mary Colbert, 'All men are liars', *Cinema Papers*, no. 106, October 1995, p. 6.

48 Colbert, 'All men are liars', p. 6.

49 Jan Chapman, *Some Significant Women in Australian Film: A Celebration and a Cautionary Tale*, Canberra: ScreenSound Australia Monograph no. 3, 2002, p. 27.

50 In Jim Schembri, 'Me Jane', *The Age*, 6 August, 1993, p. 13.

51 Jan Chapman Productions, 'Re: The Piano' [advertisement] *Variety*, 28 March–3 April, p. 13.

52 B. Ruby Rich, 'What you see is (never) what you get: the geopolitics of cinema and film festivals', an unpublished presentation at 'The Persistence of Vision: Fifty Years of the Sydney film festival', 3–4 June, Seymour Centre, University of Sydney.

53 Thomas Elsaesser, *European Cinema: Face to Face with Hollywood*, Amsterdam: Amsterdam University Press, 2005, p. 82.

54 Elsaesser, *European Cinema*, p. 87.

55 Susan Borham, 'Don't rest on past glories, warns Cannes man', *Sydney Morning Herald*, 22 March 1993, p. 2.

56    Benjamin Craig, 'History of the Cannes film festival', 2006, www.
      cannnesguide.com/basics/.

57    Elsaesser, European Cinema: Face to Face with Hollywood, p. 91.

58    'The posters: 60th festival', http://www.festival-cannes.fr/en/archives/
      2007/posters.html.

59    Wyatt, 'Economic constraints/economic opportunities: Robert Altman as
      auteur', p. 61.

60    Manohla Dargis, 'Campion invests plenty in 'In the Cut'', Los Angeles Times,
      31 October 2003, p. 108.

61    Hillel Schwarz, The Culture of the Copy, New York: Zone Books, 1996, p. 248.

62    David J. Fox, 'Mindful there's no "sure thing" at Oscar time, Piano Studio
      orchestrates a costly campaign', Los Angeles Times, 13 March 1994, p. D3.

63    Jim Schembri, 'Me Jane', p. 13.

64    Schembri, 'Me Jane', p. 13.

65    Fox, 'Mindful there's no "sure thing" at Oscar Time, Piano Studio
      orchestrates a costly campaign', p. D3.

66    William Grimes, 'After a first wave of raves, The Piano slips into a trough',
      New York Times, 10 March 1994, p. 15.

67    Janet Harbord, Film Cultures: Production, Distribution and Consumption,
      London: Sage, 2002, p. 90.

68    Michael Fleming, 'Buzz: paging Jane Campion', Variety, January
      31–February 6, 1994, p. 8

69    Touchstone home video press release dated 30 September 1994.

70    Sue Williams, 'The portrait of a certain lady', The Weekend Australian Magazine,
      Saturday 7 December, 1996, p. 55.

71    Williams, 'The portrait of a certain lady', p. 56.

72    Gary Maddox, 'Campion fired up at "career crisis" jibes', Sydney Morning
      Herald, 10 September, 1999, p. 2.

73    Maddox, 'Campion fired up at "career crisis" jibes', p. 2.

74    Maddox, 'Campion fired up at "career crisis" jibes', p. 2.

75    Sue Williams, 'Campion comes a cropper', Sun Herald, 5 September 1999,
      p. 18.

76    Maddox, 'Campion fired up at "career crisis" jibes', p. 2.

77    Shane Danielsen, 'Holy smoke, Campion faces a commercial death in
      Venice', The Australian, 6 September 1999, p. 5.

78    Sandra Hall, 'Smoke on the water', *Sydney Morning Herald*, 6 September 1999, p. 13

79    Derek Malcolm, 'Holy Smoke in your eyes', *Guardian*, 8 September 1999, p. 13.

80    David Stratton, 'Campion forces eyes open at Venice festival', *The Australian*, 17 September 1999, p. 11.

81    Alexander Walker, 'Wonder of Winslet', *The Evening Standard*, 6 September 1999, p. 3.

82    Patrick Z. McGavin 'Holy Smoke'. *Hollywood Reporter*, vol. 359, no. 23, 8 September 1999, p. 13.

# 3

---

# DISCIPLINING JANE CAMPION

## Auteurism and the knowing audience

I never think about all my films.

Jane Campion[1]

From very early in her career, Jane Campion's films have provided the cornerstone for a series of academic debates, most particularly those arising from feminist studies. But especially striking is the singular impact of *The Piano* on a broad range of academic scholarship, anywhere from disability studies to musicology to Jungian psychology and the list goes on. *The Piano* has generated an entire academic industry of its own, producing innumerable books, conference papers and scholarly articles in a multitude of languages, one which continues to manufacture publications and heated debate more than a decade after the film's release. These debates have, in turn, led many academic commentators to Campion's earlier works.

On this basis alone, it is fair to say that there is much in Campion's work that is intrinsically appealing to academics and that almost all of her films have been able to successfully cultivate and address a global 'expert' audience. And in so enthusiastically embracing her, this audience has in turn, assisted in establishing Campion as an international filmmaker, a 'deterritorialized' figure articulating the sort of universal 'issues' and principles many academics also claim to address. In this way, *The Piano*, for example, is taken up by academics for its contribution to broad debates about post-colonialism and feminism rather than for being a clever Antipodean romance in the way the contemporaneously released and underestimated New Zealand period film *Desperate Remedies* (Main and Wells, 1993) was.

Unlike popular critical opinion, academics have for the most part remained loyal to Campion's post-*Piano* films, treating them with due consideration despite their lesser box office appeal. In fact, in many ways the post-*Piano* films have extended Campion's academic reach, *Portrait of a Lady*, for example receiving considerable coverage in literary studies (and reigniting interest in *An Angel at My Table*), *Holy Smoke* inspiring debate among those concerned with spiritualism and alternative lifestyles.

But on the whole, the vast majority of academic commentators have been preoccupied with the role Jane Campion's films have played for identity-based disciplines such as gender studies, post-colonial studies and national cinema studies. Often this commentary takes the form of either/or debates in which the options for Campion are presented as limited choices (feminist/not feminist; racist/not racist), however, a large number of academics are also interested in the way in which Campion's films repeatedly return to unresolved problems of reconciliation, hybridity and collaboration which sit uneasily with accounts of her practice and her films as distinctively auteurist or simply feminist, for example.

For many academics. Campion's films are just as good to talk about as they are to watch and they stand up to the repeated viewing demanded by detailed textual analysis. All this talk has also been useful for bolstering Campion's status as an auteur. A quick scan of the chronology and bibliographic resources at the end of this book shows that long after Campion's films have completed their theatrical run, there is still a wide amount of material (books, journal articles, DVD commentaries) keeping her name in circulation (this book, of course, being no exception).

Universities themselves play an important and largely unremarked role in the film industry, particularly for filmmakers such as Jane Campion. In terms of film distribution and exhibition universities harbour a key market for art and indie cinema. In the US, for example, the campus circuit is a lucrative market for cult and specialized cinema. The successful mini-studio, New Line Cinema, emerged from this circuit distributing specialized films with accompanying academic lectures and presentations. In many cases university film societies and festivals have historically formed the basis for later art cinema distribution and exhibition initiatives. Universities are also a distinct non-theatrical market for film rentals and DVD sales in order to resource cinema studies courses, for example. Their staff, students and graduates participate in debates adjudicating the canonical status of particular films and directors. And academics are prominent in providing annotations and expert opinion for the 'rich' content such as specialized commentaries and catalogues that circulate with film and DVD releases.

Jane Campion herself has been conferred an academic title at the Sydney College of the Arts and an honorary doctorate from Victoria University in Wellington, both of which lend further credibility to her 'academic' appeal as a filmmaker. Many media interviews emphasize her academic qualifications, which include courses in anthropology, painting and then film production. Her undergraduate major in anthropology is an early source of interest for interlocutors and in one early interview she cited its influence in her filmmaking: 'I think actually that I have an anthropologist's eye. I have good observation skills.'[2] And, further: 'I think I've always been one, ever since I opened my eyes really.'[3] More recently she has reiterated this affinity with her early studies: 'I think why I ended up loving [anthropology] so much was that I've always been really curious about people's habits. Even when I was a child going to visit friend's houses, I used to love to quiz their mums about how they run everything.'[4]

More directly, Campion has spoken of her use of scholarly works in pre-production; she prepared for the adaptation of *Portrait* by reading the research of William H. Gass and Alfred Habegger and whom she quotes in the press kit for the film.[5] Campion has underscored something of her studious approach to the cinema by describing one of her films, *Holy Smoke*, as an 'essay'.[6] And not incidentally, Campion also made a film featuring an academic of sorts. Frannie of *In the Cut* is a professor of creative writing at an unnamed institution (see Figure 3.1).

Campion's ongoing identification with her time at university is an important reminder that the circulation of scholarly debate doesn't just occur in universities and among academics and neither do academics simply limit their discussion to scholarly outlets such as specialized film journals. Furthermore, many contemporary filmmakers now enter the industry with a prior degree or two under their belt and are well versed in the academic analysis of film texts. Similarly, countless film critics and trade journalists have film studies degrees and some

FIGURE 3.1 **Knowledge by degrees: creative writing professor Frannie (Meg Ryan) in** ***In the Cut***
Screen Gems/Pathé/The Kobal Collection/Bridges, James

academics also publish in these non-scholarly formats and do not confine their commentary to other academics only (this is especially true in Australia and New Zealand, which have smaller publication markets and pools of writers to draw on). And finally we can observe that a great deal of contemporary publishing on cinema occurs on the web in online fansites and blogs and that many of these writers are also familiar with academic approaches to the cinema.

If we accept that academic film consumption and commentary is also (a sometimes unintended) part of the 'long tail' of film promotion and circulation then we can better understand the types of segmentation that occur within this market. For example, among scholarly film publications, there is considerable variation between peer reviewed and non-reviewed journals, between journals that appear on a monthly basis and those that appear quarterly, between those published as 'hard copy' and those principally published online. There are journals that are aimed at both cinephiles and film scholars and that draw their authors from both groups such as *Sight and Sound*, *Film Comment*, *Film Quarterly* and the online *Senses of Cinema*. And there are journals that seldom look at films in current release and are mostly directed to other academics such as *Screen*, *Cinema Journal* or the online *Screening the Past*. And then there are magazines that include informed film commentary, these being aimed at avid cinema consumers such as *Empire*, *Première* or *Rolling Stone*.

Within these various publication outlets, academics vie to demonstrate their variation from each other. Academic publishing is the stage on which subtle interpretive differences are dramatized, in which reformulations of the canon are enacted and in which the novelty of new theoretical references and frameworks are emphasized above all other considerations. As Janet Staiger notes: 'Competition in academia and the film industry reinforces canons and canon making.'[7] For Staiger, the underlying motivation of most academics in writing about cinema is twofold: 'One rereads canonized works not only for providing another interpretation, but also, usually, to make one's name with a new methodology. One resurrects a film to claim it as an unnoticed masterpiece . . . One applies rigorous analyses of theories and methodologies to indicate fallacious reasoning of predecessors.'[8] In chapter one, we saw how this diversity of opinion does little to harm, and much to enhance, the reputation of the contemporary auteur. But there is more at stake for academics than simply reviewing one another's reading of the auteurist's film texts. In identifying, debating and interpreting Campion's 'auteurprints', her signature moments, many academic commentators divulge their own. In dwelling on Campion's multiple texts (on her films as well as the production of her auteur self), academics also self-fashion, producing their own 'selves'.

For Michel Foucault, intellectuals represent the ultimate self-fashioning 'auteurs', nothing of them (himself included): 'From the idea that the self is not given to us, I think there is only one logical consequence: we have to create ourselves as a work of art.'[9] Intellectuals are simultaneously auteurs and the objects of their own creative output, a work of art. For Foucault this project of self-formation, the 'training of oneself by oneself', is linked to knowledge – it 'implies attention, knowledge, technique.'[10] It could be suggested then that for many film scholars, their 'knowledge' of the auteur provides a compelling model of the practice of self-formation. And it follows that, as there are many tropes of auteurism, there will be corresponding and multiple tropes of academic self-formation among cinema studies scholars; ideas of the auteur's artistic freedom aligning with expectations for academic freedom; a belief in the universality of the auteur aligning with the abstraction of academic expertise; conviction in the self-sufficiency of creativity aligning with notions of the university as a detached ivory tower. And vice versa. Campion herself said:

> I don't think of stories as women's pictures or men's pictures . . . My view of how to write a script is just 'Make it interesting to yourself.' Of course you hope it's going to be watchable and workable, but you've got more chance of that if it springs from a genuine desire to communicate something personal to yourself.[11]

This seems to posit the auteur as purely nonfigurative, unmarked by social distinctions and differences and focused intently on internal structure and form. Campion proposes the narcissistic idea of the creative figure who is at one and the same time the object of her own creativity, an unattainable story of the auteur/auteurist's origins and originality. In this way, Campion posits her self as something that is known to her and yet in her creativity she eludes herself as well.

This seems close to what Foucault describes as the quality of self-detachment required by intellectuals – not in terms of academic abstraction but an elaboration of 'self by self', an intellectual self-recognition achieved through practice rather than reflection per se.[12] Donald E. Hall, in *The Academic Self*, acknowledges the unlikelihood for academics in achieving anything resembling clarity on our selves. Instead, Hall proposes the academic self as perpetually novel, created and sustained by constant acts of reflexivity. For Hall, the impulse to 'question, reinterrogate, unsettle and dissipate familiarities should drive our work as intellectuals, and we – *our selves* – should hold no privileged position vis-à-vis that critical engagement. That we cannot see our 'selves' clearly means that we must energetically solicit the articulated perspectives of others who can add immeasurably to our partial views, even if those views will, in fact, never be complete.'[13] Because academic self-knowledge can never be fully achieved we should actively enter into interdisciplinary dialogue to better understand where and how our agency is limited and activated. The point of academic self-reflexivity therefore is not to add further layers of confessional biography to auteurist studies, for example.

McKenzie Wark, addressing the partiality of self-recognition in a different context, identifies the role of celerity figures like Campion in shaping a sense of communal or social belonging (rather than difference per se), in particular fostering a notion of belonging that exceeds our ordinary experience and identifies our partiality:

> We may not like the same celebrities, we may not like any of them at all, but it is the existence of a population of celebrities, about whom to disagree, that makes it possible to constitute a sense of belonging. Through celebrating (or deriding) celebrities it is possible to belong to something beyond the particular culture with which each of us might identify.[14]

Wark highlights the way in which disparate communities of commentary, linked together by the figure of the celebrity auteur, might lend each other an alternative 'perspective'. Specifically in relation to the question of academic belonging, Wark's observations about the role of the celebrities such as Campion in turning insight outwards, suggests that institutional and disciplinary affiliations might also usefully be expanded and diffuesed by a common interest in a specific filmmaker such as Campion.

Academic and disciplinary modes of behaviour are arguably the key components of scholarly communities. We form our initial academic subjectivity, or selfhood, through the disciplinary engagements of our earliest academic career.[15] Writing about fan cultures (including academic fans), Matt Hills admits a 'sneaking suspicion that academic writers are more attached to their discipline than their "subject"'.[16] Certainly this has often been the case for how Campion's work, especially The Piano has been mobilized through a series of overtly tactical scholarly debates. There is even an exchange of articles that was consciously called 'the Screen debate' which is made up of least five articles, the first three of which were published in 1995.[17] In the following years two further articles appeared in the journal picking further at the threads of disciplinary dispute. Dana Polan identifies another strand of commentary in which the figure of Baines is the locus for a series of debates about The Piano's feminist credentials.[18] And there is another renowned series of articles written by Leonie Pihama, Lynda Dyson and bell hooks, which engage in discussion of The Piano's status as a post-colonial text.[19] What is telling in many of these contributions is the way in which the film serves either as a pretext for reconsideration of disciplinary divisions or in which its success or failure is measured on the basis of its conformity to disciplinary expectations. In looking across these various debates, however, what is remarkable is the way in which Campion and her film texts are by implication characterised as being post-disciplinary, multidisciplinary and transdisciplinary in nature, simply in being so variously debated.

It is possible to see in these assorted disciplinary debates about Campion another way of thinking about the modalities of contemporary academic work. Thomas Osborne has recently argued for the emergence of a new type of academic practice that arises broadly out of the impact of contemporary media on academic life and the embedding of knowledge in the media themselves. It is easy to imagine that this form of academic practice bears an especially pertinent relationship to those of us working on and therefore as I would argue, within these media. Thomas elaborates from the identification of academics as 'legislators' (those who are concerned with the formation of correct opinions which result in authoritative statements); 'interpreters' (those concerned with the production of understanding derived from the analysis of cultural texts); and 'experts' (those who produce useful information). To these forms of epistemic conduct and intellectual subjectivity, he adds one further figure: the 'mediator':

> The mediator is not simply a 'media' intellectual, but also someone for whom ideas are more like instruments than principles; a motivator of syntheses that 'work', and have purchase, rather than ideals that dimly reverberate; an expert as much in the contexts and fields in which ideas operate as in the intellectual content of ideas themselves.[20]

Mediators produce ideas in relation to others, mediation is 'integrally public, collective and interactive'.[21] Mediation occurs in academic spaces in which people can argue and debate. Osborne observes that the figure of the academic mediator is becoming more prevalent and visible and that there is an elective affinity between this type of academic practice and various transformations in contemporary culture and politics, in particular, around changes in the social organization of media consumption.[22]

## CINEMA'S KNOWING AUDIENCES

There exists very little academic work in cinema studies explicitly examining the features and preferences of academics as media consumers, in particular as a movie market segment. One notable exception to this absence of academic discussion is Pierre Bordieu's classic ethnographic research conducted in France in the 1960s, which links cinema-going preferences to class position and academic qualification.[23] Bordieu for example, finds that the frequency of cinema going is highest among the most educated and lowest amongst the least educated but that the scale of these differences in consumption cannot explain a larger disparity in specific cinema knowledges such as the ability to identify film directors. For Bordieu, this indicates that: 'Knowledge of directors is much more closely linked to cultural capital than is mere cinema-going . . . At equivalent levels of education, knowledge of directors increases with the number of films seen . . . [but] assiduous cinema-going does not compensate for absence of educational capital.'[24] Bordieu explains these observations by suggesting that such competences arise from unintentional learning:

> [m]ade possible by a disposition acquired through domestic or scholastic acquisition of legitimate culture. This transposable disposition, armed with a set of perceptual and evaluative schemes that are available for general application, inclines its owner towards other cultural experiences and enables him or her to perceive, classify and memorize them differently. Where some only see 'a western starring Burt Lancaster', others 'discover an early John Sturges' or 'the latest Peckinpah'. In identifying what is worthy of being seen and the right way to see it they are aided by their whole social group . . . and by the whole corporation of critics mandated by the group to produce legitimate classifications and the discourse necessarily accompanying any artistic enjoyment worthy of the name.[25]

For Bordieu, there is an identifiable aesthetic disposition that can be associated with elite cultural groups defined by their social capital such as academics, the authority of which is premised on the privileging of specific, distinctive types of knowledge such as attributions of authorship. Auteurist knowledge, for Bordieu, is a defining feature of academic authority. These habits of cultural consumption conversely serve to legitimate social distinctions and perpetuate divisions between elite and non-elite consumption, which still exist beneath much film scholarship, despite the many changes that have occurred in both cinema consumption and academic life since Bordieu undertook his research.

In addition to the cultural disposition of elites such as academics identified by Bordieu, the elevated status of academics as 'authorized knowers' is both embedded in the ego strength of the scholar and the status of their organizational affiliation.[26] Universities, like many institutional communities, are characterized by their collective and individual values and by their beliefs and structures. Kathryn Hegarty has noted the many implications and challenges that result from these sources of academic self-hood in a changing social environment in which intellectuals and researchers are just as likely to be found working in government, in the media, and in business rather than universities:

> If the constituent element of academic culture is identity, it will inform all those practices in which academics are involved. Amongst these is the process of determining a role and function for higher education in the 21st century, as knowledge itself becomes the stock in trade of many organizations. Universities have to find new ways to articulate their relevance and to maintain their own unique commitment and contribution.[27]

There is significant trepidation in the current setting in which universities find it increasingly difficult to explain their distinctiveness as institutions centred on the production of knowledge. The spectre of academy's proximity to other knowledge-rich organizations and the concomitant loss of their 'critical distance' from the society that sustains them has produced alarmist commentary. Mark Considine suggests that for the university sector 'to lose the primary distinction around which identity is organised is to succumb to a state of emergency'.[28] More specifically, it is interesting to note that the latest revival of interest in academic auteurist study has occurred as the film industry makes room for emerging non-academic 'knowing audiences'. Most recently, for example, has been the rise of 'smart' cinema, in which the chief pleasure for the audience lies in their ability to recognize, to 'know', a sequence of inter-textual references.

Alternatively, other commentators have found changes to the social positioning of the academy to be an opportunity to produce a new vision of the university. Bill Readings' discussion in *The University in Ruins* reiterates an emphasis on 'dissensus' – the profound differences in the professional allegiances and identifications of academics who collectively might instead form a heteronomous community, which, he says, 'does not pretend to have the power to name and determine itself; it insists that *the position of authority cannot be authoritatively occupied*'.[29]

This question of how to occupy or evacuate a position of authority has also been a troubling matter at the more specific level of academic practice and inflects much contemporary academic auteurist writing in a doubled sense. First, there is the problem of the authority claimed by the auteur herself and then there is problem of the authority of the auteurist. Furthermore, if auteurist film academics position themselves as a 'knowing audience', they do so twofold: both in occupying a place of authority in relation to the films and filmmakers under their microscope but also in their own orientation to self-production, in revealing that they also 'know' auteurism as a creative practice which produces both the auteur and the auteurist.

Janet Staiger has written on her difficulties with auteurist authorization in her reflections on the politics underlying academic acts of canon creation. Staiger rejects political pluralism as a solution for academics seeking to negotiate their positions of authority, arguing that the exercise of 'power' is an unavoidable aspect of the political choices entailed in canonizing activity. Instead, Staiger proposes an alternative approach that emphasizes the capacities of academics to combine both an inward looking self-reflection and an outward looking orientation to social improvement:

> Our evaluative procedures relate to our interpretive strategies; interpretative strategies result from how we are constructed as subjects and which interpretive strategies we learn. What art works we have

available are a product of these causes. Canons are 'inevitable' only as a consequence of prior choices. This is not a question of shepherds leading the sheep but making sure all of us are shepherds (of whatever variety) and none of us sheep. Thus the issue of the politics of film canons is one of consciously (as far as possible) choosing methods of interpreting the experience of films so as to improve our human condition.[30]

For Staiger, by not being sheep, we prove to be more human as film scholars. Here, Staiger deploys a 'self-evident' academic truism: that animals, in this instance, sheep, are not self-conscious or self-determining (but humans are). Whereas sheep are indistinct, academics can and must assert their distinctiveness and individuality; whereas sheep are pliant, academics should be critical and wilful; and whereas sheep do not understand their own self-hood as the product of an historical process, academics can and must aspire to recognize that their self-formation is a contingent aspect of their ongoing rationalizing activity. But, in making these observations, Staiger preserves a distinction between those who are capable of rational self-reflection (academics) and those who are not (woolly minded non-academics). Here, Staiger reiterates a typical division within otherwise amorphous conceptions of culture consumers; between the rational discernment of academic writing and the 'emotional', non-serious attachments of enthusiasts, a division that has been subject to recent reconsideration.

It is easy to overstate the distinction between the non-rational subjectivity of fans and the rational self of academics. Many of the academics engaged in the foundation of cinema studies programmes at universities were upfront fans and cinephiles before they began and then throughout their academic careers. Contemporary auteur theory and studies emerges in part from this history. Richard Dyer, in his work on stars, noted with more than a hint of personal poignancy, the relationship between analysis and affect in his own work. In his concluding comments to Stars, he describes how he could still find

FIGURE 3.2 **On the up:** Ada (Holly Hunter) and Flora (Anna Pasquin) in *The Piano*
Jan Chapman Prods/CIBY 2000/The Kobal Collection

himself catching his breath at the sight of Marilyn Monroe, sighing over the beauty of Montgomery Clift, admiring the strength of Barbara Stanwyck: 'I don't want to privilege these responses over analysis, but equally I don't want, in the rush to analysis, forget what it is that I am analyzing.'[31] A substantial component of the project of feminist film theory also brought the relationship between the professional and the affective to the fore of its analytic ambit.

But it is specifically in relation to auteurist studies that the division between academic rationality and everyday fandom falls over. William D. Routt in a luminous historical overview of the development of early auteurist criticism, has written about the role of 'love' as an underlying feature of auteurist appreciation and auteur practice. Not only does Routt identify an emotional undercurrent in auteurist commentary he also identifies its role in aligning the auteurist with the object of their affection, 'Love', Routt says, 'is a state common to both auteurist and auteur'.[32] In auteurist writing, according to Routt, the critic–viewer becomes the auteur's collaborator and double:

> [I]t seems that auteurism, by elevating the individual artist to supremacy in film making, paradoxically raised the viewer to a position of creative power . . . the auteurist speaks about a film *as* its auteur *through* its spectator.[33]

The expressions of the auterist are not intended to exercise cultivated preference or even understanding. The auteurist recreates rather than dissects the films she gazes at and in so doing she is both self-forming and self-effacing. For Routt, auteurist criticism ultimately substitutes love for understanding:

> It betrays its object by loving it too well, by seeing it too quickly, seeing through it, betrays it by the impatience of seeing at all, instead of just looking, being content to look, staring into thin air. Love is certain, knows its own worth. Love is the best there is or can be. And understanding? Thin, shivery understanding, full of self-loathing, knowing only ignorance, tentativeness, hope. Strike a match for understanding so that she may warm her hands once more and see where love is, and see where she so wants to be.[34]

Routt's evocative account of the interplay between emotional attachment and interpretation in auteurist writing begs the question of what happens when the auteurist does not find an auteur who reciprocates with articulations of cineastic love, such as Campion, an auteur for example who repeatedly professes ambivalence? In Routt's terms there are at least two alternatives to the way of looking premised on the mutual love of auteur and auteurist: in which the auteurist invokes a type of 'aspirational' understanding which reaches further and more intently towards its object within otherwise unreciprocated relationship or in which the auteurist appropriates a type of ambivalence, neither *a priori* or *a posterior* to the text, but approaching the auteur and her films without judgement, as intrinsically and deliberately polysemic, located soley at the level of the phenomenal. These are both valid options for the contemporary auteurist: hyperbolic unreciprocated love (and sometimes loathing) or operative ambivalence and it is possible to identify both, sometimes in combination in many academic approaches to Campion's films.

## BEYOND ACADEMIC SELF-CARE: LOVING THE PIANO TO BITS

Almost as an aside, in an interview, Jane Campion remembers that one of her proposed titles for *The Piano* was *The Sleep of Reason*.[35] It is tempting to wonder what impact this designation might have had on subsequent academic discussion of the film. An array of viewer assessments of Campion's films seem to inspire passionate 'ownership' on the part of her many fans. The intensity of feeling, positive and negative, toward *The Piano* expressed by many viewers including reviewers and academics is a case in point (see Figure 3.3). Critics and fans alike have been moved to hyperbole in what Gail Jones has described as the film's capacity to 'alienate and entrance'.[36]

FIGURE 3.3 Toronto 2003: fans waiting to glimpse the stars at the première of *In the Cut*

Photo by Donald Weber/Getty Images

Sue Gillett's fluent description of her response to her first viewing of *The Piano* captures the intense emotional tenor of her experience:

> *The Piano* affected me very deeply. I was entranced, moved, dazed. I held my breath. I was reluctant to re-enter the everyday world after the film had finished. *The Piano* shook, disturbed, and inhabited me. I felt that my own dreams had taken form, been revealed. I dreamed of Ada the night after I saw the film. These were thick, heavy and exhilarating feelings.[37]

For Gillett, the film returns her to a state of unconscious awareness, the 'sleep of reason' perhaps. Similarly for Lizzie Franke viewing *The Piano* was also about bringing her emotions to the fore:

> For a while I could not think, let alone write about *The Piano* without shaking. Precipitating a flood of feelings, *The Piano* demands as much a physical and emotional response as an intellectual one . . . I wanted to rush at the screen and shout and scream.[38]

Franke's emphasis on the physicality of her response was echoed in many other accounts of the film. For example, for Vivian Sobchack, various kinds of feelings overwhelmed her thoughts on watching the film:

> However intellectually problematic in terms of its sexual and colonial politics, Campion's film moved me deeply and touched me throughout, stirring my bodily senses and my sense of body. The film not only 'filled me up' and often 'suffocated' me with feelings that resonated in and constricted my chest and stomach, but it also 'sensitised' the very surfaces of my skin – as well as its own – to touch. Throughout *The Piano*, my whole being was intensely concentrated and, rapt as I was in what was there on the screen, I was also wrapped in a body that, here, was achingly aware of itself as a sensuous, sensitised, sensible material capacity.[39]

Sobchack proposes her academic self as sensate *despite* her intellectual misgivings about the film. It may also be possible that is precisely because of what she believes to be *The Piano's* intellectually problematic status that enables her 'feelings' to come to the fore. For Sobchack, the film's enigmatic opening scenes bind her in a bodily sense to the idea of being emotionally 'touched':

> Despite my 'almost blindness' the 'unrecognisable blur', the resistance of the image to my eyes, *my fingers knew what I was looking at* – and this in advance of the objective 'reverse' shot that followed and put those fingers in their proper place . . . What I was seeing was, in fact, *not* an unrecognisable image, however blurred and indeterminate in my vision, however much my eyes could not 'make it out'. . . My experience of *The Piano* was thus a heightened instance of our common sensuous experience of the movies: the way we are in some carnal modality able to touch and be touched by the substance of images, to feel a visual atmosphere envelop us, to experience weight and suffocation and the need for air, to take flight in kinetic exhilaration and freedom even as we are relatively bound to our ears, to be knocked backwards by a sound, to sometimes even smell and taste the world we see upon the screen.[40]

Sobchack was not the only member of the audience whose viewing of the film resulted in a revelatory physical experience of film consumption. On watching the finger severance scene, Laleen Jayamanne found, for example, that she experienced an inexplicable pain in her hand.[41] For Sobchack and Jayamanne, *The Piano* invites us to share its material surfaces and to thus become aware of our own materiality as spectators, therefore outwardly producing a novel self-awareness. What begins as an experience of self-absence, in which the academic viewer is wholly subjugated to the film text, overrun by physical and emotional feelings, results in a radical insertion of the academic self in the written scholarly text.

From these, admittedly small, sample accounts of academic appreciations of *The Piano*, it might be possible to pick out some of the important identificatory features of Campion's films for her academic fans:

- an extraordinary viewing experience – distant from the everyday world and the everyday experience of cinema
- overwhelmingly sensuous, embodied experience of spectatorship
- emotionally moving and exhilarating ('wanted to rush at the screen and shout and scream')
- inspires strong personal identification ('I felt that my own dreams had taken form, been revealed')
- explanations for academic pleasure can be found in the film text, specifically in particularly resonant images or in response to 'problematic' content
- belief that the academic viewer is in a unique position of mediation; between sentiment and intellect, between interpretation and understanding; between identification and reflection, between physical self-presence and emotional self-absence and so on.

What is especially striking about the writing of these academic fans, however, is how closely they resemble the descriptions that non-academic fans give of their own self-hood. For Matt Hills, what characterizes many fans' accounts of their 'becoming a fan' is a striking self-absence. Theirs is a presentation of moments of 'self-suspensions and radical hesitation'. The fan cannot 'rationally' account for their experience, words fail. Matt Hills outlines several fan studies in which fans describe, with difficulty, their own 'becoming a fan' stories in terms of an epiphany, a dramatic and drastic departure from one point to another: a 'radical, enduring change in orientation . . . a dramatic opening of oneself to another's experience . . . a lasting and profound transition from an "old" viewpoint . . . to a "new" one, filled with energy and insight'.[42] Self-identified cult film fan and academic, Mark Kermode for example, tells of how he: '[S]ensed from the very beginning that there was something incomprehensibly significant about the actions being played out on-screen, something which spoke to me in a language I didn't quite understand . . . I felt from the outset that beyond the gothic trappings these movies had something to say to me about my life. I just didn't have any idea what.'[43]

In admitting that there is a more porous relationship between fandom and academia, it is possible to see that there are at least two resultant self-identified groups which differ in emphasis: the 'academic–fan' (a scholar who admits they are also a fan, occasionally drawing on their fandom as a source of honor within their discipline) and the 'fan–academic' (a fan who uses academic theorizing within their fan writing). Matt Hills has written on the way these two positions have been categorically split in both theoretical terms but also through practical logics of belonging and self-identification.[44] For Adrian Martin there are further distinctions that characterize cinema fandom – between cinephiles (who like to read) and film 'nerds' who are openly anti-intellectual and as a rule do not read but are engaged in frequent writing (principally of lists and inventories).[45]

As Matt Hills puts it, these approaches share their status as outsiders and outcasts in common. They are both, by definition, mediators:

> [T]he scholar–fan and the fan–scholar are necessarily liminal in their identities (that is, they exist and transgress between the regulative norms of academic and fan imagined subjectivities). This 'between-ness' is what underpins the defensiveness and anxiety of both groups, since both are marginalized within their respective primary communities. Equally, neither fan–scholars, nor scholar–fans can 'properly' belong to the other, secondary community unless they temporarily adopt its institutional norms of writing and practice.[46]

There is then a sense in which the distinction between the two is simply preserved for practical purposes – through differences in the social value attributed to distinct cultural spaces (those that read and write for *Empire* versus those read and write for *Screen*, for example). This distinction itself seems increasingly less plausible, despite the best efforts of government initiated, academic publication ranking exercises, designed to quarantine scholarly research from mainstream publication efforts. Lizzie Franke's account of watching *The Piano*, cited earlier in this chapter, appeared both in *Sight and Sound* and an academic publication. Academics who identify as mediators will continue to pursue a variety of outlets, especially those which operate on less lengthy timeframes in which to engage with pressing industrial and intellectual issues.

## ARRESTED ACADEMICS AND THE IMAGE OF THE AUTEUR

Many of the academic accounts of *The Piano* describe responses that occur 'despite' a lack of clarity about the film's formal or narrative purpose. It is possible, instead, to consider that the identifiably 'enigmatic' qualities of *The Piano*, and many of Campion's other films, has been crucial to providing scholars an opportunity to consider their academic 'selves' differently. Against an abstract rationality imposed by conventional academic modes of production, the auteur becomes an ally of the oppositional energies and sentiments of experience; of the human senses, dramatizing and inspiring qualities like curiosity, memory, a hunger for seeing, hearing and connection.

For Barbara Klinger, in seeking to understand *The Piano*'s hold on (mostly academic) viewers, one answer lies in a generic feature of the art film and in the specific qualities of *The Piano* itself: 'the spectacular, enigmatic and captivating image'.[47] In Campion's films – particularly in her visual direction – the same stunning, ambiguous symbolic images (see Figure 3.4) that, as we saw in chapter one, became a source of criticism for critics no longer struck by their arresting qualities, suggest to Klinger a lingering affective power:

> We can consider the arresting image, then, as the 'money shot' of the art film insofar as it delivers a payoff for one of the genre's chief expected pleasures: contact with highly aestheticised, ambiguous and affecting imagery.[48]

FIGURE 3.4 **Ada (Holly Hunter) plays in** *The Piano*
Jan Chapman Prods/CIBY 2000/The Kobal Collection

Klinger's notion of the arresting image certainly provides insight into some of the academic accounts of *The Piano* as well as Campion's other films. Kathleen McHugh, for example, ends her book on Campion by contemplating the succession of arresting images in her *oeuvre* as conclusive evidence of Campion's auteurist credentials:

> [W]hat stays, what persists in a Campion film, beyond narrative, are the images, that like Ada's will in *The Piano*, are so strange and strong: a young girl with a Beatles mask practicing kissing with her girlfriend; a sapling uprooted by a woman in the middle of the night, its roots a ghostly echo of her legs in a diaphanous nightgown; jackaroos dancing together under the stars in the outback; a woman, her skirts high over her head, tethered underwater to her piano; another woman, trapped, her shoes confiscated, devising an escape from footwear made out of ribbons and books. This last image is an apt visual metaphor for the unwieldy and contradictory ingredients of feminine aspiration, mobility, and desire and with it, I will close.[49]

This closing image of *The Piano*, one of the film's several 'conclusions' has proved especially intriguing to many academic commentators, including Klinger herself who notes its personal effect on her repeated viewing of the film:

> This epilogue is, then, especially moving and provocative: its visual and aural presentation impart a compelling lyrical quality, while its unexpected and inexplicable representation of Ada's death, portrayed with some longing, create an enigma. Indeed, the mysteries of the interpretive and affective dimensions of this image have become a mainstay of my viewing of *The Piano*, from my first encounter with the film through each subsequent screening.[50]

Gail Jones also describes the power of this image in terms of its incomprehensibility:

> This is a death and not-death, a cinematic moment of meditation, a moment of hallucinatory vivacity and complicated rhetoric, captured in an eerie, and in some ways incomprehensible, image.[51]

In these commentaries, academics find themselves submerged beneath a representation that seems as tantalizing as it is out of reach to them and there appears ever so briefly in this image of self-suspension, a momentary alignment between the academic, the auteur and the film text.

The characteristic feature of enigma and ambiguity in Campion's cinema has been noted by a wide array of academics and not just in relation to her manipulation of visual style. Claudia Gorbman, for example, has written on the role of ambiguity in *The Piano*'s soundtrack. Gorbman asks: 'What are we to make of Ada's playing?':

> In *The Piano*, Stewart, wishing to make up his mind about Ada's playing, can only react to it with wide-eyed puzzlement. Baines responds erotically, recognizing Ada's sexuality in her playing . . . The faces of the

FIGURE 3.5 Isabel Archer (Nicole Kidman) thinking hard in *Portrait of a Lady*
Polygram/Propaganda/The Kobal Collection/Teller, Jurgen

> Maori listeners are impassive, and Stewart's female relations seem troubled by the music's passionate idiosyncrasy. On the one hand, there is no diegetic listener whom the film identifies as an authentic or qualified judge; on the other hand, unlike established musical stars, Holly Hunter is not a known quantity as a performer of music. *The Piano* provides few cues, casting Ada's playing on a sea of indeterminacy. Her piano music is 'a sound that creeps into you', in all its pain, artlessness, and ambiguity.[52]

Valerie Hazel focuses on the importance of enigma in *The Piano* in terms of the film's treatment of speech. In her reading, the limits of the body must be rethought in light of the complexities of the film's presentation and performance of the relationship between voice and articulation. According to Hazel, *The Piano* questions 'the adequacy of the tradition which sees voice as a transparent intermediary between the self and the world'.[53] In decentring the voice as the principal form of instrumental communication, the film focuses on other methods for producing and mediating meaning:

> In *The Piano*, different modes of articulation reinscribe the boundaries of the human body . . . To be articulate is to make something of oneself available to the other, to be joined to another in an attachment whose insecurities also describe a field of possibility. Within this displacement of the conventions of articulation, the operation of the voice itself is exposed: no longer in any sense the vehicle of intentional communication or thought, it too is a form of attachment which puts the boundaries between subject and object into question.[54]

In conclusion, Hazel asks what we might make of a notion of voice which 'no longer claims the guarantee of identity, nor authenticates the self and experience, but brings us to these things as enigma?'[55] The murkier aspects of *The Piano* pre-empt and participate in academic debates about identification, sensate experience and articulation. The experience of inexplicable enigma, challenges the academics reliance on *a priori* critical and disciplinary frameworks for analysis or evaluation but it also displaces their *a posteriori* disposition for interpretation as well.

For Klinger, there is a further specifically temporal dimension to the power of the enigmatic in Campion's *Piano*:

> These arresting images achieve affective power because they thrust the contradictions to the surface and refuse to resolve them. In sustaining this tension, the images animate the clashes and anomalies that bedevil female subjectivity. This sense of anomaly is critical to the emotions conjured by the arresting image. Just as the vision of the submerged woman and the piano is surreal in its odd and surprising juxtaposition of elements, the representation of female subjectivity, shaped by collisions between past and present, between oppressed and liberated versions of the self, is incongruous, uncomfortable and moving.

Here, Klinger reveals the work of the film text in revealing the (female) self as the product of a process of temporal mediation located between past and present. Again, it is possible to see *The Piano* itself as discursive on this question of the temporality of knowledge: In a scene within a scene, the play of Bluebeard is performed. Bluebeard's wife is decapitated for her curiosity, for seeking out the knowledge of what occurred to Bluebeard's previous four wives (and which she now realizes will occur to her). In effect, she is punished for knowing too early – for spoiling the surprise perhaps (see Figure 3.6). The scene is structurally important prefiguring Ada's own act of 'door opening', the unlocking of sexual desire and Stewart's consequent rage that has him removing her finger as punishment.

Klinger is also arguing that there is something about the elusivity of arresting images that particularly appeals to women, using psycho-analytic theory, her own viewing experience and audience studies to elaborate her point. Klinger recognizes that it is precisely the ideological ambiguities contained within these images that is their most powerful inducement:

> By blurring clean ideological lines, they lure the viewer into an episte-mological quest, a protracted attempt to clarify and resolve their con-tradictions. At a deeper level, though, their troubled ideologies appeal to a

FIGURE 3.6 **Knowing too early: the nativity play in** *The Piano*
Jan Chapman Prods/CIBY 2000/The Kobal Collection

certain realpolitik of the female subject: they objectify the trauma and complexity of the acquisition of identity in circumstances domination, demonstrating that this process does not result in a linear sweep of the old by the new. The process itself haunts the genealogy of identity formation represented in the films and in the female viewer's own experience, meaning that subjectivity is forever populated with visions of past selves and possibilities. The arresting images . . . offer particularly poignant crystallizations of this theme.[56]

Klinger aligns the enigmatic image in The Piano with the elaboration of a specifically female subjectivity arising from both the text and women's viewing of the film. In contrast, Kimberely Chabot Davis argues against any essentialist reading of the film in her detailed empirically based study of academic and feminist responses to The Piano.

For Davis The Piano plays between two genres, classic Hollywood melodrama and avant-garde or art cinema and that it is the film's mediation of these two which opens a space for multiple identifications. Davis suggests that The Piano is a hybrid genre, both 'popular' and 'elite' in a way that typifies many postmodern texts; and therefore it engenders multiple responses associated with these generic features, mixing critical detachment (associated with elite texts) and over-whelming feeling (associated with melodrama). These observations are based on an assumption about the way popular texts are viewed with affective immediacy and immersion while elite texts apparently favour detachment. Davis, elaborating from these presumptions, argues that The Piano opens up a space for sentimental postmodernism – in which viewers, such as the cademics she surveys, can accommodate both reading styles:

> While questioning the representational logic of realist classical cinema, The Piano promotes critical distance but avoids a more extreme Brechtian alienation effect by combining this distance with the emotional engagement of melodrama. This hybrid text allows viewers to think while feeling, to be soothed and disturbed at the same time, and to question familiar paradigms while still acknowledging the emotional value of traditional social formations and identities.[57]

Despite any misgivings about the instability of the binary division on which Davis's analytic architecture rests, she makes several important observations based on her interviews with academic and feminist viewers of The Piano. First, she emphasizes that there is a multiplicity of responses to the film, including its presentation of textual and visual ambiguity:

> Some of my audience group were alienated by this ambiguity because they desired the answers they are accustomed to receiving from 'entertainment', while others enjoyed the interpretive challenge.[58]

Second, she identifies the importance of disciplines *as well as* social or personal experiences in forming the basis for how the academics inter-preted the film, questioning the idea that academics simply respond to texts without prior influence. Davis also finds that identification is not necessarily an unconscious process, as suggested by psychoanalytic theoretical frameworks, but can involve a conscious negotiation between self and other, a cognitive choice:

> The widely divergent responses to *The Piano* among the women I interviewed highlight the fact that identification is an ideological process, rather than one that simply devolves from the female body or psyche. Feminist viewers of *The Piano* recognized that their identification and/or disidentification with the protagonist Ada was influenced by their own adherence to particular feminist ideologies, such as difference feminism, postmodern anti-essentialist feminism, victim's rights feminism, power feminism, lesbian separatism, Marxist feminism, or combinations thereof.[59]

In opposition to film theories that propose viewer identification as a process of self-recognition, Davis finds a large number of viewers of The Piano were able to cross boundaries of 'difference', identifying instead with their social others: 'For example, male feminist viewers of The Piano identified with the silent woman Ada rather than with the controlling male characters.'[60] Furthermore, Davis also finds a type of ambivalent identification, entailing 'an awareness of difference that prevents a colonizing incorporation yet leaves room for sympathy and connection. For example, many of the male feminists in my study identified with Ada's struggles against patriarchy yet did not forget their own complicity to patriarchy; nor did they presume to understand all that women experience.'[61] Davis describes how these same men identified with Ada in an 'excorporative way' recognizing the other with respect but retaining the power to transform the self.

Davis's findings represent a challenge to examinations of Campion's Piano that isolate the impact of its textual effect on female subjectivity alone. It may be, instead for instance, that Klinger's theorization of the power of the arresting image of The Piano on women, applies very well, perhaps better, to explaining the phenomenon of Campion's academic fans (including Klinger herself). Many academic writings on The Piano focus on an 'arresting image' – and surely moments in the cinema that give pause for thought are indeed a 'money shot' for those who presume to earn a living, or even take pleasure, by thinking about films. Perhaps this is why, when for many media critics Campion's images are no longer 'arresting', they still work for many academics, and that for many academics her texts remain central to their study of the cinema and are repeatedly chosen as the site from which to self-fashion? (See Figure 3.7.)

## CONCLUSION

The Piano is perhaps without precedent in establishing an international academic audience. The durability, breadth and tenor of the film's impact on academic publication and teaching are suggestive for a study of academics as an audience segment and, more specifically, in relation to the terms of 'fan' culture. This chapter prompts many questions: What is so appealing to academics about Jane Campion's films? To what extent can we generalize from the diversity of academic selves to

FIGURE 3.7 Colonial conflicts and post-colonial debates: George Baines (Harvey Keitel) in *The Piano*

Jan Chapman Prods/CIBY 2000/The Kobal Collection

describe the features of an academic audience for (Jane Campion) films? What role does Campion the auteur play in academic self-fashioning? How might a reading of academic commentary on Campion reveal and challenge these processes of self-formation? What is the impact of academic identity in film studies for understanding and writing about filmmakers such as Campion?

Academics, critics, festival aficionados, fans, publicists, cultural bureaucrats are all what we might call 'authenticating audiences'. In answering the question of what lies at the heart of the attraction between Campion films (particularly *The Piano*) and academic audiences, it is possible to look to the specific qualities of Campion's texts: to their use of 'arresting' images; their ambiguous use of sound; their ideological complexity; their hermeneutic uncertainties; and their generic hybridity. But it is also important to look past the auteur's films, to consider the mediating role of the filmmaker, as a colleague and competitor in diverse contemporary 'knowledge' practices. Although we can recognise that each works in a different location and from within a different discourse we can also see that the both the contemporary auteur and the film academic are mutually imbricated and that both share a cultural role as trans-mediators, each professionally focused on realisation rather than specialisation.

Perhaps instead of a theorisation of the 'post-auteur' what is really required is a theory of the 'post-auteurist'. Certainly, what is currently required, and which is beginning to emerge, is a shift in conventional academic thinking about the auteur, from a concern centred on intentions (where she is coming from?) or the opportunity for interpretation (where she is going?) to the self-recognition of the academic *in relation* to the auteur (where are we at with Campion; where does she fit in?). Other shifts in thinking about the auteur are also becoming evident as the tempo of academic practice changes. Rather than writing about the auteur in terms of the *a priori* choices proposed by the disciplinary (and subdisciplinary) 'programmes' of various forms of film scholarship or conversely rather than making use of those writing and teaching practices in which textual interpretation is superimposed as an *a posteriori* critical activity, the mobile industriousness of contemporary academic work moves commentary on Campion quickly along from one point in time to another.

And so we are reminded that the contemporary auteur is always already present and also never finished, irrespective of the status of their film texts or the explanations made of them. This book for example, will appear in circulation prior to the release of Campion's latest film *Bright Star*. But as I write, this film is already the subject of pre-emptory critical evaluation and has a tangible 'public' role in the ongoing unfolding of Campion's career, picking up on many themes evident in previous media and the industry representations of Campion and her films. *Bright Star*, promoted as a film about cruel fate and poetic love, is based in part on letters written between John Keats and Fanny Brawne, emphasizing Campion's propensity for explicit inter-textuality, more specifically thematically linking the film to Campion's previous works such as *Mishaps: Seduction and Conquest* and also highlighting the importance of written correspondence in *The Piano* and *Holy Smoke*. The film boasts a wide array of financiers from a variety of national industries and is, in part, funded by television interests. It features Australian and British stars (with Abby Cornish already being talked up in media as a potential award winner) and brings Campion together with producer–collaborator Jan Chapman again.

The prescient, premature public reception of *Bright Star*, well before its release in cinemas, reminds us that Campion's visions are always already 'mediated'. In this circuitous context, the contemporary auteur makes her self available to academics in a way that also enables us to orient and conduct our selves in a world indelibly marked by media images and practices of mediation.

## NOTES

1    Mick Brown, 'Where there's smoke', *Courier Mail*, 11 September 1999, p. 11.

2    Michel Ciment, 'Two interviews with Jane Campion', in Rafaele Caputo and Geoff Burton, *Second Take: Australian Film-makers Talk'*, Sydney: Allen &

Unwin, 1999, p. 49. Also see the lengthy review of Campion's *The Piano* that draws extensively on her background in anthropology; Alan A. Stone, 'The Piano', *Boston Review*, 24 February 1998, reprinted in Margolis, *Jane Campion's The Piano*, Cambridge: Cambridge University Press, 2000, pp. 179–84.

3    Eric Harrison, 'If it's Campion, think again: Holy Smoke, the latest in director's provocative film treatises, twists romance and religion', *LA Times*, 3 December 1999, p. F2.

4    Stephanie Bunbury, 'Cutting in on Campion', *Sunday Age – Agenda*, 16 November 2003, p. 18.

5    William Gass, 'The high brutality of good intentions', in Robert D. Bramberg (ed.), *The Portrait of a Lady: An Authoritative Text, Henry James and the Novel, Reviews and Criticism*, New York: W. W. Norton & Company, 1995; and Alfred Habegger, *Henry James and the 'Woman Business'*, Cambridge: Cambridge University Press, 1989.

6    Joy Press, 'Campion: Holy Smoke was an essay about love, about belief systems', *Village Voice*, 22–28 October 2003, p. 52.

7    Janet Staiger, 'The politics of film canons', in Diane Carson, Linda Dittmar and Janice Welsch (eds), *Multiple Voices in Feminist Criticism*, Minneapolis: University of Minnesota Press, 1994, p. 192.

8    Janet Staiger, 'The politics of film canons', p. 203.

9    Michel Foucault, 'On the genealogy of ethics: an overview of a work in progress', in Paul Rabinow (ed.) *The Foucault Reader*, New York: Pantheon Books, 1986, p. 351.

10   Foucault, 'On the genealogy of ethics', p. 360.

11   Errigo, Angie, 'Jane Campion: Antipodean director', *Empire*, no. 53, 1993, p. 64.

12   Foucault, 'The concern for truth' in *Politics, Philosphy, Culture: Interviews and Other Writings, 1977–1984* (trans. Alan Sheridan et al., ed. Lawrence D. Kritzman), New York: Routledge, 1988, p. 264.

13   Donald E. Hall, *The Academic Self: An Owner's Manual*, Columbus: Ohio State University Press, 2002, p. xviii, original emphasis.

14   McKenzie Wark, *Celebrities, Culture and Cyberspace*, Sydney: Pluto Press, 1999, p. 33.

15   Hegarty, 'Shaping the self'.

16    Matt Hills, *Fan Cultures*, London: Routledge, 2002, p. xiii

17    *Screen*, vol. 36, no. 3 (1995); and Suzy Gordon, 'I clipped your wing, that's all': auto-erotism and the female spectator in The Piano debate', *Screen*, vol. 37, no. 2, 1996.

18    Dana Polan, *Jane Campion*, London: British Film Institute, 2001, pp. 42–53. The debate includes articles by Naomi Segal and Carol Jacobs.

19    Leonie Pihama, 'Are films dangerous? A Maori woman's perspective on The Piano', *Hecate*, vol. 20, no. 2, 1994; Lynda Dyson, 'The return of the repressed? Whiteness, femininity and colonialism in The Piano,' *Screen*, vol. 36, no.3, Autumn 1995, pp. 267–76; Leonie Pihama, 'Ebony and ivory: constructions of Maori in The Piano', in Harriet Margolis (ed.), *Jane Campion's The Piano*, Cambridge: Cambridge University Press, 2000; bell hooks, 'Gangsta culture – sexism and misogyny', in *Outlaw Culture: Resisting Representations*, London: Routledge, 1994, pp. 115–23.

20    Thomas Osborne, 'On mediators: intellectuals and the ideas trade in the knowledge society', *Economy and Society*, vol. 33, no. 4, November 2004, p. 435.

21    Thomas Osborne, p. 443.

22    Thomas Osborne, 'On mediators: intellectuals and the ideas trade in the knowledge society', *Economy and Society*, vol. 33, no. 4, November 2004, pp. 430–47.

23    Pierre Bordieu, 'The aristocracy of culture' (trans. Richard Nice), *Media Culture and Society*, vol. 2, no. 3, 1980, pp. 225–54.

24    Bourdieu, 'The aristocracy of culture', pp. 232–3. Knowledge of actors, by way of contrast, varies consistently with the number of films seen.

25    Bourdieu, 'The aristocracy of culture', p. 233.

26    John Kornfeld, Perry M. Marker, Martha Rapp Ruddell, Thomas Cooke and Phyllis Fernlund, 'Through the looking glass: self-study in an era of accountability'. *Teacher Education Quarterly*, vol. 30, no. 7, 2003, pp. 7–22.

27    Kathryn Hegarty, 'Shaping the self to sustain the other: mapping impacts of academic identity in education for sustainability', *Environmental Education Research*, vol. 14, no. 4, 2008.

28    Mark Considine, (2006) Theorizing the university as a cultural system: distinctions, identities, emergencies. *Educational Theory*, vol. 56, no. 3, 2006, p. 256.

29    Bill Readings, *The University in Ruins*, Cambridge, MA: Harvard University Press, 1996, p. 187, original emphasis.

30    Staiger, 'The politics of film canons', p. 206.

31    Richard Dyer, *Stars*, London: BFI Publishing, 1982, pp. 184–5.

32    William D. Routt, 'L'évidence', in Adrian Martin (ed.) *Film – Matters of Style. Continuum, The Australian Journal of Media and Culture*, vol. 5, no. 2, 1992, p. 61.

33    William D. Routt, 'L'évidence', p. 56.

34    William D. Routt, 'L'évidence', p. 62.

35    Raffaele Caputo and Geoff Burton, *Second Take*, p. 78.

36    Gail Jones, *The Piano*, Sydney: Currency Press, 2007, p. 7.

37    Sue Gillett, 'Lips and finger: Jane Campion's The Piano', *Screen*, vol. 36, no. 3, 1995, p. 286.

38    Originally reviewed in *Sight and Sound*, vol. 3, no. 11, November 1993, pp. 50–51; and also in Margolis (ed.) *Jane Campion's The Piano*, p. 170.

39    Vivian Sobchack, 'What my fingers knew: the cinesthetic subject and vision in the flesh', *Senses of Cinema*, no. 5, 2000, http://www.sensesof cinema.com.au.

40    Sobchack, 'What my fingers knew'.

41    Laleen Jayamanne, 'Post-colonial gothic: the narcissistic wound of Jane Campion's *The Piano*', in *Toward Cinema and its Double: Cross-cultural Mimesis*, Bloomington: Indiana University Press, p. 48.

42    Cavicchi, 1998, p. 59.

43    Kermode, 1997, p. 57.

44    Matt Hills, *Fan Cultures*, London: Routledge, 2002.

45    José David Cácaeres and Alejandro Diaz, 'Guys, did you get past page 80 of volume 1 of *The Movement Image*?': *Miradas de cine* interviews Adrian Martin', *Cinemascope*, no. 7, January–April 2007, www.cinemascope.it.

46    Matt Hills, *Fan Cultures*, pp. 19–20.

47    Barbara Klinger, 'The art film, affect and the female viewer: *The Piano* revisited', *Screen*, vol. 47, no. 1, 2006, p. 20.

48    Klinger, 'The art film, affect and the female viewer', p. 24.

49    Kathlen McHugh, *Jane Campion*, Urbana: University of Illinois Press, 2007.

50    Klinger, 'The art film, affect and the female viewer', p. 24.

51    Gail Jones, *The Piano*, p. 72.

52    In Margolis, pp. 56–7.

53    Valerie Hazel, 'The politics of voice in Jane Campion's *The Piano*', p. 38.

54    Valerie Hazel, 'The politics of voice in Jane Campion's *The Piano*', p. 38.

55    Valerie Hazel, 'The politics of voice in Jane Campion's *The Piano*', p. 38.

56    Klinger, pp. 34–5.

57    Kimberley Chabot Davis, *Postmodern Texts and Emotional Audiences*, West Lafayette, FL: Purdue University Press, 2007, p. 65.

58    Kimberley Chabot Davis, *Postmodern Texts and Emotional Audiences*, p. 64.

59    Kimberley Chabor Davis, 'An ethnography of political identification: the Birmingham school meets psychoanalytic theory', *Journal for the Psychoanalysis of Culture and Society*, vol. 8, no. 1, 2003, p. 6.

60    Kimberly Chabot Davis, 'An ethnography of political identification', p. 7.

61    Kimberly Chabot Davis, 'An ethnography of political identification', p. 8.

# 4

## JANE CAMPION
## ON JANE CAMPION

One more interview

The following comments, gathered together in thematic order, were made in a wide-ranging phone interview conducted between the author and Jane Campion in August 2005. The interview took place early in the research for this book and, as a result, it does not address some of the issues subsequently explored in this analysis of Campion's contemporary auteurism. It does, however, look in detail at the critical factors that assisted in the development of Campion's career and her own approach to the creative process of filmmaking and, as such, many of her responses will be of enormous interest especially to filmmakers starting out in the industry.

### GETTING STARTED

It feels very fragile at the beginning. I feel a lot of compassion for people starting off on their so-called 'careers' or on their working life because it just feels like an impregnable wall in front of them and they don't know how they can possibly get that first step and I can remember feeling like that too. I think I felt that by the time I'd finished at film school, or even when I went into film school, it was going to be an opportunity for me to find out myself, number one, what I could do.

I knew I was passionate about film but I really didn't know if I had enough talent or ability to offer that would be interesting to anyone or even myself. So the film school was an opportunity to see what sort of things I would do and then I did feel quite calm about the idea that even if I liked what I could do, if nobody else liked it, well that would be the answer; that the answer was that what I wanted to do nobody wanted and that would be OK for me. Then I thought maybe I'll grow flowers or I'll start a business in something else.

While I was at the film school, a couple of women came and talent scouted at the end of my third year for people that might work in their newly formed Women's Film Unit which was established to help women get a beginning in their careers and they chose me to do their special project. They were very, very supportive and they loved the work I'd been doing which was kind of a shock to me so that was very encouraging. I was pretty tired after film school, but I thought I'm just not going to say no to anything that comes my way where I've got complete creative control. In fact, I didn't have complete creative control on that project which was probably the only one I haven't ever had complete creative control on because you know what women are like; they never trust you; they just want everything. And so I had a much better idea for *After Hours*, but the powers that were at the time didn't think it was a good idea, and in the end I wasn't happy with that film.

Even though I was happy enough doing it, *After Hours* was a film with a social purpose and I feel very uncomfortable about that kind of work. It just rubs against my principles of art making, so I guess that was a lesson. I think anything that you can take away from a film, like an epitaph or something, indicates a failed film. I prefer to think of films as meditations, a beautiful meditation that your mind naturally comes back to because it trusts the material (see Figure 4.1).

## WHAT HELPED

I do think that the support from the Australian government was crucial to me having any chance at all, particularly as a woman.

FIGURE 4.1 An uncomfortable experience: Jane Campion on the set of *After Hours*
Courtesy Film Australia

The fact of Gillian Armstrong, her great courage, as the first women's film director I saw. When they let her do, when she did, *My Brilliant Career* I thought: 'My god, are women going to be allowed to direct movies?' Because that was really a question before then. And she did it and you thought: 'They're going to let you; it's amazing.'

All the affirmative action directed towards giving women opportunities in the eighties. There were a lot of women that did the politics for that, who didn't necessarily end up making the films but they made it possible for people like me. They put a lot of energy into creating the real obligation for a sense of equality.

The women who set up those schemes really helped me out in a sense. And people like [Australian film critic] David Stratton who was supportive to me early on. He was so consistently supportive. I don't really even know him personally. And Pierre Rissient who was the scout for the Cannes festival, really focused on trying to support me. Those people do make a difference.

I don't think that same support exists for young women now. I think the eighties were a hard won, special time where people were skiting about having a woman film director or someone who was a woman in their group and there was a sort of male guilt at the time about it. But I think that's all gone now and I don't think that things are better at all anymore, as hard as it was then for women in general. But it's not one of my issues in particular because I'm really happy about being a woman and wouldn't want to be a man anyway. I think they've got so much to deal with; I don't know how they manage at all.

And overseas there are just so few women film directors. I don't know if they just don't like the film world. There's many reasons why women don't pursue a film career, that the sort of toughness of it is may be something that men are more used to.

## CANNES (1986)

The whole thing appeared to me from being there like a great failure, but the people that work these festivals, like Pierre Rissient, they don't care what the audience is doing; they care about who's there from which magazine and what they're going to say and so he'll just run around and find out what they were saying and say: 'Oh no, no, no, it's a great success.'

Going to Cannes was kind of a fluke, because he came out to look at some feature films and didn't find any and so he had time and he started to say: 'Well, have you got anything in your archive, maybe some short filmmakers or something we haven't seen before'; anyway that's how I heard about it at the Film Commission. So they gave him one of my short films to look at. I don't know which one it was first . . . it was either *Peel* or *Passionless Moments* or *A Girl's Own Story* and he said: 'Oh, I like this; is there anything else by her?' and they brought up another one and he said: 'I like this too, is there anything else?' and then they brought up the third and he said: 'Well, I really like all of them and I want to make a programme of them; is there anything else she's doing now?' And they said she's making *Two Friends* at the ABC and he said: 'Oh well, it's a TV movie and most unlikely we'll be interested, but maybe I'll have a look when it's finished.'

And he rang me up at 7.00 am in the morning just saying: 'This is Pierre Rissient you don't know me, but I am this guy from Cannes and may I have permission to take your films.' And this is out of the blue. Cannes. I didn't even know about it really. I just said: 'Yes, thank you very much, thanks for your kind comments.' And he said, 'Well it's in May' and I said, 'I won't be able to come because I'm on a holiday' and he said, 'Ooh, but you have to come.' But he was very, very sweet and very, very helpful and kind and he was instrumental in getting me to Cannes in the first place and later for selecting *Sweetie* for Cannes in competition. He can select but he can't decide. (See Figure 4.2.)

And then he was also instrumental in getting the funding for *The Piano* from CIBY 2000. We thought it was a joke, it was so easy. We didn't believe them for a long time because he just told the plot to the guy who was in charge of finding the films for CIBY 2000, he didn't even give him a script to read; he just told them the plot on the plane from Paris on the way over to see us in London where we were at the time

FIGURE 4.2 Getting started: brother/father (Tim Pye), sister/aunt (Katie Pye) and son/nephew (Ben Martin) in *Peel*
Courtesy AFTRS

and we thought how would a guy decide on that basis. And Pierre told me: 'Don't worry Jane, I left out any boring bits and he seemed very pleased.' And the guy who was making decisions was one of those really handsome, charming French guys; he was kind of good natured and uninterested, and we thought, 'He can't be serious.'

But he was and a lot of stuff is like that in life and business. I think really our frame of reference is always school; it's like the headmaster, but a lot of headmasters are kind of slack; they make decisions off the hip. And that's been my experience, that quite often people make decisions for the most odd reasons and don't weigh them up that well. Like when the financing of *Sweetie* happened, it was by these couple of guys in Melbourne who seemed to want to just give the impression of being able to make snap decisions, to see my face drop; that's how I saw it anyway. They had read the script and told me that even though it was supposed to be funny but they couldn't see anything funny in it and in fact it was really boring and it put them to sleep. So I thought: 'Oh well, what am I doing here guys.'

And so they asked if I could tell them the story again but after I started I saw them going a bit cross-eyed after about 2 minutes, so I went: 'And . . . that's the end.' And they were just so relieved that I didn't talk for too long. It seemed to me that they sort of rushed. They were trying out office chairs at the time or we were all trying them out and we went off into the other room and when we came back and they said: 'You've got your money babe.' And I was just like, 'Are they real?'

And then when they saw *Sweetie* finished that was pretty funny; they wanted to watch it with the lights on and drink champagne all the way through because they were terrified of being bored. And then when it ended they said, 'Right, well, we should resell this story onto LA', but fortunately, by this time, it had been accepted into Cannes and I could see they thought that was a swell idea. (See Figure 4.3.)

FIGURE 4.3 **Sweetie (Genevieve Lemon)**
Arenafilm Pty Ltd

## AUTHENTICITY

Despite the hype, I see a lot of authenticity in the cinema. I think that when we say authenticity what we mean is people applying themselves to understanding life. That's what attracted me to film in the first place. I thought it was a place where you could, in an exciting way, engage with that. If you go and see something like *Apocalypse Now*, I think that's a very good example of a sort of authenticity.

The film industry's a mini-version of life anyway. There's all sorts of nonsense and crookery and swaggery and stuff happening and then some amazing moments. Sometimes something beautiful happens and it's just so great. These are the moments that keep me doing it and keep me going to see movies.

## AUTEURISM

There is an attitude held by some people in the industry that the auteur is a very bossy, selfish person who has to have everything their way and won't share, whereas I don't hold that view at all. There has to be a director anyway and in that sense I don't really know the difference between an auteur and normal director. I think most really good directors have an auteur aspect to them, even if they aren't writing the material.

I think I've always been interested in auteur cinema so it always seemed natural. It's like novelists; it's not shocking that there is the auteur novelist. I love reading so it just seems natural that someone decides to write something or make something and there's a real satisfaction in them having, as much as possible, a cohesive voice.

I've only started to realize how common my motifs are to myself. I think I've been very preoccupied with the idea of who a woman is in the world and women and love and sex.

There's the type of 'Jane Campion film' credit that your agent earns for you. It's always on the contract and what it signifies to me is really nothing. I'm always quite embarrassed when I see the credit come up since it's so not true because so many people work on the films. I don't feel a responsibility to a 'Jane Campion film'. I don't have any idea about what I'm going to give. I guess, in a deep way I feel a responsibility to myself. Like if I take on a project that isn't the right one for me I won't be able to get enough energy to do it.

FIGURE 4.4 **An early promotional portrait**
Courtesy Film Australia

## POINTS OF DIFFERENCE

I think I'm the same and different. When I talk to people and I listen to other filmmakers or students talking about themselves trying to get work together, the thing that I constantly hear and recognize is that what's really difficult for people is dealing with the fear that they have about their work. Quite often that feeling is so great, it completely obscures them; they kind of lose themselves in their fear and they can't really do the work. I hear this very, very constantly. Whereas I have got some kind of capacity that when I'm engaged in a project or an idea, I have enough sense of love or charm for it, that I don't think about what could go wrong. So when I get excited about an idea I can't think negatively. I just think it's only going to work out well; of course it's going to work out. I mean it's not like I have a completely idiotic view; I can be critical as well but on the whole I think, yes, I've got to fix this and that but it will work out. And then it's not until it's really completed that I start to freak and be able to see the other sides or the negative positions that people could take on it. What I've said doesn't sound like very much but it's probably the single best quality I've got.

Common sense is also very underestimated. The very word makes it sounds like it's just hanging around everywhere, but it's quite rare; that sort of practical ability to find a middle line. The quality of my enthusiasm being greater than my fear and my common sense are the two only real qualities that I have that distinguishes myself as someone who can have an ongoing career as a filmmaker. And to know what's achievable. All those sort of very dull things. I'm really practical. I'm very, very deeply practical and have great capacity to work out what can fit into what size box. I think so many people are creative; everybody is and I'm just only as creative as anybody else, but just with those different qualities of being fearless at the right time and having lots of common sense.

## DO FILMS SPEAK (FOR THEMSELVES OR ON BEHALF OF DIRECTORS)?

I think it's true that the work is the work, but we're just naturally curious animals and I think for myself, if I've read something I've loved or seen something I loved, I love to read anything about it, sort of to augment my understanding or curiosity, how do they do it.

I would rather say, 'the film *has* a . . .' rather than say 'the film argues or thinks something' because, in the end, the director may have not achieved what they really wanted to say and so then the film is what's left.

Sometimes a film might be more than the sum of the parts, perhaps, but it can be less too; often a lot less. What would that be? You would have to spell *Gestalt* backwards! It's actually pretty hard work to make a good film as many people find out.

## 'READING' FILMS

I don't know outside of myself what's right or wrong. I hardly know for myself. I look at someone like Tarantino and I think well, he's a genius. He's very good at reading cinema and he's got all sorts of new levels of irony that haven't even been thought about before. I don't know if he gets it through 'reading' films but he gets it through a very compulsive obsessive interest in film and it certainly makes him a very special filmmaker. I mean I think if I look at some filmmakers that I love anyway, like Gus Van Sant, and I don't know if he really reads a lot. I don't know what he does. I think he paints. It seems to me right now that Gus Van Sant is having experiments where he's putting entertainment in a lesser position than just creating little units of truth or experimenting with long shots, pieces of action that are unmanipulated or apparently unmanipulated. So those sorts of things interest me.

I don't know how come those guys are doing that. I think in Gus's case he's very independent and that's just what he loves and it's what gets him up in the morning. And I think it's like having the independence of mind to choose what it is you love and go ahead and do it, like a great gardener, or a great chef; they go their own way and they have the confidence to do it because they know what they're doing.

## MEASURING SUCCESS

I'm very clear about whether I like what I've done or whether I feel it's good and generally there's some parts of it which I feel really thrilled about having found and other parts that I don't like so much. So I guess I feel like as long as I've applied myself in the best way I know how I'm very satisfied with myself.

The results are like a mixed bag. Sometimes you get really surprised and thrilled but there's always the results and there's always some things that you wouldn't have expected and that you like and things that were maybe not so great, you'd hoped had come out better.

Sometimes something beautiful happens and it's just so great. These are the moments that keep me doing it and keep me going to see movies.

## CREATIVITY

There's a few aspects to creativity. I suppose there's two sorts of minds – there's the unconscious mind and the mind which can refine and sift through ideas that can work together that come up through your unconscious thinking and critique them, but that sort of thinking mind, the one you've trained, is really a bit of a monkey. It's not that bright and it's not going to come up with anything very, very clever so all the big leaps of faith and all the really interesting stuff is just going to just pop into your head without any effort whatsoever, but you just have to recognize them and set it to work, to give it tasks. And so developing your relationship with your unconscious creative thinking and believing in it really is the big deal, and then having developed some critical thinking you have to use that to refine it. People have got instinct but instinct doesn't really exist without some kind of critical thinking.

## MANAGING CREATIVITY

I think I stored up from all those years of education a lot of stuff, like 10 years of anthropology, fine arts and then film. I was peaking and going to see everything and having my own opinions. I was a student so I had plenty of time to think, but then I had a period of about 20 years or 15 years of doing, doing, doing and I didn't have really a time to go back, unpack my head to the point where I really knew things could come in. So for a while, at the end of the day I was starting to work with a bit of a full suitcase, and the same old suitcase, and that's why I stopped working for a while, because I wanted to chuck the whole lot out and see what came up. (See Figure 4.5.)

I think it has been successful. I didn't think I would want to do anything much, but I found that after a year or so and then I was doing things like embroidering pillow slips and very crafty simple stuff,

FIGURE 4.5 Working with a full suitcase: middle Janet (Alexia Keogh) from *An Angel at My Table*

Courtesy hibiscus Films Ltd

horses and stuff for my daughter; doing like my mum and my sister and friends, so really not asking anything of myself. And then without really any effort I'd just notice what I was interested in. Like, 'Oh, I'm really interested in filling the paddock with horses', watching them behave together or something and I'd just think, oh, so that's what I like.

So it was like I was rediscovering myself and it was a bit scary to begin with to think that I'm not telling myself what I should be interested in; this is actually what I do like. Now I'm writing another project and it's a project that I couldn't imagine anybody would possibly be interested in. Even the fact that I was interested in it, I found amazing. But I just have to go, 'Well that is what I love' and so off I go and do it. And yes, I do think it's been really helpful to me to unpack. I feel a sense of a new phase. What can you do but do what you are, especially if you've given yourself the time to be what you are.

## CREATIVITY: ISOLATION VS. INTERCONNECTION

I think it's both. I think the idea is that you connect at a higher level or in a better way or you really offer people something, so when you connect with people you're offering them something that I fantasize as being worthwhile; something that I want to give. And, of course, the process of doing it means that you do need to focus quite a long time on what you're doing and that takes you out of normal social life, thank god.

I think when I was younger I was really wanting to be everything, have everything. I never wanted to give anything up, but I've also been somebody that really likes time alone and that's got stronger, that impulse really. I really love to be alone now.

I'm also very sociable, kind of extremely so. Like I love a good time and that's why being a filmmaker has been good. It's an unusual blend of characteristics I have. Someone who likes time alone, someone who loves a kind of fun. For me, I could probably do without the fun but I don't think I could do without the time alone now.

## KEY TO SUCCESSFUL COLLABORATIONS

I've learned the hard way. I think the best trick is to hire really amazing people; people who are just very sorted out and who are very good at what they do and also to work with people you love and you respect and who are friends (your producers, for instance). And just make a decision that you're not going to split off from each other; that you will really support each other at those hard moments or especially in front of other people.

A relationship is challenging and complicated. Inevitably, each film brings everybody to their edge. It's one of those things, it's like everybody wants to know that they've given it everything and therefore they get to the point where they're just too cranky at some stage or another and then you just take a step back from that person and go well, they've just reached a limit there. It requires a very forgiving attitude once you've got those fabulous people. You just presume that they're all doing their best.

And I'm also really outside of that. I never think anybody is purposefully fucking up or making mistakes. I always just think a mistake is a mistake. I also say everything, so I've learned that on a set, I'm not going to try and think of a nice way to say things. I just say it without blaming, I try to do it without blaming and just say look, this room doesn't look right to me, can I have some help here or whatever, because anything bottled up, it just doesn't work in the work, to get all peculiar or complicated. I think if they just know that whatever I say it's just about the work and if I say it wrong, I'm sorry, I'll apologize but we're all here to do the work and our feelings and all the rest of it we are putting in service to that in the mean time. And also I do believe it's about having fun. The atmosphere on the set is very important to me because you want the actors to feel very comfortable and playful, because when people are playful they're at their best.

People are willing to take creative risks if they know that you're not going to have a bad opinion of them and that you're going to support them. I mean all good actors know that they are in a relationship with

FIGURE 4.6 Jane Campion lines up a shot
The Kobal Collection

you based on their talent. It can't be worked out beforehand and that's how you get your best work but you'll also do shit, but you just need a director there to remove that later. (See Figure 4.6.)

## DEVELOPING OTHER PERSONAL SKILLS AND TALENTS

I think I wouldn't mind being a cinematographer. That would be good!

I love writing and I love novels and I would like to write a novel but as it's just happened, I developed my skills as filmmaker and now when I go to think about writing a novel, it just seems like my skills as filmmaker are rarer than my skills as a novelist. So I think: 'Oh well, I'll do film while I still can.'

The novelizations were really a scam. For the novelization of *The Piano*, I wrote one chapter and then it was cut up into pieces and incorporated through the rest of the book. I didn't really want to bother, but they did and they were willing to pay me and it seemed like a good enough job and I really didn't do much for it except have the story in the first place. Anna [Campion's sister and collaborator on Holy Smoke] did all of the Holy Smoke novel but of course I developed with her the ideas for the film, so that's in it, but really she did all the writing.

There are other skills and talents that I feel that I'm interested in developing that are what I would call deep ones; which is about having the courage to relax more, have more faith in the process all the time.

I was thinking recently about how you do your research on a scene or a subject that you're going to be writing about as a filmmaker – or if it's a directing thing you do your storyboard and you think about how you're going to shoot it you do everything you possibly can work-wise (and there is a lot that you can do). But once you've done that it's really simple; *you have to just let go* and there's nothing more you can do, except see how it comes out. See how it comes together in you and with the day and with the people.

As I'm writing a scene I can prepare, I've got all the material, I know what the scene has to be and then yes, I write it out. OK, the first time it mightn't come out so it's like diving for pearls; then you have another go. But you will get one if you just keep going once you've got your stuff together. It's that kind of space; it will come out this way or that way. There's nothing more you can do except to have a few goes.

So I think for me it is about having faith in the process. I've seen it in myself and I've seen others when they are trying to get some guarantee on that process and what happens is kind of an obsession with slickness or complex shots that make them feel successful or clever (or myself more clever!). Things that you are doing because you're insecure and you want a guarantee because the creative process doesn't have any easy guarantees. But they sort of are there in a weird way, when you realize that once you've done all you've done, you just have to go with it. It's like preparing for a party. You just have to let the party happen. It's all grace really. Some things will work, some things won't. And some of it will always work. I think even if you try and write a scene that doesn't quite work out the whole way; at least you'll know it hasn't worked out and you have to try again. Now that is a step forward. (See Figure 4.7)

FIGURE 4.7 Doing it to be loved: the young Sweetie (Emma Fowler)
Arenafilm Pty Ltd

## CHANGES IN APPROACH

Changes? I think that I'm just getting older. Getting older is one of the great glories of life; feeling that shift in perspective and things that are important to you. Like what other people think is very unimportant to me now; whereas before I was really desperate about being accepted. I wanted to go my own way but be accepted for it.

The thing that I found difficult is I really did want approval but you're just not going to get it, not on a universal scale. I mean you can win all the Oscars you like and still people will hate what you do, you know. And I think that realizing that you're going to be hated and publicly hated is one of the hardest things for filmmakers because that's not why you do it; you do it to be loved, of course. Now I just think there's a sort of percentage thing. You realize that inevitably a large percentage of people will hate what you do and if it's good, some people will love it. And those people are maybe quite passionate and furious; passionate for you or furious against you and that may even change over time and so I no longer take it very seriously.

As I get older I certainly don't take a particularly serious view of life. It's kind of best lived lightly. I'm not even interested in myself much; the story of me as I developed it; I'm over it. I don't know . . . I just enjoy very simple things these days.

# CHRONOLOGY

| YEAR | KEY EVENTS IN AUSTRALIA/ NEW ZEALAND | KEY EVENTS IN FILM INDUSTRIES | JANE CAMPION |
|------|------|------|------|
| 1952 | Sir Keith Arthur Murdoch (chairman of *Herald and Weekly Times*) dies (Australia) | Australian Council of Film Societies (a grouping of state federations of film societies) hold first film festival in Olinda (outer suburban Melbourne) | Richard and Edith Campion (parents) establish touring theatrical company, the New Zealand Players Anna Campion (sister) born |
| 1953 | | The Television Act is passed by parliament, setting regulations for the broadcast of television in Australia David Gulpilil born (Australia) | |
| 1954 | SEATO created Pauline Parker and | Village Theatres (later Village Roadshow Group) | Born 30April in Waikanae on the |

| | | | |
|---|---|---|---|
| | Juliet Hulme murder Parker's mother (NZ) | founded First Sydney Film festival | north coast of Wellington (NZ) |
| 1955 | | *The Wild One* is banned for second time in NZ | |
| 1956 | Olympic Games are held in Melbourne (Aust) Department of Trade formed (Aust) | Television broadcasts begin (Aust) | |
| 1957 | | Variety show hosted by Graham Kennedy, *In Melbourne Tonight* begins (Aust) | Janet Frame's first novel *Owls Do Cry* published |
| 1958 | | Inaugural year of the Australian Film Institute awards | |
| 1959 | | First TV serial drama, *Autumn Affair*, begins (Aust) | |
| 1960 | Reserve Bank of Australia is formed First Adelaide Festival (Aust) | Regular TV broadcasts begin in Auckland (NZ) | New Zealand Players closes |
| 1961 | NZ joins IMF Capital punishment abolished (NZ) Government limits the amount of credit available to investors (Aust) | Peter Jackson born (NZ) | Edith Campion awarded an MBE for services to NZ theatre Michael Campion (brother) born |
| 1962 | Western Samoa becomes independent of NZ NZ Maori Council established Aborigines gain the right to vote in all states except Queensland (Aust) | *Vincent Report* completed with its findings supporting increased government funding of film (it is, however, not widely publicized) (Aust) | |
| 1963 | | First locally written TV programme, *All Earth to Love*, is broadcast (NZ) | |

1964   Reintroduction of compulsory military service (Aust)
       OZ editors are charged with obscenity in Australia
       Beatles tour Australia
       Rupert Murdoch starts *The Australian* newspaper

       Russell Crowe born (NZ)
       John O Shea's *Runaway* about adolescent alienation is released (NZ)
       Excerpts of *Vincent Report* (1962) published, with film industry pushing for its recommendations (Aust)

1965   Australia commits troops to Vietnam
       Aborigines gain right to vote in Queensland (Aust)
       Australian Conservation Foundation established

1966   Opening of international airport (Auckland) (NZ)
       National Library of NZ created
       Ban on the employment of married women in the public service lifted (Aust)
       Robert Menzies retires as longest serving PM. Succeeded by Harold Holt (Aust)
       Decimal currency introduced (Aust)

       First popular NZ musical, *Don't Let it Get to You*
       NZ's longest running TV series, *Country Calendar*, begins
       Daily news reports by satellite enabled (Aust)

       Appears in Barry Barclay's *All That We Need* as a flower girl

1967   Referendum grants Aborigines full citizenship (Aust)
       Referendum extends hotel closing hours to 10 pm (NZ)
       Decimal currency introduced (NZ)
       First NZ-born Governor General appointed (NZ)
       Gough Whitlam becomes

       First issue of *Cinema Papers* (Aust)
       *Ulysses* released to segregated audiences (NZ)
       First exchange of satellite signals between Australia and UK

leader of the Labour Party
(Aust)
Australian Council for the
Arts established
PM Harold Holt disappears
presumed drowned (Aust)

| 1968 | Australia signs the nuclear non-proliferation treaty | Lucy Lawless born (NZ) Formation of government body Australia Council of the Arts | |
| 1969 | Vote extended to 20 year olds (NZ) National Party wins fourth election in a row (NZ) | Formation of industry-based lobby group Australia Film Council | |
| 1970 | Largest demonstrations in history held against Vietnam War (Aust) Publication of Germaine Greer's *The Female Eunuch* (Aust) | First university film course offered (NZ) Australian Film Development Corporation Bill passed, from which the Australian Film Development Corporation and the Australian Film Development Fund were formed | Richard Campion produces *Green Are the Islands* at Expo 70 (Osaka) Around this time family moves to a farm |
| 1971 | Australia and NZ announce they will withdraw troops from Vietnam First Aboriginal member of parliament (Aust) Nation-wide protests against Springbok tour (Aust) Ten pound subsidized immigration ends (Aust) Exchange rate expressed in US dollars not British pounds sterling (Aust) | Formation of the Sydney Women's Film Group R (18+) film classification introduced in Australia The NZBC produces the first NZ drama series, *Pukemanu* Warkworth satellite station opened (NZ) | |

| 1972 | Labour government elected (NZ)<br>First Labour government since 1949 elected (Aust)<br>Equal Pay Act passed (NZ)<br>Commonwealth Arbitration Commission rules that women should be paid the same wage for the same job (Aust) | First Wellington Film Festival (NZ)<br>Establishment of the South Australian Film Corporation (Aust)<br>*The Adventures of Barry McKenzie* released and is a huge box office success (Aust) | |
| --- | --- | --- | --- |
| 1973 | NZ rugby tour of South Africa cancelled<br>Sydney Opera House opened (Aust)<br>Federal voting age dropped from 21 to 18 (Aust)<br>First Australian to win Nobel Prize for literature (Patrick White)<br>Twenty-five percent cut in protective tariffs introduced (Aust)<br>Inflation hits 13% (Aust)<br>Australia signs trade pact with China | First intake of students at Australian Film and Television School (AFTS) and at Swinburne College of Technology in Melbourne<br>First live international TV broadcast (NZ) | |
| 1974 | PM Norman Kirk dies (NZ)<br>Christchurch Common-wealth Games | First national women's film event: Womenvision (Aust)<br>Rudall Hayward dies (NZ)<br>Introduction of colour TV (NZ) | |
| 1975 | Sacking of Australian PM<br>Liberal Party win election (Aust)<br>Women tram workers win the right to drive trams (Melbourne)<br>Robert Muldoon begins | Establishment of Australian Film Commission<br>Second TV channel begins broadcasting (NZ)<br>First government-sponsored presence at | BA (anthropology major), Victoria University, Wellington (NZ) |

| | | | |
|---|---|---|---|
| | 19 years as PM (NZ) Homosexuality legalized in South Australia Australia Council established | Cannes (Aust) NZBC dissolved and replaced by TV One, TV Two and Radio NZ Introduction of colour TV (Aust) | |
| 1976 | Metric system for measurement introduced (NZ) Cigarette advertising banned on TV and radio (Aust) Murdoch buys *The Times*, *The Sunday Times* and *The NY Post* (Aust) | Establishment of the Women's Film Fund (administered by AFC) (Aust) Special Broadcasting Service established (Aust) Establishment of Victorian Film Corporation (Aust) | Travels in Europe, lives in Italy Enrols on diploma of fine arts course, Chelsea School of Arts, London |
| 1977 | Advance Australia Fair becomes national anthem (Aust) | *Sleeping Dogs* is seen by the biggest ever audience for a local film and is the first NZ film released in the US Interim NZ Film Commission established Establishment of state government film bodies in New South Wales, Queensland and Tasmania (Aust) | Edith Campion publishes a collection, *A Place to Pass Through and Other Stories* Around this time works as an assistant to a commercials and documentary filmmaker |
| 1978 | First Gay and Lesbian Mardi Gras held in Sydney (Aust) Unemployment reaches 7.5% (Aust) | NZ Film Commission begins production subsidies Natural History Unit established in Dunedin (NZ) Establishment of Western Australian Film Council Capital investment for film write-off period reduced from 25 to 2 years (Aust) | |

| 1979 | Women win right to maternity leave (Aust) | *Catalogue of Independent Women's Films* published (Aust) Release of *My Brilliant Career* (Gillian Armstromg) | BA (painting) Sydney College of Arts (Aust) Edith Campion publishes a novel, *The Chain* |
|---|---|---|---|
| 1980 | Federal government deregulates interest paid by banks (Aust) | Len Lye dies (NZ) The NZFC is represented at Cannes in its first major film market initiative Broadcasting Corporation of NZ (BCNZ) formed to manage both TV channels SBS begins broadcasting (Aust) *Breaker Morant* (Aust) | *Tissues* |
| 1981 | Springbok rugby team tours NZ sparking civil unrest Australia's Trevor Chappell bowls underarm delivery for the last ball of the 1-day series cricket final at the Melbourne Cricket Ground to secure a win over New Zealand | Introduction of 10BA tax incentives (Aust) NZ Film Archive established Annus mirabilis for the NZ film industry with three influential films released: *Goodbye Pork Pie*, *Picture*, *Smash Palace* | Enrols AFTS *Mishaps of Seduction and Conquest* |
| 1982 | CER signed with Australia coming into effect March 1983 Australian dollar falls below parity with US dollar for first time Economy in recession (Aust) Freedom of Information Act (Aust) | Anna Paquin born (NZ) *The Scarecrow* is first NZ film to be selected for Director's Fortnight at Cannes | *An Exercise in Discipline – Peel* First volume of Janet Frame's autobiography *To the Island* published Campion visits Janet Frame in NZ |
| 1983 | Unemployment hits 10.7% (Aust) Bob Hawke elected PM | *Patu!*, first feature film by woman (NZ) *Utu*, a film about the | *Passionless Moments* *A Girl's Own Story* screens at |

| | | |
|---|---|---|
| (Aust)<br>Australian dollar floated | Maori land wars (NZ)<br>133/33 adjustment to<br>10BA (Aust) | Melbourne and Sydney film festivals and wins awards at both. Also picks up 4 AFI Awards<br>*Peel* screens at Melbourne and Sydney film festivals |
| 1984 | Labour elected, Lange PM (NZ)<br>Deregulation of NZ economy begins<br>NZ ratifies UN Convention on the Elimination of All Forms of Discrimination against Women<br>Australian banking system deregulated | Establishment of Women's Film Units in Victoria and NSW (Aust)<br>AFTS launches on-the-job training scheme for women in film industry<br>Release of *Silver City* (Aust)<br>*Vigil* becomes first NZ feature selected in competition at Cannes<br>National Film and Sound Archive established as a separate collecting institution (Aust) | Graduates AFTS<br>*After Hours* screens at Melbourne and Sydney Film Festivals winning prizes for best short fiction at both<br>*Passionless Moments* screens at Melbourne Film Festival, winning award for unique artistic merit. Also wins AFI Award for best experimental film<br>Edith and Richard Campion divorce |
| 1985 | NZ refuses nuclear ships to enter ports<br>French DGSE agents blow up Greenpeace ship in Auckland harbour killing one person<br>NZ dollar floated<br>Keri Hulme wins Booker prize (NZ)<br>Government grants free- | Closure of Sydney Film-maker's Co-Op (Aust)<br>AFC appoints a Director of Affirmative Action<br>*The Quiet Earth* (NZ) | Shoots *Dancing Daze* (Ep. 5)<br>Shoots *Two Friends*<br>*Girl's Own Story* wins Critic's Prize at Amsterdam Film Festival<br>*Passionless Moments* voted most popular short film at |

hold title for Uluru and
surrounds to Mutitjullu
people (Aust)
Austrade established
Murdoch becomes a US
citizen
      Sydney Film
Festival

1986

US suspends its ANZUS
obligations to NZ and
informs NZ it will not
defend it against attack
*Whale Rider* published (NZ)
Homosexual Law reform
bill passed (NZ)
Pope visits NZ for first time
Constitution Act ends right
of Britain to pass laws for NZ
The Australia Act makes
Australian law independent
of British parliamentary
and legal systems

*Crocodille Dundee* (Aust)
120/20 adjustment to
10BA (Aust)

*Dancing Daze* screens
on ABC TV
*Two Friends* screens
on ABC TV and at
Cannes, Sydney,
Melbourne and
Edinburgh film
festivals
*Girl's Own Story* and
*Passionless Moments*
screen at Cannes
*Peel* wins Palm
d'Or at Cannes
film festival

1987

Maori Language Act
makes Maori an official
language (NZ)
Anti-nuclear legislation
enacted (NZ)
Labour wins election (NZ)
Australian Stock Exchange
formed from state
exchanges

*Ngati* (Barry Barclay) first
fiction feature film
written and directed by
Maori. Selected for
Critic's Week at Cannes
Peter Jackson's *Bad Taste*
(NZ)

Begins writing
*The Piano*
Begins develop-
ment for *Angel at
My Table*
*Two Friends* wins
Golden Plaque
(Television) at the
Chicago film
festival and three
AFI awards

1988

Unemployed exceeds
100,000 (NZ)
Bastion Point land returned
to Maori (NZ)
Australian bicentenary

*Mauri* (Merata Mita) first
fiction feature film
directed by Maori woman
Film Finance Corporation
established (Aust)
BCNZ replaced by state-
owned enterprise, TV

Publishes 'Big shell'
(short story)
*The Audition* (actor)
Begins production
on *Sweetie*
Mother is
hospitalized in

| | | New Zealand 10BA adjustment to flat 100% write-off (Aust) | Dunedin for depression |
|---|---|---|---|
| 1989 | PM Lange resigns (NZ) Sunday trading begins (NZ) | Deregulation of TV in NZ. Third TV channel begins and TVNZ loses its monopoly (NZ) | *Sweetie* theatrically released in Australia Campion wins Australian Film Institute's Byron Kennedy Award for excellence and contribution to Australian cinema Short films theatrically released in US *Sweetie* released as video rental in Australia |
| 1990 | National Party wins election. James Bolger is PM (NZ) First female governor general (NZ) Welfare payments reduced (NZ) Australia in recession Telecom NZ privatized | Pay TV begins (NZ) | *An Angel at My Table* premières at the Venice film festival winning seven awards including Silver Lion and the Elvira Notari Award (best woman director) Voted most popular film at Sydney Film Festival *Sweetie* wins the Australian Critic's Award, LA Film Critic's Award and best foreign film award at the Spirit of Independence Awards (USA) |

| 1991 | Unemployed exceeds 200,000 (NZ) Welfare payments reduced further (NZ) | Overseas ownership of broadcasting companies legislated and a Canadian company takes over TV3 (NZ) *Proof* (Aust) | *Angel at My Table* available to purchase on video in UK |
|------|------|------|------|
| 1992 | NZ gets seat on UN Security Council Citizenship Act is amended to remove allegiance to the British Crown (Aust) Unemployment hits 11.5% (Aust) Disability Discrimination Act (Aust) | *Shortland Street*, first daily TV drama, begins (NZ) *Strictly Ballroom* and *Romper Stomper* (Aust) | Marries Colin Englehert *Angel at My Table* available as video rental in Australia |
| 1993 | Helen Clarke becomes leader of Labour Party (NZ) Paul Keating is elected PM (Aust) Native Title Act grants Aborigines right to claim compensation for loss of land (Aust) Unemployment hits 12.2% (Aust) Privacy Act (NZ) | *Desperate Remedies* (Peter Wells/Stewart Main) selected for Un Certain Regard at Cannes (NZ) Anna Paquin becomes the first New Zealander to win an Oscar (best supporting actress for *The Piano*) Film New Zealand established to promote NZ locations to offshore productions US-owned Renaissance begins 6-year production residency for *Hercules* and *Xena: Warrior Princess* (NZ) | *The Piano* theatrically released Wins Palm d'Or (best film) Cannes Wins Academy Award (best original screenplay) Son Jasper born (dies after 12 days) *Sweetie* video available to purchase in UK *The Piano* novelization published |
| 1994 | | *Once Were Warriors* (Lee Tamahori) becomes most successful feature film in NZ grossing more than $6m box office (NZ) *Heavenly Creatures* wins the | Daughter Alice born Rudall Hayward Award, New Zealand Film & Television Awards |

| | | | |
|---|---|---|---|
| | | Silver Lion at Venice Film Festival (NZ) | *Angel at My Table* and *The Piano* videos available to purchase in Australia<br>*The Piano* video available to purchase in UK<br>Anna Campion releases her feature film *Loaded* |
| 1995 | | TV screening of *Forgotten Silver* (Peter Jackson/ Costa Botes)<br>First UK/NZ co-production *Loaded* (Anna Campion)<br>Sam Neill's retrospection on NZ cinema, *Cinema of Unease* | *Screen* journal debates *The Piano* |
| 1996 | NZ government settles biggest indigenous land claim<br>John Howard becomes PM (Aust) | *Love Serenade* (Aust) | *The Portrait of a Lady* theatrically released<br>Invited to close the Venice Film Festival<br>*Two Friends* released at Film Forum in New York<br>*Angel at My Table* and *The Piano* released on video in USA |
| 1997 | Jenny Shipley becomes first female PM of NZ<br>Tasmania is the last state to legalize homosexuality (Aust)<br>Telecommunications Act deregulates telecoms (Aust)<br>First Telstra float (Aust) | TV4 begins daily broadcasts (NZ)<br>*Gonski Review* released (Aust) | President of the International Jury of the Venice Film Festival<br>Barbara Hershey nominated as Best Supporting Actress at the Academy |

|      |                                                                                                                                                                                                      |                                                                                                                            | Awards<br>*Sweetie* video available to purchase in USA<br>*The Portrait of a Lady* available to purchase on video and DVD in USA and video rental in Australia<br>*Henry James Review* special issue on *Portrait of a Lady*<br>Signed 3-year, first-look agreement with Propaganda Films to begin after fulfilment of terms of agreement with Miramax |
| ---- | ---------------------------------------------------------------------------------------------------------------------------------------------------------------------------------------------------- | -------------------------------------------------------------------------------------------------------------------------- | ------------------------------------------------------------------------------------------------------------------------------------------------------------------------------------------------------------------------------------------------------------------------------- |
| 1998 | Re-election of Howard government (Aust)<br>Referendum to establish Australian Republic lost                                                                                                         | Fox Studios Australia open facilities in Sydney (Aust)                                                                     | *The Piano* released on DVD in USA and in ALL region format                                                                                                                                                                                                                     |
| 1999 | Labour party wins election. Helen Clarke becomes PM (NZ)<br>Broadcasting Services Amendment (Online Services) Act stipulates online content regulation (Aust)                                      | Peter Jackson begins shooting *Lord of the Rings* trilogy (NZ)<br>Closure of tax provisions for film and TV investment (NZ) | *Holy Smoke* theatrically released<br>*Holy Smoke* novelization published<br>*Soft Fruit* (executive producer)<br>Women in Hollywood Icon Award<br>Honourary Doctorate of Literature, Victoria University, Wellington                                                           |

| | | | The Portrait of a Lady video available to purchase in Australia The Piano released on DVD in UK Wexman's book of edited interviews released Coombs and Gemmel's edited collection of essays published |
|---|---|---|---|
| 2000 | Sydney hosts Olympic Games (Aust) Digital Agenda Copyright Act (Aust) | Chopper (Aust) Government funding cut to Australian Film Institute announced (Aust) | Appointed Adjunct Professor, Sydney College of the Arts WIN Award, Wimfemme film festival (Women's Image Network), US Holy Smoke available as rental video in Australia Holy Smoke released on DVD in US The Portrait of a Lady video available to purchase in UK Book of essays on The Piano released Pocket Essential book on Campion released |
| 2001 | NZ and Nauru announce they will take Afghani asylum seekers stranded in Australian waters | Worldwide release of The Fellowship of the Ring setting global box office records (NZ) | Holy Smoke video available to purchase is US The Portrait of a Lady |

| | | | |
|---|---|---|---|
| | John Howard is re-elected for third term as PM (Aust) | | released on DVD in UK and Australia; disc includes documentary and booklet *Angel at My Table* released on DVD in Australia; disc includes six deleted scenes and US trailer Dana Polan's book on Campion released |
| 2002 | Helen Clarke wins second term as NZ PM NZ PM apologizes to Samoa for mistakes during colonial rule Bomb in Bali kills 88 Australians | Due to funding cuts AFI closes its distribution arm (Aust) | *Holy Smoke* video and DVD available to purchase in UK; disc includes commentary track featuring Kate Winslet and co-writer Anna Campion and TV spots *Angel at My Table* released on DVD in UK; disc includes Jane Campion interview, trailer, stills, Janet Frame biography, filmographies |
| 2003 | Senate passes first ever vote of no confidence in PM over handling of war with Iraq (Aust) Governor general resigns (Aust) | Television Local Content Group established (NZ) NZ Screen Council established Large Budget Screen Production Fund | *In the Cut* theatrically released Announces time out from feature film production *Holy Smoke* released |

| | | established (NZ) National Film Archive controversially taken over by Australian Film Commission TVNZ Bill stipulates both commercial and public service objectives for TVNZ TVNZ Charter implemented | on DVD in Australia |
|---|---|---|---|
| 2004 | NZ parliament passes civil unions legislation for gay couples Janet Frame dies John Howard wins fourth terms as PM (Aust) Australia–US Free Trade Agreement | Maori TV Service established (NZ) *The Lord of the Rings* wins 11 Academy Awards Melbourne Central Studios opens (Aust) | *In the Cut* video and DVD available to purchase in USA UK, and Australia; disc includes producer and director commentary, making of documentary, slang dictionary. US version restores censorship cuts Sue Gillett's book on Campion released |
| 2005 | Helen Clarke wins third election (NZ) | 1909 cinema screens in Australia | *Angel at My Table* released on DVD in US by Criterion; disc includes commentary by Jane Campion, actress Kerry Fox and cinema- tographer, Stuart Dryburgh, six deleted scenes, a |

theatrical trailer, a
documentary on
the film's
production, a stills
gallery and an
audio interview
with Janet Frame
*The Piano* released on
DVD in Australia;
disc includes
commentary from
producer and
director, 'Inside the
Piano' featurette
Presides over the
Istanbul film
festival at which
Harvey Keitel is
given a lifetime
achievement award

2006   Queen of Maori        *Kenny* (Aust)          *Water Diary*
       population dies (NZ)                            *Abduction: The Megumi*
       Commonwealth Games                              *Yokota Story*
       held in Melbourne (Aust)                        (executive
       Oil treaty signed with                          producer)
       East Timor (Aust)                               *Sweetie* released on
                                                       DVD by Criterion;
                                                       disc includes *Peel*,
                                                       *Passionless Moments*, *A*
                                                       *Girl's Own Story* as
                                                       well as a 1989
                                                       interview with film
                                                       critic Peter
                                                       Thompson
                                                       *The Piano* released on
                                                       DVD in UK;
                                                       'special edition'
                                                       disc includes
                                                       commentary from

| | | | director and producer, trailer, extended interview with Jane Campion and Jan Chapman, interview with Michael Nyman, making of documentary |
|---|---|---|---|
| 2007 | Kevin Rudd elected ending 11 years of Liberal Party rule (Aust) | *Happy Feet* (Aust) | *The Lady Bug* screens as part of the *Chacun Son Cinéma* portfolio production commissioned for the Cannes film festival's 60th anniversary Edith Campion dies aged 83 Kathleen McHugh's book on Campion released Gail Jones' book on *The Piano* released |
| 2008 | Australian government apologizes to Aborigines for past and present discrimination | Merger of Australian Film Commission, Film Finance Corporation and Film Australia into Australian Screen Authority | National Film and Sound Archive of Australia becomes independent statutory body Production begins on *Bright Star* |

# FILMOGRAPHY

This section lists all the films Jane Campion has worked on as a director, writer or producer as well as films such as interviews and 'making of' documentaries that feature Campion. Key cast and crew members, awards and a synopsis are included for major films.

## FEATURE FILMS

### *Bright Star (in production)*

*Production companies*: BBC Films, Film Finance Corporation Australia, Pathé Renn Productions, UK Film Council in association with Hopscotch International and NSW Film and Television Office

*Producers*: Jan Chapman, Caroline Hewitt

*Writer*: Jane Campion

*Cinematographer*: Greig Fraser

*Key cast members*: Abbie Cornish, Kerry Fox, Paul Schneider, Ben Whishaw

### Synopsis

Traces the passionate and short-lived love affair between poet John Keats and 'the girl next door', Fanny Brawne. The film's title is drawn from a poem written by Keats in 1819, just before his death, in which he describes the tenor of his love for Brawne:

**Bright Star, would I were Stedfast**
Bright star, would I were stedfast as thou art –
Not in lone splendour hung aloft the night
And watching, with eternal lids apart,
Like nature's patient, sleepless Eremite,
The moving waters at their priestlike task
Of pure ablution round earth's human shores,
Or gazing on the new soft-fallen mask
Of snow upon the mountains and the moors –
No – yet still stedfast, still unchangeable,
Pillowed upon my fair love's ripening breast,
To feel for ever its soft fall and swell,
Awake for ever in a sweet unrest,
Still, still to hear her tender-taken breath,
And so live ever – or else swoon in death.

## In the Cut (2003)

Running time: 119 minutes
Production companies: Pathé Productions, Screen Gems, Pathé International (Paris), Red Turtle
Producers: Laurie Parker, Effie T. Brown (executive), Francois Ivernel (executive), Nicole Kidman, Ray Angelic (associate)
Writers: Jane Campion; Susanna Moore (novel and screenplay)
Cinematographer: Dion Beebe
Music: Ray Evans, Hilmar Orn Hilmarsson, Jay Livingston
Key cast members: Kevin Bacon (uncredited), Nick Damici, Jennifer Jason Leigh, Sharrieff Pugh, Meg Ryan, Mark Ruffalo

## Synopsis

Based on Susanna Moore's best selling novel of the same name, In the Cut is the story of Frannie (Meg Ryan), a New York professor of creative writing, who becomes embroiled in a murder investigation after she witnesses a sexual encounter involving a suspected killer. Frannie begins a consuming affair with the investigating police officer, Detective Malloy (Mark Ruffalo), all the time unsure if he is not actually the killer.

## Holy Smoke (1999)

Running time: 114 minutess
Production company: Miramax International
Producers: Jan Chapman, Julie Goldstein (executive), Mark Turnbull (associate), Bob Weinstein (executive), Harvey Weinstein (executive)
Writers: Jane Campion, Anna Campion
Cinematographer: Dion Beebe
Music: Angelo Badalamenti
Key cast members: Pam Grier, Julie Hamilton, Harvey Keitel, Sophie Lee, Tim Robertson, Kate Winslet
Awards: Venice International Film Festival; Elvira Notari Prize; nominated for Golden Lion, 1999

## Synopsis

On a holiday in India, Ruth (Kate Winslet) has a spiritual experience, falls under the thrall of a guru named Baba and decides to start a new life as his disciple. Her alarmed family in Australia arrange for an American exit-counsellor, P. J. Waters (Harvey Keitel) to liberate her from what they believe is a cult. Ruth is tricked into traveling to the outback so that PJ can undertake his 3-day, three-step programme. Instead, Ruth turns the tables on PJ engaging him in an intense and intimate combat.

## The Portrait of a Lady (1996)

*Running time:* 144 minutes
*Production companies:* Polygram Filmed Entertainment, Propaganda Films
*Producers:* Monty Montgomery, Steve Golin
*Writer:* Laura Jones
*Cinematographer:* Stuart Dryburgh
*Music:* Wojciech Kilar
*Key cast members:* Martin Donovan, Barbara Hershey, Nicole Kidman, John
   Malkovich, Mary Louise Parker, Shelley Winters
*Awards:* Los Angeles Film Critics Association, Best Production Design
   (Janet Patterson) and Best Supporting Actress (Barbara Hershey)
   1997; National Society of Film Critics Best Supporting Actor (co-
   winner, Martin Donovan) and Best Supporting Actress (Barbara
   Hershey) 1997; Venice Film Festival, Francesco Pasinetti Award (Best
   Film); National Union of Film Journalists

### Synopsis

Dispensing with a large amount of Henry James's novel, this adaptation
begins when Isabel Archer (Nicole Kidman) is sent to Europe and
encounters a series of suitors. She turns down an offer of marriage from
the rich Lord Warburton (Richard E. Grant) in order to pursue her
travels, made possible by her sickly cousin Ralph Touchet (Martin
Donovan) who arranges for her financial independence. Seduced
instead into disastrous marriage by the suave and manipulative Gilbert
Osmond, an American expatriate living in Italy (John Malkovich),
Isabel realizes too late she has exercised her independence in defiance
of better judgment.

### The Piano (1993)

*Running time:* 120 minutes
*Production companies:* New South Wales Film and Television Office, Jan
   Chapman Productions, CIBY 2000, Australian Film Commission

Producers: Jan Chapman, Alain Depardieu (executive), Mark Turnbull (associate)

Writer: Jane Campion

Cinematographer: Stuart Dryburgh

Music: Michael Nyman

Key cast members: Holly Hunter, Harvey Keitel, Sam Neill, Anna Paquin, Kerry Walker

Awards: Cannes Film Festival, Palm d'Or, Best Film shared award with Jan Chapman (tied with Chen Kaige for Farewell My Concubine), Best Actress (Holly Hunter) 1993; Academy of Motion Pictures Arts and Sciences, Academy Award for Best Original Screenplay, Best Actress (Holly Hunter), Best Supporting Actress (Anna Paquin), nominated for Best Director, 1993; Vancouver International Film Festival, Most Popular Film, 1993; Golden Globe Awards, Best Actress (Holly Hunter), Best Motion Picture Drama, 1993; Cesar Awards, France, for Best Foreign Film, 1993; Los Angeles Film Critics Association Awards, Best Director, Best Cinematography (Stuart Dryburgh), Best Screenplay, 1993; National Society of Film Critics Awards, US, for Best Screenplay, 1993; New York Film Critics Circle Awards for Best Director and Screenplay, 1993; Writers Guild of America, Best Screenplay, 1993; Australian Film Institute Awards, Best Film (Jan Chapman), Best Achievement in Direction, Best Screenplay, Best Performance by an Actress in a Leading Role (Holly Hunter), Best Performance by an Actor in a Leading Role (Harvey Keitel), Best Achievement in Cinematography (Stuart Dryburgh), Best Original Music Score (Michael Nyman), Best Sound (Gethin Creagh, Tony Johnson, Annabelle Sheehan, Lee Smith, Peter Townend), Best Achievement in Production Design (Andrew McAlpine), Best Achievement in Costume Design (Janet Patterson), Best Achievement in Editing (Veronika Jenet), 1993; Film Critics' Circle of Australia, Best Film, Best Director, Best Supporting Actress (Anna Paquin), Best Screenplay, Best Music Score (Michael Nyman), 1993; American Independent Spirit Award, Best Foreign Film, 1994; UK Critic's Circle, Best Film, Best Actress (Holly Hunter); Chicago Film Critics, Best Foreign Film,

Best Screenplay, Best Music; BAFTA, Best Costume Design (Janet Patterson), Best Production Design (Andrew McAlpine), 1994; Producer's Guild of America, Best Producer (Jan Chapman)

### Synopsis

Ada (Holly Hunter) a mute Scottish woman is brought to New Zealand with her 10-year old daughter Flora (Anna Paquin) and their piano to marry Stewart (Sam Neil) a colonial settler. But it is her neighbour, Baines (Harvey Keitel), an illiterate whaler who lives with the local Maori community, who responds to her piano playing and kindles her passion. Baines purchases Ada's beloved piano from Stewart and negotiates a deal with her in which she can 'earn' the piano back one black key at a time in exchange for 'lessons'.

## An Angel at my Table (1990)

*Running time:* 158 minutes

*Production companies:* Hibiscus Films, New Zealand Film Commission, Television New Zealand, Australian Broadcasting Corporation, Channel 4

*Producers:* Bridget Ikin, Grant Major, John Maynard

*Writer:* Laura Jones

*Cinematographer:* Stuart Dryburgh

*Music:* Don McGlashan

*Key cast members:* Iris Churn, Karen Fergusson, Kerry Fox, Alexia Keogh, Jessie Mune, Kevin J. Wilson

*Awards:* Venice International Film Festival, Silver Lion and Special Jury Prize, Fipresci Prize for Best Film, Elvira Notari Prize (Best Woman Director), Agia Scuola Prize, Cinema and Ragazzi Award for Best Film for Young Audiences, OCIC Award by Christian journalists, Ciak D'Ora Award for Most Popular Film of Festival (shared), 1990; American Independent Spirit Awards, Best Foreign Film, 1990; Sydney Film Festival, highly commended and voted Most Popular Film, 1990; Film Critics' Circle of Australia, Best Foreign Feature film, 1990; Toronto International Film Festival, International Critics' Award (FIPRESCI), 1990; Festival of Festivals, International Critics' Prize, 1990; Valladolid Film Festival, Spain, Best Actress (Kerry Fox), 1990; New Zealand Film and Television Awards, Best Film, Best Director, Best Screenplay, Best Female Performance (Kerry Fox), 1990; Berlin Film Festival, Otto Dibelius Film Prize, Most Popular Film in the Forum, Otto Debelius Prize (from International Jury), 1991; Union of Film Critics, Belgium, Best Film, 1991; screened at Toronto International and Berlin Film Festivals; Los Angeles Film Critics Association, New Generation Award, 1990

### Synopsis

Based on the life of acclaimed New Zealand author Janet Frame as recorded in her three-volume autobiography. Frame grew up in a poverty-stricken family and experienced tragedy at an early age. Always socially awkward she is misdiagnosed with schizophrenia, committed to an institution and subjected to years of electroshock therapy, before eventually achieving recognition for her talents as a writer.

### Sweetie (1989)

*Running time:* 100 minutes
*Production companies:* Arenafilm, Australian Film Commission, New South Wales Film and Television Office
*Producers:* John Maynard, William Mckinnion (co-producer)
*Writers:* Jane Campion, Gerard Lee
*Cinematographer:* Sally Bongers
*Music:* Martin Armiger
*Key Cast members:* Dorothy Barry, Karen Colston, Jon Darling, Genevieve Lemon, Tom Lycos
*Awards:* Georges Sadoul prize for Best Foreign Film, 1989; Australian Film Institute Awards, Best Original Screenplay (shared with Gerard Lee), 1989; Los Angeles Film Critics' Association, New Generation Award, 1990; Australian Film Critics' Association Award for

Best Film, Best Director, Best Actress (Genevieve Lemon), 1991; American Independent Spirit Awards, Best Foreign Film, 1991

### *Synopsis*

Shy and awkward Kay (Karen Colston) meets the man of her destiny, Louis (Tom Lycos), and they live in predictable routine until her sister, Dawn (Genevieve Lemon), nicknamed Sweetie, turns up. Dawn is delusional and extroverted, consumed with the idea of realizing her childhood dreams of a career in show business and encouraged in this by her overly attentive father, Gordon (Jon Darling). The family dynamic is further complicated as their mother, Flo (Dorothy Barry), arranges her separation from Gordon.

## *Two Friends (1986)*

TV feature
*Running time:* 76 minutes
*Production company:* Australian Broadcasting Corporation
*Producers:* Jane Campion, Jan Chapman
*Writer:* Helen Garner
*Cinematographer:* Julian Penney
*Music:* Martin Armiger
*Key cast members:* Kris Bidenko, Steve Bisley, Emma Coles, Peter Hehir, Stephen Leeder, Kris McQuade
*Awards:* Chicago International Film Festival, Gold Plaque (Television), 1987; Australian Film Institute Award, Best Telemovie, Best Director, Best Screenplay, 1987

### *Synopsis*

Based on a Helen Garner short story, this film retrospectively presents the waning friendship between two teenage girls, Kelly (Kris Bidenko) and Louise (Emma Coles), once inseparably close but eventually estranged as a result of differing parental expectations.

## SHORT FILMS

### *The Lady Bug (2007)*

Running time: 3 minutes
Writer: Jane Campion
Cinematographer: Greig Frasier
Music: Marc Bradshaw
Key cast members: Erica Englert, Clayton Jacobson, Genevieve Lemon,
    Marney McQueen

### *Synopsis*

Campion's contribution to a collective film, *To Each His Cinema* (Chacun Son Cinéma), commissioned by the Cannes Film Festival to mark its 60th anniversary. The festival invited a group of internationally diverse auteur directors (33 filmmakers from 25 different countries) to respond to the theme of cinema going. *The Lady Bug* is an experimental interplay between movement (an insect played by Erica Englert who just wants to dance in front of the big screen) and soundtrack (a dialogue of captured conversational snippets about gender and cinema).

### *The Water Diary (2005)*

Running time: 18 minutes
Production companies: LDM Productions, Big Shell Publishing
Producers: Marc Oberon, Lissandra Haulica, Christopher Gill
Writer: Jane Campion
Cinematographer: Greg Frasier
Music: Mark Bradshaw
Key cast members: Ian Abdulla, Di Adams, Justine Clark, Russell Dykstra,
    Alice Englert, Harry Greenwood, Chris Haywood, Clayton Jacobson,
    Miranda Jakich, Tintin Kelly, Genevieve Lemon, Isidore Tillers

### Synopsis

Commissioned by the UN and invited to dramatize the UN Millennium Goals, which address a series of global issues such as poverty, hunger and child mortality. One of eight films (to be collectively titled 8), *Water Diary* focuses on environmental sustainability telling its story about both the incidental and traumatic impact of drought through the eyes of a child (played by Campion's daughter, Alice).

## Dancing Daze (1985)

TV episode (no. 5 in series)
*Running time:* 50 minutes
*Production company:* Australian Broadcasting Corporation (ABC)
*Producer:* Jan Chapman
*Writer:* Debra Oswald
*Cinematographer:* Chrissie Koltai
*Music:* Martin Armiger
*Key cast members:* Paul Chubb, Lance Curtis, Melissa Docker, Kate Green, Norman Kaye, Meryl Tankard

### Synopsis

Anita (Melissa Docker), who has devoted her life to ballet, fails to win a place in a ballet company. In the meantime, the contemporary dance troupe, the Greens, learn that their rehearsal space and showcase venue is to be taken from them unless they can convince a theatre entrepreneur to book them. All appears lost when one of their key dancers, Phoebe (Meryl Tankard), is injured, but Anita steps in to save the day and the venue.

## After Hours (1984)

Running time: 29 minutes
*Production company:* Women's Film Unit of Film Australia
*Producer:* Janet Bell

*Writer:* Jane Campion

*Cinematographers:* Laurie McInnes, Michael Edols

*Key cast members:* Anna Maria Monticelli, Russell Newman, Danielle Pearse, Don Reid

*Awards:* San Francisco Film Festival, Certificate of Merit & Honorable Mention, 1985; Sydney Film Festival, finalist, Greater Union Awards, 1985; Melbourne Film Festival, Best Short Fiction, 1985; Australian Teachers of Media Award, highly commended, 1986; selected for screening at Oberhausen Film Festival, 1985, Cannes Film Festival, 1986

### Synopsis

A sensitive portrayal of a young office worker who alleges sexual abuse by her employer. She loses her job as a result of her claims. This dramatized situation looks at the ways in which an employee can be victimized in an office environment without those around being aware of the situation. It pursues notions of truth such as legal truth, truth of experience and who possesses truth. It also studies sex and desire, not as an expression of love, but as a burden. In this scenario, both the fellow workers and the boyfriend of the young girl fail to understand her situation, somehow blaming her for what happened. The investigator for the case has a difficult task in extracting evidence from people associated with the manager and is left with many unanswered questions. [Film Australia]

### Passionless Moments (1983–84)

*Running time:* 12 minutes

*Production company:* Australian Film and Television School

*Producers:* Jane Campion, Gerard Lee (executive director)

*Writers:* Gerard Lee, assisted by Jane Campion

*Cinematographer:* Jane Campion

*Key cast members:* Anne Berriman, Sean Callinan, Paul Chubb, Elias Ibrahim, Paul Melchert, Jamie Pride, Yves Stenning

*Awards*: Australian Film Institute Award, Best Experimental Film, 1984; Melbourne Film Festival, special award for unique artistic merit (for 'delicious teasing irony'), 1984; Sydney Film Festival, Most Popular Short Film, 1985; selected for screening at Edinburgh Film Festival, 1984, Cannes Film Festival, in 'un certain regard', 1986

### Synopsis

This film documents a much neglected aspect of the human condition, known by psychologists as 'passionless moment'. [AFTRS]

## Mishaps: Seduction and Conquest (1983–84)

*Running time*: 16 minutes
*Production company*: Australian Film and Television School
*Producer*: Jane Campion
*Writer*: Jane Campion
*Cinematographers*: Sally Bongers, Nicolette Freeman, George Petrykowski, Paul Cox
*Key cast members*: Stuart Campbell, Richard Evans, Deborah Kennedy

### Synopsis

In 1924 a British party of climbers made a second attempt to conquer Mount Everest. It ended in tragedy. Among the climbers was George Mallory. Here we record his letters to his brother Geoffrey and Geoffrey's replies . . . Obsessed with a different kind of conquest. [AFTRS]

## A Girl's Own Story (1983–84)

*Running time*: 27 minutes
*Production company*: Australian Film and Television School
*Producer*: Patricia L'Huede
*Writer*: Jane Campion
*Cinematographer*: Sally Bongers
*Music*: Alex Proyas

*Key cast members*: Joanne Gabbe, John Godden, Geraldine Haywood, Marina Knight, Gabrielle Shornegg

*Awards*: Australian Film Institute Awards, Best Direction, Screenplay, Cinematography (for Sally Bongers), 1984; Sydney Film Festival, Rouben Mamoulian Award for Best Short Film in the Greater Union Awards, 1984; Melbourne Film Festival, special award for unique artistic merit (for 'compelling stylistic innovation'), 1984; Amsterdam Film Festival, First Prize Cinestud and voted Best Film by critics, Cinestud (Press Prize), 1985; selected for screening at Wellington, Auckland, Cannes Film Festivals in 'un certain regard'.

### Synopsis

Set in the Beatlemania of the 1960s, this is a stylized account of girl-hood, where perversion is innocent, family is strange and adulthood lonely. [AFTRS]

## Peel – An Exercise in Discipline (1982–83)

*Running time*: 9 minutes

*Production company*: Australian Film and Television School

*Producer*: Ulla Ryghe

*Writer*: Jane Campion

*Cinematographer*: Sally Bongers

*Key cast members*: Katie Pye, Ben Martin, Tim Pye

*Awards*: AFI nominations for Best Short Fiction Film and Editing, 1983; Melbourne Film Festival, Diploma of Merit, 1983; Sydney Film Festival, finalist in Greater Union awards, 1983; Cannes Film Festival, Palme d'Or for Best Short Film, 1986

### Synopsis

A red-headed family's drive in the country begins an intrigue of awesome belligerence and obstinacy. [AFTRS]

## *Tissues (1980)*

### *Synopsis*

About a father who is arrested for child molestation.

## PRODUCED BY JANE CAMPION

### *Abduction: The Megumi Yokota Story (2006)*

Documentary
*Running time:* 85 minutes
*Production companies:* BBC, Safari Media
*Producers:* Jane Campion, Patty Kim, Chris Sheridan
*Directors:* Patty Kim, Chris Sheridan
*Writer:* Patty Kim
*Cinematographer:* Chris Sheridan
*Music:* Shoji Kameda
*Awards:* Slamdance Film Festival, winner audience award Best
Documentary, 2006; Omaha Film Festival, winner audience award
Best Documentary, 2006; Austin Film Festival, Documentary Film
Award, 2006

### *Synopsis*

A documentary tracing the story of a teenage girl abducted by North
Korea.

### *Soft Fruit (1999)*

Feature film
*Running time:* 100 minutes
*Production company:* Soft Fruit Ltd
*Producers:* Jane Campion (executive), Helen Bowden
*Director:* Christina Andreef
*Writer:* Christina Andreef

*Cinematographer:* Laszlo Baranyai

*Music:* Antony Partos

*Key cast members:* Jeanie Drynan, Russell Dykstra, Linal Haft, Sacha Horler, Genevieve Lemon, Alicia Talbot

*Awards:* Sydney Film Festival, audience award for Most Popular Australian Film, 1999; San Sebastian, International Critics Prize (FIPRESCI), 1999; Turin, Jury Prize, 1999; AFI Awards, Best Actor (Russell Dykstra), Best Supporting Actress (Sacha Horler), 1999; Film Critics' Circle of Australia, Best Original Screenplay, 1999; Australian Screen Composers' Guild, APRA Award for Best Original Music for a Soundtrack CD, 1999

### Synopsis

Four siblings gather from across the globe to care for their dying mother (Jeannie Drynan) and fulfil her final wishes.

## FEATURING JANE CAMPION

### Making Sweetie (2006)

'Making of' documentary

*Running time:* 23 minutes

*Production company:* Criterion Collection

*Executive producers:* Peter Becker, Fumiko Takagi, Jonathan Turell

### Synopsis

A video conversation between stars Genevieve Lemon and Karen Colston.

### Making of The Water Diary (2005)

'Making of' documentary

*Running time:* 5 minutes

*Director:* Pauline Goasmat

*Music:* Gilles Lakoste

### Synopsis

Impressionistic compilation of scenes in production.

## Making of The Water Diary (Teaser) (2005)

Promotional short
Running time: 2 minutes
Director: Pauline Goasmat
No other credits available

### Synopsis

Shows the set-up of one dollyshot which obscures the action being recorded, with Jane Campion in frame (but unrecognizable) calling the shot.

## In the Cut: Behind the Scenes (2003)

'Making of' documentary
Running time: 16 minutes
Production company: Columbia Tristar Home Entertainment

## The Making of An Angel At My Table (2002)

'Making of' documentary
Running time: 11 minutes
Created by: Bridget Ikin, Tiara Lowndes

## With the Filmmaker: Portraits by Albert Maysles (2001)

Documentary
Running time: 120 minutes
Production companies: Genko Film Company, IFC Originals
Producer: Antonio Ferrera
Writer/director: Albert Maysles
Cinematographer: Albert Maysles

### Synopsis

Documentary special that focuses on four filmmakers and their personal visions: Jane Campion, Wes Anderson, Robert Duvall and Martin Scorcese.

## Conversations in World Cinema – Jane Campion (2000)

Documentary
Running time: 28 minutes
Production company: Sundance Channel
Producers: Scott Hopper, Keith Keity (associate)
Cinematographer: Simon Riera
Host: Richard Pena

### Synopsis

Chronicles Jane Campion's foray into filmmaking and subsequent success as a director. In an interview, she speaks about the films that she saw her in her childhood and the impression they made on her, her experiences at art school and being a woman within that environment. Discusses the processes of script writing, her relationship with actors and with cinematographers. Contains short excerpts from her films. [NZ Film Archive]

## Women Film Desire: A Journey through Women's Cinema (2000)

Documentary
Running time: 60 minutes
Production companies: ARTE France, RTBF, The Factory, Saga Films, Sylicone
Director: Marie Mandy

### Synopsis

Interviews women filmmakers from five continents about how they film love, desire and sexuality.

## Portrait: Jane Campion and the Portrait of a Lady (1996)

'Making of' documentary
Running time: 54 minutes
Production company: Polygram
Producer: Monty Montgomery
Directors: Peter Long, Kate Ellis

### Synopsis

Behind-the-scenes documentary that focuses in particular on the actor–director relationship.

## Cinema of Unease: A Personal Journey by Sam Neill (1995)

Documentary
Running time: 52 minutes
Production company: Top Shelf Production for the British Film Institute
Producers: Paula Jalfon, Grant Campbell
Directors: Sam Neill, Judy Rymer
Writers: Sam Neill, Judy Rymer
Cinematographer: Alun Bollinger
Music: Don McGlashan

### Synopsis

This is the New Zealand contribution to the British Film Institute's Century of Cinema series. The 'unease' belongs not so much to expatriate Neill, who does admit to being conflicted about his country, but to the national cinema, the history of which Neill demonstrates via clips and commentary.

## Inside the Piano (1993)

'Making of' documentary
Running time: 16 minutes

Production companies: Jan Chapman Productions, CIBY 2000
Producer: Colin Englert
Director: Colin Englert

## Audition (1990)

Short documentary film
Running time: 24 minutes
Producer: David Hazlett
Director: Anna Campion
Writer: Anna Campion
Cinematographer: David Attewell
Key cast members: Edith Campion, Jane Campion

### Synopsis

An exploration of family dynamics. Jane Campion, in pre-production on *An Angel at My Table* auditions her reluctant mother, Edith, a once famous New Zealand actress and theatre entrepreneur, for a small role as a school teacher in *An Angel at My Table*. The film captures the tension between the mother's resistance to Jane's inducements and in turn Jane's resistance to her mother's stultifying pessimism.

## The Grass is Greener: Interview with Jane Campion (1990)

Documentary
Running time: 23 minutes
Production companies: Rymer/Bayly Watson
Director: Greg Stitt
Cinematographer: Bayly Watson
Music: Jan Preston

### Synopsis

Jane Campion discusses her childhood, training at the Australian Film and Television School, the current period of directing *An Angel at My*

*Table* trilogy and living and working in Sydney. Contains excerpts from the latter film along with *Peel*, *A Girl's Own Story*, *Two Friends* and *After Hours*. [NZ Film Archive]

## The Film School Years: Interview with Peter Thompson (1989)

Documentary
Running time: 22 minutes
Production company: AFTRS
Producer: Jason Wheatley
Interviewer: Peter Thompson

### Synopsis

Jane Campion talks about her films and about her relationship with the film school. Includes excerpts from *A Girl's Own Story* and *Sweetie*.

## All That We Need (1966)

Drama/documentary
Running time: 25 minutes
Production company: Pacific Films
Producer: John O'Shae
Director: Barry Barclay
Writer: Barry Barclay
Cinematographer: David Gribble
Music: Steve Robinson, Simon Morris
Key cast members: Jane Campion (flower girl), John Reid, Keith Richardson, Bill Stalker, Jeremy Stephens, Bill Toft

### Synopsis

A dramatized documentary highlighting the 'energy crisis', which focuses on a New Zealand city, its citizens, a mask maker and an actor whose work has been affected by the crisis. [NZ Film Archive]

# BIBLIOGRAPHIC RESOURCES

This section is intended to provide students, scholars and fans with an overview of publications by and about Jane Campion, as well as identifying key books and articles that concern her movies. The references are divided into three broad sections: published primary sources that directly relate to Campion's films (the scripts, novels and novelizations as well as key source materials) organized alphabetically by film title; significant secondary sources (a comprehensive listing of analytical writings about Jane Campion and her films, including non-English-language publications, important interviews and media reviews and unpublished research theses); and, finally, a brief listing of archival holdings with items that relate to aspects or periods of Campion's career.

## SCRIPTS, NOVELS AND NOVELIZATIONS

### An Angel at My Table

Frame, Janet, *An Angel at My Table*, London: The Women's Press, 1984.
—— *An Angel at My Table* (intro. Jane Campion), Sydney, NSW: Random House, 2008.
—— *The Envoy from Mirror City*, London: The Women's Press, 1984.

—— To the Is-Land, London: The Women's Press, 1984.

—— Un angelo alla mia tavola: autobiographia (intro. Anna Nadotti; trans. Lidia Conetti Zazo; including an interview with Jane Campion), Rome: Einaudi, c1996.

Jones, Laura, An Angel at My Table: The Screenplay from the Three-Volume Autobiography of Janet Frame, London and Sydney: Pandora, 1990.

## *Bright Star*

Gittings, Robert, Letters of John Keats: A Selection (Oxford Letters & Memoirs), Oxford: Oxford University Press, 1970.

Keats, John, 'Bright Star! Would I were stedfast as thou art', in Selected Poems (Penguin Classics), London: Penguin, 2007.

Motion, Andrew, Keats, Chicago: University of Chicago Press, 1997.

Rodriguez, Andres, Book of the Heart: The Poetics, Letters, and Life of John Keats (Studies in Imagination), Great Barrington, MA: Lindisfarne Books, 1993.

## *Holy Smoke (novel)*

Campion, Anna, and Jane Campion (trans. Lilē Ioannidou), Hieros kapnos, Athens: Nea Synopa, Ekdotikos Organismos Livanē, 2000.

Campion, Anna, and Jane Campion (trans. Bert Meelker), Holy Smoke, Baarn: de Prom, 1999.

Campion, Anna, and Jane Campion (trans. Marja Alopaeus), Holy Smoke: Pyhässä pilvessä, Jyväskylä: Gummerus, 2000.

Campion, Anna, and Jane Campion (trans. Linda Bravo), Holy Smoke, Madrid: Espasa, 2000.

Campion, Anna, and Jane Campion (trans. Marii Makarovoi), V blazhennom ugare. Za illi' u 'minatorom, Moscow: Inostranka, 2002.

Campion, Anna, and Jane Campion (trans. Silvia Morawetz), Holy Smoke: Roman, Munich: Piper, 2000.

Campion, Anna, and Jane Campion, Holy Smoke: A Novel, New York: Hyperion, 1999.

Campion, Anna, and Jane Campion (trans. Mona Lagerström), Holy Smoke: avprogrammeringen: roman, Stockholm: Pan Pocket, 2000.

Campion, Anna, and Jane Campion (trans. Uri Lotan), 'Ad she-yetse 'ashan, Savyon: Stardast multimedyah, 1999.

Campion, Anna, and Jane Campion (trans. Petr Handl), *Jako dým*, Bígl: Aradan, 2000.

Campion, Anna, and Jane Campion (trans. Atsuko Saitō) *Hōri sumōku*, Tokyo: Shinchosha, 2001.

## *In the Cut*

Moore, Susanna, *In the Cut*, London: Picador, 1996.

## *The Piano: A Novel (novelization)*

Campion, Jane, and Kate Pullinger (trans. Samiyah Falu Abbud), *al-Biyānū*, Abu Dhabi: al-Mujtama' al-thaqafi, 2000.

Campion, Jane, and Kate Pullinger, *De Piano*, Amsterdam: Rainbow, 1997.

Campion, Jane, and Kate Pullinger (trans. Tjadine Stheeman), *De Piano*, Rainbow Pocketboeken, 238, Amsterdam: M. Muntinga, 1995.

Campion, Jane, and Kate Pullinger (trans. Ulla Warren), *Anmeldelse*, Copenhagen: Lindhardt og Ringhof, 1994.

Campion, Jane, and Kate Pullinger, *Piano*, Helsinki: Gummerus, 1998.

Campion, Jane, and Kate Pullinger (trans. K. Serap Yönter), *Piyano*, Istanbul: Altin Kitaplar, 1995.

Campion, Jane, and Kate Pullinger, *Piano*, Jakarta: Gramedia Pustaka Utama, 1995.

Campion, Jane, and Kate Pullinger, *Dœ pīanō: dontrī hœng chīwit*, Krung Thēp: Samnakphim Čhēndœ Phrœt, 1995.

Campion, Jane, and Kate Pullinger, *The Piano: A Novel*, London: Bloomsbury, 1993.

Campion, Jane, and Kate Pullinger (trans. Francesco Saba), *Lezioni di piano*, Milan: Bompiani, 1994.

Campion, Jane, and Kate Pullinger (trans. Carin von Enzenberg), *Das Piano: Der Roman*, Munich: Piper, 1994.

Campion, Jane, and Kate Pullinger (trans. Atle Bjørge), *Pianoet*, Oslo: Aventura, 1995.

Campion, Jane, and Kate Pullinger, *Le piano*, Paris: Grand livre du mois, 1994.

Campion, Jane, and Kate Pullinger (trans. David Collins), *Le piano*, Paris: J. C. Lattès, 1994.

Campion, Jane, and Kate Pullinger (trans. Petra Štechová), *Piano*, Prsten, sv. 1, Prague: Mladá fronta, 1995.

Campion, Jane, and Kate Pullinger (trans. Lena Lundgren), *Pianot: roman*, Stockholm: Tiden, 1994.

Campion, Jane, and Kate Pullinger (trans. Daiman Lin), *Gang qin shi he ta de qing ren: The Piano*, Taipei: You shi wen hua shi ye gong si, 1993.

Campion, Jane, and Kate Pullinger (trans. Atsuko Saito), *Piano Resson*, Tokyo: Shinchosha, 1993.

Campion, Jane, and Kate Pullinger (trans. Krzysztof Zarzecki), *Fortepian*, Torun: C & T, 2000.

Campion, Jane, and Kate Pullinger (trans. Krzysztof Zarzecki), *Fortepian*, Warsaw: Odeon, 1994.

## The Piano (Screenplay)

Campion, Jane (trans. Stephanos Kokkales), *Mathēmata pianou*, Athens: To kleidi Ekd. Organismos Livane, 1994.

Campion, Jane (trans. Barbara de Lange), *De Piano*, Baarn: Bodoni, 1994.

Campion, Jane, *La lección de piano*, Buenos Aires: Emecé Editores, 1994.

Campion, Jane, *The Piano: Screenplay*, London: Bloomsbury, 1993.

Campion, Jane (trans. Mario Biondi), *Lezioni di piano. Bompiani cinema, 2*, Milan: Bompiani, 1993.

Campion, Jane (trans. Peter Pfaffinger), *Das Piano: das Drehbuch zum Film*, Munich: Heyne, 1994.

Campion, Jane, *La leçon de piano: scenario*, Paris: Union Générale d'Éditions, 1994.

Campion, Jane, *P´iano: '93 K´annŭ Yŏnghwaje gŭrangp´ ŭri susangjak!*, Seoul: Sŏjŏkp´o, 1993.

Campion, Jane (trans. Lee Jung Gue), *Bada we ui piano*, Seoul: Paleun, 1999.

Mander, Jane, *The Story of a New Zealand River*, Auckland: Godwit, 1994.

## Portrait of a Lady

James, Henry, *The Portrait of a Lady*, London: Penguin, 1984.

Jones, Laura, and Henry James, *The Portrait of a Lady: Screenplay Based on the Novel by Henry James*, Hollywood, CA: Script City, 1994.

—— *The Portrait of a Lady: Screenplay Based on the Novel by Henry James*, London: Penguin, 1997.

—— *The Portrait of a Lady: Screenplay Based on the Novel by Henry James*, New York: Penguin, 1996.

## *Sweetie*

Lee, Gerard, and Jane Campion, *Sweetie: The Screenplay*, St Lucia, QLD: University of Queensland Press, 1991.

## *Other writing by Jane Campion*

Campion, Jane, 'Big shell', *Rolling Stone*, no. 426, 1988, pp. 74–6.
Campion, Jane, 'In search of Janet Frame', *Guardian*, 19 January 2008, http://books.guardian.co.uk/print/0,,332118204–99930,00.html.

# KEY BOOKS AND ARTICLES

Abramovitz, Rachel, *Is that a Gun in Your Pocket? Women's experience of power in Hollywood*, New York: Random House, 2000.

Adams, Phillip, 'The subtlety of the subtext', *The Weekend Australian Magazine*, 18 January 1986, p. 11.

Anantnarayan, Parvathy. *Silence, Alterity and Synoptic Understanding*, thesis (PhD), University of Louisiana at Lafayette, 2006.

Andrew, Geoff, 'Nicole Kidman and Jane Campion: after treading water in mainstream Hollywood fare like "Batman Forever", Nicole Kidman has taken a step to the left in Jane Campion's Portrait of a Lady', *Time Out*, no. 1382, 1997, pp. 22–5.

—— 'Sisteract', *Time Out*, no. 1366, 1996, p. 75.

Ansen, David, and Charles Fleming, 'Passion for "Piano"', *Newsweek*, vol. 121, no. 22, 31 May 1993, p. 52.

Ardener, Edwin, 'Belief and the problem of women', in Shirley Ardener (ed.), *Perceiving Women*, London: Malaby Press, 1975.

Applebaum, Stephen, 'Great expectations: Kate Winslet on Holy Smoke, gurus and peeing in public' (interview), *Empire Online*, 30 March 2000, www.empireonline.com/interviews/interview.asp?IID=136.

Ashby, Justine, 'Jane Campion', in Yvonne Tasker (ed.), *Fifty Contemporary Filmmakers*, London: Routledge, 2002, pp. 90–8.

Attwood, Fiona, 'Weird lullaby: Jane Campion's *The Piano*', *Feminist Review*, vol. 58, no. 1, 1998, pp. 85–101.

Babington, Bruce, *A History of the New Zealand Fiction Film*, Manchester: Manchester University Press, 2007.

Bachmann, Dieter, *Jane Campion. Neuseeland. Kino von der anderen Seite*, Zurich: TA-Media AG, 1996.

Bagnall, Diana, 'Jane's addiction', *The Bulletin with Newsweek*, vol. 117, no. 6203, 1999, p. 100.

Bailey, Rachael Decker. *'The Finest Entertainment': Conscious Observation on Film in Adaptations of Henry James' The Portrait of a Lady, The Wings of the Dove, and Washington Square*, thesis (MA), Brigham Young University, 2006.

Baker, David, 'Mud-wrestling with the angels: *The Piano* as literature', *Southern Review*, vol. 30, no. 2, 1997, pp. 180–201.

Ball, Anna, 'Writing in the margins: exploring the borderland in the work of Janet Frame and Jane Campion', *eSharp: Electronic Social Sciences, Humanities, and Arts Review for Postgraduates*, vol. 5, pp.1–18.

Barber, Lynden, 'Reel women', *The Weekend Australian Review*, 25 April 1998, pp. 4–6.
—— 'Angel with an eccentric eye', *Sydney Morning Herald*, 8 September 1990, p. 75.

Barlowe, Jamie, '"On which (we) looked up at her": Henry James's and Jane Campion's Portrait(s) of a Lady', in Mica Howe and Sarah Appelton (eds), *He Said, She Says: an RSVP to the male text*, Madison, NJ: Fairleigh Dickinson University Press; London: Associated University Presses, 2001, pp. 221–37.

Basting, B., 'Sie betreten jetzt das menschliche Herz. Jane Campion, die Anthropologin hinter der Filmkamera', *DU*, no. 10, 1996, pp. 34–43.

Battisti, Chiara, 'A re-reading of Bluebeard's fairy tale in Jane Campion's The Piano' in Angelo Righetti (ed.), *Theory and Practice of the Short Story: Australia, New Zealand, the South Pacific*, Verona: University of Verona, 2006, pp. 165–79.

Bauer, Dale M., 'Jane Campion's symbolic *Portrait*', *Henry James Review*, vol. 18, no. 2, 1997, pp. 194–6.

Bauer, Denise, 'Jane Campion's The Piano: a feminist tale of resistance', in Deborah Johnston and Wendy Oliver (eds), *Women Making Art: women in the visual, literary, and performing arts since 1990*, New York: Peter Lang, 2001, pp. 211–26.

Beck, Sandra, *I am Curious about Women: feministische Aspekte in den Filmen der neuseeländischen Regisseurin Jane Campion*, Alfeld: Coppi-Verlag, 2001.

Behan, Erin L., *Refracting the Gaze in Cinema: a feminist exploration of Jane Campion's The Piano*, thesis (MA), Georgia State University, 2001.

Bell, Philip, 'All that patriarchy allows', *Metro Magazine*, no. 102, 1995, pp. 57–60.

Bentley, Greg, 'Mothers, daughters, and (absent) fathers in Jane Campion's *The Piano*', *Literature/Film Quarterly*, vol. 30, no. 1, 2002, pp. 46–58.

Bentley, Nancy, '"Conscious observation of a lovely woman": Jane Campion's *Portrait* in film', *Henry James Review*, vol. 18, no. 2, 1997, pp. 174–9 (also published in Susan M. Griffin (ed.), *Henry James Goes to the Movies*, Lexington: University Press of Kentucky, 2002).

Bernard, Jami, 'Communication as Eros in *The Piano*', in Peter Keough (ed.), *Flesh and Blood: the National Society of Film Critics on sex, violence, and censorship*, San Francisco: Mercury House, 1995.

Berry, Jason M., *Gender and Narrativity: the films of Jane Campion*, thesis (MA), Clemson University, 1999.

Bihlmeyer, Jaime, 'The (un)speakable femininity in mainstream movies: Jane Campion's *The Piano*', *Cinema Journal*, vol. 44, no. 2, 2005, pp. 68–88.

Bilbrough, Miro, '*The Piano*: Jane Campion interviewed by Miro Bilbrough', *Cinema Papers*, no. 93, 1993, p. 4–11.

Bird, Carmel, 'Freedom of speech', in Cassandra Pybus (ed.), *Columbus's Blindness and Other Essays*, St Lucia, QLD: University of Queensland Press, 1994, pp. 190–8.

Blaze, Margaret K., *Life doesn't have to End at Thirty: some advice from Kate Chopin, Margaret Drabble, Margaret Atwood, Jane Campion and Janet Frame*, thesis (MA), University of Wyoming, 1995.

Bloustien, Geraldine, 'Jane Campion: memory, motif and music', *Continuum*, vol. 5, no. 2, 1992, pp. 29–39.

Bogdan, Deanne, Hilary E. Davis and Judith Robertson, 'Sweet surrender and trespassing desires in reading: Jane Campion's *The Piano* and the struggle for responsible pedagogy', *Changing English*, vol. 4, no. 1, 1997, pp. 81–104.

Boni, Stefano, et al. (eds), *Jane Campion*, Turin: Scriptorium, 1994.

Boudreau, Kristin, 'Is the world then so narrow? Feminist cinematic adaptations of Hawthorne and James, *Henry James Review*, vol. 21, no. 1, 2000, pp. 43–53.

Bousquet, Marc, 'I don't like Isabel Archer', *Henry James Review*, vol. 18, no. 2, 1997, pp. 197–9.

Bradley, John R., *Henry James on Stage and Screen*, New York: Palgrave, 2000.

Brooks, Ann, *Postfeminisms, Feminism, Cultural Theory and Cultural Forms*, London: Routledge, 1997.

Brown, Caroline, 'The representation of the Indigenous Other in *Daughters of the Dust* and *The Piano*', *NWSA Journal*, vol. 15, no. 1, 2003, pp. 1–19.

Brown, Georgina, 'Down under and dirty', *Village Voice*, 21 May 1991, p. 58.

Brown, Mick, 'Where there's smoke', *Courier Mail Weekend Arts*, 11 September 1999, p. 11.

Brugiamolini, Fabiola, Stefano Gambelli and Lorenzo Capulli, *Le donne riprendono l'infanzia, ovvero Regie al femminile e maternità da Jane Campion a Francesca Archibugi*, Figlio figlia, 3. Roma: D. Audino, 1995.

de Bruyn, Oliver, 'Jane Campion – *In the Cut* – Le secret derrière la porte', *Positif*, no. 514, 2003, p. 19.

Bruzzi, Stella, 'Review of *Holy Smoke*', *Sight and Sound*, vol. 10, no. 4, 2000, p. 48.

—— 'Review of *Portrait of a Lady*', *Sight and Sound*, vol. 7, no. 3, 1997, p. 60.

—— *Undressing Cinema: clothing and identity in the movies*, London: Routledge, 1997, pp. 57–63.

—— 'Jane Campion: costume drama and reclaiming women's past', in Pam Cook and Philip Dodds (eds), *Women and Film: a Sight and Sound reader*, London: Scarlet Press, 1995, pp. 232–42.

—— 'Tempestuous petticoats: costume and desire in *The Piano*', *Screen*, vol. 36, no. 3, 1995, pp. 257–66.

—— 'Replaying *The Piano*', *Sight and Sound*, vol. 4, no. 3, 1994, p. 64.

—— 'Bodyscape' (with comments from *The Piano*'s crew), *Sight and Sound*, vol. 3, no. 10, 1993, pp. 6–10.

Bussi, Elisa, 'Voyages and border crossings: Jane Campion's *The Piano*', *Critical Studies*, no. 14, 2000, pp. 161–73.

Cairns, Barbara, *Shadows on the Wall: a study of seven New Zealand feature films*, Auckland: Longman Paul, 1994.

Calder, Alex, 'From post-colonialism to settlement studies: on the consequences of buying land in Old New Zealand and *The Piano*', *New Literatures Review*, no. 39, 2003, pp. 125–40.

Calhoun, John, 'Interior landscapes', *American Cinematographer*, vol. 84, no. 11, 2003, pp. 76–8, 80–2, 84–5.

Campbell, Russell, 'Dismembering the Kiwi bloke: representations of masculinity in *Braindead*, *Desperate Remedies*, and *The Piano*', *Illusions*, no. 24, Spring, 1995.

Campion, Anna, 'Diary and notes for *Holy Smoke*', *Melbourne Herald-Sun*, 30 January 2000, pp. 99–100.

Campion, Jane, and Catherine Brelliat, 'Costume – insider's view: CINEMA: MY OWN VISION – Intervista reccolta da Deborab Young', *Vogue Italia*, no. 685, 2007, p. 620.

Canby, Vincent, 'In the end literature conquers all', *New York Times*, 4 October 1990, p. C26.

Cantwell, Mary, 'Jane Campion's lunatic women', *New York Times*, 19 September 1993, pp. 40–4; 51.

Caputo, Raffaele, and Geoff Burton (eds), *Second Take, Australian Film-makers Talk*, St Leonards, NSW: Allen & Unwin, 1999.

Carroll, Fiona M., *Deconstructing Domestic Violence: (what's that piano doing on the beach?)*, thesis (MA), University of Adelaide, 1997.

Çelebi, Hatice, *Structural and Functional Analysisof Henry James's Novel the Portrait of a Lady with a Comparison of Jane Campion's Adaptation of the Novel*, Ankara: METU, 2003.

Chandler, Karen Michelle, 'Agency and social constraint in Jane Campion's *The Portrait of a Lady*', *Henry James Review*, vol. 18, no. 2, 1997, pp. 191–3.

Cheshire, Ellen, *Jane Campion: the pocket essential guide*, London: Harpenden, 2000.

Chion, Michel, '"Mute music" in three films by Jane Campion (The Piano), Krzystof Kieslowski (Trois Couleurs Bleu), and Roman Polanski (The Pianist)', in Lawrence Kramer, Richard D. Leppert and Daniel Goldmark (eds), *Beyond the Soundtrack: representing music in the cinema*, Berkeley: University of California Press, 2007, pp. 86–98.

—— *David Lynch* (trans. Robert Julian), London: British Film Institute, 1995.

Chumo, Peter, 'Keys to the imagination: Jane Campion's *The Piano*', *Literature/Film Quarterly*, vol. 25, no. 3, 1997, pp. 173–6.

Ciment, Michel, 'Jane Campion and *Positif*', Part II in Raffaele Caputo and Geoff Burton (eds), *Second Take, Australian Film-makers Talk*, St Leonards, NSW: Allen & Unwin, 1999, pp. 43–89.

—— 'The function and state of film criticism', in John Boorman and Walter Donohue (eds), *Projections 8: film-makers on film-making*, London: Faber & Faber, 1998, pp. 35–42.

Clover, Carol, 'Ecstatic mutilation', *The Threepenny Review*, no. 57, 1994, pp. 20–22.

Cochrum, Connie Gigi, *Women's Voices: myth, gender, power, patriarchy and language*, thesis (MA), San Francisco State University, 2001.

Colloque C.O.R.A.I.L., *La Femme: entre tradition et modernité dans le Pacifique Sud: actes du huitième Colloque C.O.R.A.I.L. 1995/* publiés sous la direction de Sonia Faessel,

Noumea: Université Française du Pacifique and C.O.R.A.I.L.; Paris: L'Harmattan, 1996.

Cook, Pam, 'Passionless moments', *Monthly Film Bulletin*, vol. 57, no. 678, 1990, p. 210.

Coombs, Felicity, and Gemmell, Suzanne, *Piano Lessons, Approaches to The Piano*, Sydney: John Libby, 2000.

Cordaiy, Hunter, 'Jane Campion interviewed by Hunter Cordaiy', *Cinema Papers*, no. 81, 1990, pp. 32–6.

Corrigan, Timothy, *A Cinema without Walls: movies and culture after Vietnam*, New Brunswick: Rutgers University Press, 1991.

Crawford, Anne-Marie, and Martin, Adrian, '*Sweetie*', *Cinema Papers*, no. 75, 1989, pp. 56–7.

Cummings, Richard, '*The Piano* Revisited', *Sight and Sound*, vol. 4, no. 2, 1994, p. 72.

Dalton, Mary M., and Kirsten James Fatzinger, 'Choosing silence: defiance and resistance without voice in Jane Campion's *The Piano*', *Women and Language*, vol. 26, part 2, 2003, pp. 34–9.

Dapkus, Jeanne R., 'Sloughing off the burdens: parallel/antithetical quests for self actualisation', *Literature/Film Quarterly*, vol. 25, no. 3, 1997, pp. 177–87.

Davis, Michael, 'Tied to that maternal "thing": death and desire in Jane Campion's *The Piano*', *Gothic Studies*, vol. 4, no. 1, 2002, pp. 63–78.

Dayal, Samir, 'Inhuman love: Jane Campion's *The Piano*', *Postmodern Culture*, vol. 12, no. 2, 2002, http://www.iath.virginia.edu/pmc/text-only/issue.102/12.2dayal.txt.

D'Cruz, Doreen, 'Textual enigmas and disruptive desires in Jane Campion's *Sweetie*', *Australian Feminist Studies*, vol. 21, no. 49, 2006, pp. 7–22.

Delichatsios, Angela Michelle, *The Drawbacks of Feminist Psychoanalytic Film Theory: Jane Campion's Sweetie and The Piano as a case study*, thesis (BA), Harvard University, 1995.

Demers, Annick, *Parcours du féminin dans l'oeuvre cinématographique de Jane Campion*, Montreal: Université du Québec à Montréal, 2000.

Denby, David, 'Creep shows', *The New Yorker*, 27 October 2003, vol. 79, no. 32, p. 112.

Dennis, Jonathan, and Bieringa, Jan (eds), *Film in Aotearoa New Zealand*, 2nd edn, Wellington: Victoria University of Wellington Press, 1996.

Di Drusco, Fabia, 'Let's talk with Peter Weir and Jane Campion', *L'Uomo Vogue*, no. 353, 2004, p. 318.

Dupont, Joan, 'The Cannes festival: Jane Campion, on drought and isolation', *International Herald Tribune*, 31 May 2006, http://www.iht.com/articles/2006/05/26/news/dupont.php.

Dupont, Mary Anderson, *The Tragic Heroine 'Lives to Swim Another Day': Jane Campion's The Piano and Kate Chopin's The Awakening*, thesis (MA), University of St Thomas (Saint Paul, MN), 1994.

DuPuis, R., 'Romanticizing colonialism: power and pleasure in Jane Campion's *The Piano*', *Contemporary Pacific*, vol. 8, no. 1, 1996, pp. 51–80.

Dyson, Lynda, 'The return of the repressed? Whiteness, femininity and colonialism in *The Piano*', *Screen*, vol. 36, no. 3, 1995, pp. 267–76.

Eggleton, David, 'Grimm fairytale of the south seas', *Illusions*, no. 23, 1994, pp. 2–5.

Enker, Debi, 'The girl's own story', *Cinema Papers*, no. 60, 1986, pp. 47–8.

Errigo, Angie, 'Jane Campion: Antipodean director', *Empire*, no. 53, 1993, pp. 63–4.

Feinstein, Howard, 'The Jane mutiny', *Guardian Unlimited*, 2 April 1999, http://film.guardian.co.uk/Feature_Story/Guardian/0,,39226,00.html#article_continue.

Felperin, Leslie, '*In the Cut*', *Sight and Sound*, vol. 13, no. 12, 2003, pp. 37–8.

Ferrier, Liz, 'Vulnerable bodies: creative disabilities in contemporary Australian film', in Ian Craven (ed.), *Australian Cinema in the 1990s*, London: Frank Cass, 2001, pp. 57–78.

Francke, Lizzie, 'On the brink', *Sight and Sound*, vol. 6, no. 11, 1996, pp. 6–9 (also published in Ginette Vincendeau (ed.) *Film/Literature/Heritage*, London: British Film Institute, 2001).

—— Review of *The Piano* in *Sight and Sound*, vol. 3, no. 10, 1993, pp. 50–2.

Frankenberg, Ronnie, 'Re-presenting the child: the muted child, the tamed wife and the silent instrument in Jane Campion's *The Piano*' in Alan Prout (ed.) and Jo Campling (consultant ed.), *The Body, Childhood and Society*, New York: St Martin's Press, 2000.

Fraser, Kennedy, 'Portrait of the director', *Vogue*, Jan. 1997, p. 144.

Freiberg, Freda, 'The bizarre in the banal: notes on the films of Jane Campion', in Annette Blonski, Barbara Creed and Freda Freiberg (eds), *Don't Shoot Darling: women's independent film making in Australia*, Richmond, VIC: Greenhouse, 1987, pp. 328–33.

French, Lisa, *Centering the Female: the articulation of female experience in the films of Jane Campion*, thesis (PhD), RMIT, 2007.

Fuller, Graham, and Lizzie Francke, 'Sex and self-anger', *Sight and Sound*, no. 11, 2003, pp. 16–19.

Gabler, Neal, 'The Oscars: Hollywood's fade to black', *Los Angeles Times (Part M)*, 25 February 2007, p. 1.

Garcia, Maria, 'In the Cut', *Film Journal International*, vol. 106, no. 11, 2003, p. 56.

Gatti, Ilaria, *Jane Campion*, Recco Genova: Le mani, 1998.

Gelder, Ken, 'Jane Campion and the limits of a literary cinema', in Deborah Cartmell and Imelda Whelan (eds), *Adaptations: from text to screen, screen to text*, London: Routledge, 1999, pp. 157–71.

Gentry, Ric, 'Painterly touches', *American Cinematographer*, vol. 78, no. 1, 1997, pp. 50–7.

Gillett, Sue, *Views from Beyond the Mirror: The films of Jane Campion*, St Kilda, VIC: Australian Teachers of Media, 2004.

—— 'A pleasure to watch: Jane Campion's narrative cinema', *Screening the Past*, no. 12, 2001, http://www.latrobe.edu.au/www/screeningthepast/first release/fr0301/sgfr12a.html.

—— 'Lips and fingers: Jane Campion's *The Piano*', *Screen*, vol. 36, no. 3, 1995, pp. 277–87.

—— 'More than meets the eye', *Senses of Cinema*, http://www.sensesof cinema.com/contents/00/1/sweetie.html.

—— 'Never a native', *Senses of Cinema*, http://www.sensesofcinema.com/ contents/00/5/holy.html.

—— 'Angel from the mirror city', *Senses of Cinema*, http://www.sensesofcinema. com/contents/00/10/angel.html.

—— 'Engaging medusa: competing myths and fairytales in *In the Cut*', *Senses of Cinema*, http://www.sensesofcinema.com/contents/04/31/in_the_cut.html.

Glaessner, Verina, 'A girl's own story', *Monthly Film Bulletin*, vol. 57, no. 678, 1990, p. 209.

Goldson, Annie, 'Piano recital', *Screen*, vol. 38, no. 3, 1997, pp. 275–81.

—— 'Piano lessons', in Jonathan Dennis and Jan Bieringa (eds), *Film in Aotearoa New Zealand*, 2nd edn, Wellington: Victoria University of Wellington Press, 1996, pp. 195–8.

Goldsworthy, Kerryn, 'What music is', *Arena Magazine*, no. 7, 1993, pp. 46–8.

Goode, Pam, 'Foundational romance, history and the photograph in *The Piano* and *Far and Away*, *Span: Journal of the South Pacific Association for Commonwealth Literature & Language Studies*, nos 42–3, 1996, pp. 52–64.

—— 'The journey's end: settler romance in *The Piano* and *Far and Away*', thesis, University of Auckland, New Zealand, 1996.

Goodridge, Mike, *Directing*, Boston: Focal Press, 2002.

Gordon, R., 'Portraits perversely framed: Jane Campion and Henry James', *Film Quarterly*, vol. 56, no. 2, 2002, pp. 14–24.

Gordon, Suzy, '"I clipped your wing, that's all": auto-erotism and the female spectator in *The Piano* Debate', *Screen*, vol. 37, no. 2, 1996, pp. 193–205.

Gotting, Peter, 'The next Campion? Just me, myself, I', *Sydney Morning Herald*, 6 May 2000, p. 7.

Green, Jesse, 'That was no "lady": pilfering literature; what benumbs a legend most? Why do film makers add insult to injury by invoking the authors whose works they are debasing?', *New York Times*, 11 May 1997, p. H23.

Greenberg, Harvey, 'The Piano', *Film Quarterly*, vol. 47, no. 3, 1994, pp. 46–50.

Griffin, Susan M., *Henry James Goes to the Movies*, Lexington: University Press of Kentucky, 2002.

Griffith University, Brisbane City Gallery, and Queensland College of Art, *Women on Art: free public lecture series*, Brisbane: Queensland College of Art, 1998.

Grunberg, Serge, 'Australia: from the desert to Hollywood', *Metro Magazine*, no. 100, 1994–95, pp. 27–31.

Halliwell, Martin, 'Transcultural aesthetics and the film adaptations of Henry James', in Deborah Cartmell, et al., *Classics in Film and Fiction*, London: Pluto Press, 2000.

Hardy, Ann, 'The last patriarch', *Illusions*, no. 24, 1994, pp. 6–13.

—— '*Sweetie*: A song in the desert', *Illusions*, no. 15, 1990, pp. 7–13.

Hardy, Linda, 'Natural occupancy', in Suvendrini Perera (ed.), *Asian and Pacific Inscriptions: identities, ethnicities, nationalities*, Bundoora, VIC: Meridian, 1995, pp. 213–27.

Harris, Meridy Joan, *Exploring a Feminist Aesthetic in Mainstream Cinema: the case of Jane Campion and The Piano*, University of Kent at Canterbury, 2001.

Haslem, Wendy, 'Towards a darker vision', *RealTime OnScreen*, no. 17, 1997, pp. 17–18.

Hawker, Philippa, 'Jane Campion' (interview), *Cinema Papers*, no. 73, 1989, pp. 29–30.

—— 'A tale of friendships . . . a few little surprises', *The Age Green Guide*, 24 April 1986, p. 9.

Hausknecht, Gina, 'Self-possession, dolls, Beatlemania, loss: telling the girl's own story', in Ruth O. Saxton (ed.), *The Girl: constructions of the girl in contemporary fiction by women*, New York: St Martin's Press, 1998, pp. 21–4.

Hazel, Valerie, 'Disjointed articulations: the politics of voice and Jane Campion's *The Piano*', *Women's Studies Journal*, vol. 10, no. 2, 1994, pp. 27–40.

Hebb, Janine A., *Lasting Impressions: contemplating Jane Campion and cinefeminist readings in motion picture film*, thesis (MA), University of Hawaii at Manoa, 1994.

Hendershot, Cyndy, '(Re)visioning the gothic: Jane Campion's *The Piano*', *Literature/Film Quarterly*, vol. 26, no. 2, 1998, pp. 97–108.

Henke, Suzette, 'Jane Campion frames Janet Frame: a portrait of the artist as a young New Zealand poet', *Biography*, vol. 23, no. 4, 2000, pp. 651–69.

Heron, Erena, *Translating Place: landscape, film and film landscape*, Auckland: University of Auckland Press, 2002.

Hoeveler, Diane L., 'Silence, sex and feminism: an examination of *The Piano*'s unacknowledged sources', *Literature/Film Quarterly*, vol. 26, no. 2, 1998, pp. 109–16.

hooks, bell, 'Gangsta culture – sexism and misogyny', in *Outlaw Culture: Resisting Representations*, London: Routledge, 1994, pp. 115–23.

Hopgood, Fincina, 'Inspiring passion and hatred: Jane Campion's *In the Cut*', *Metro Magazine*, no. 139, 2004, p. 28.

—— 'Jane Campion', *Senses of Cinema Great Directors: A Critical Database*, http://www.sensesofcinema.com/contents/directors/02/campion.html.

Horne, Philip, 'The James Gang', *Sight and Sound*, vol. 8, no. 1, 1998, pp. 16–19.

—— 'Valuing the honour of the thing', *Times Literary Supplement*, 7 March 1997, p. 20.

Hsiang, Jen-Hui, *Sound in Silence: Ada's voices in Jane Campion's The Piano*, thesis (MA), Tamkang University, 1996.

Hurd, Mary G., *Women Directors and their Films*, Westport, CN: Praeger, 2007.

Hutcheson, Tearlach Dubh, *Interpretive Keys to Jane Campion's The Piano*, thesis (MA), University of Colorado at Denver, 1996.

Izod, John, 'The Piano, the animus, and the colonial experience', Journal of Analytical Psychology, vol. 41, no. 1, 1996, pp. 117–36.

Izzo, Donatella, 'Setting a free woman free: the Portrait(s) of a Lady', Q/W/E/R/T/Y: Arts, Litteratures & Civilisations du Monde Anglophone, no. 8, 1998, pp. 169–79.

Jacobs, Carol, 'Playing Jane Campion's Piano: politically', Modern Language Notes, vol. 109, 1994, pp. 757–85.

Jacobs, Gilles, Les Visiteurs de Cannes: cineastes à l'œuvre, Paris: Hatier, 1992.

James, Caryn, 'A distinctive shade of darkness', New York Times, 28 November 1993.

Janstova, Patricia, Empirical Testing of Auteur Theory via Content Analysis: a study of Jane Campion films, thesis (MAPCT & M), Cleveland State University, 2006.

Jayamanne, Laleen, 'Post-colonial gothic: the narcissistic wound of Jane Campion's The Piano', in Toward Cinema and its Double: cross-cultural mimesis, Bloomington: Indiana University Press, pp. 24–48.

Johnson, Barbara, The Feminist Difference: literature, psychoanalysis, race and gender, Cambridge, MA: Harvard University Press, 1998.

Johnston, Sheila, 'Peter Weir/Jane Campion: directors cut to the chase', The Independent, 9 July 2004, p. 7.

Jones, Gail, The Piano, Sydney: Currency Press, 2007.

Kaplan, Cora, Victoriana: histories, fictions, criticism, Edinburgh: Edinburgh University Press, 2007.

Kaplan, E. Ann, Women and Film: both sides of the camera, New York: Methuen, 1983.

Kauffmann, Stanley, 'On films: a passion in the desert: Jane Campion's "Holy Smoke" is portentous and predictable', New Republic, no. 4438, 7 February 2000, pp. 26–7.

—— 'On films: the portrait retouched – The Portrait of a Lady – Jane Campion's risky modernization of Henry James', New Republic, no. 4275, 23 December 1996, p. 28.

—— 'The Piano', New Republic, 13 December 1993, vol. 209, no. 24, pp. 30–1.

Kaufman, Cynthia, 'Colonialism, purity and resistance in The Piano', Socialist Review, vol. 24, nos 1–2, 1995, pp. 251–5.

Kelly, David, 'The lady in the frame: two portraits by Henry James and Jane Campion', Senses of Cinema, http://www.sensesofcinema.com/contents/01/18/lady_frame.html.

Kerr, Sarah, 'People are talking about — movies – three unlikely souls cross paths in 21 Grams, while a woman courts disaster in Jane Campion's controversial In the Cut', *Vogue*, Nov. 2003, p. 352.

Kirchmann, Kay, 'Silence and physicality', *Ballett International/Tanz Aktuell*, Heft 8, 1994, pp. 33–9.

Klawans, Stuart, 'The Piano', *The Nation*, vol. 257, no. 19 (6 December, 1993), p. 705.

Klinger, Barbara, 'The art film, affect and the female viewer: *The Piano* revisited', *Screen*, vol. 47, no. 1, 2006, pp. 19–42.

Knight, Christine, 'Ada's piano playing in Jane Campion's *The Piano*', *Australian Feminist Studies*, vol. 21, no. 49, 2006, pp. 23–34.

Konow, David, 'Rough cut: Jane Campion and Susanna Moore on In the Cut', *Creative Screenwriting*, vol. 10, no. 5, 2003, pp. 69–73.

Kramer, Lawrence, *Critical Musicology and the responsibility of Response: selected essays*, Aldershot: Ashgate, 2006.

—— 'Recognizing Schubert: musical subjectivity, cultural change, and Jane Campion's *The Portrait of a Lady*', *Critical Inquiry*, vol. 29, part 1, 2002, pp. 25–52 (also published in *Journal for Research in Mathematics Education*, vol. 33, no. 5, 2002).

Langdell, Cheri Davis, 'Pain of silence: Emily Dickinson's silences, poetic persona and Ada's selfhood in *The Piano*', *Emily Dickinson Journal*, vol. 5, no. 2, 1996, pp. 196–201.

Lewis, Judith, 'Wholly Jane', *LA Weekly*, http://www.laweekly.com/ink/09/film-lewis.shtml.

Lurie, Susan, 'A twentieth-century portrait: Jane Campion's American girl', in John Kucich and Dianne Sadoff (eds), *Victorian Afterlife: postmodern culture rewrites the nineteenth century*, Minneapolis: University of Minnesota Press, 2000, pp. 83–100.

Mabry, Rochelle, 'Fighting fire with fire: reclaiming phallocentric conventions in feminine costume dramas', *West Virginia University Philological Papers*, no. 48, 2001–02, pp. 196–201.

MacDonald, Scott (ed.), *A Critical Cinema 3: interviews with independent filmmakers*, Berkeley: University of California Press, 1998.

Maddox, Gary, 'Cannes opening a snow-capped peak for director', *Sydney Morning Herald*, 8 May 2004, p. 3.

—— 'For film-maker Campion, it's a wrap – for now', *Sydney Morning Herald*, 7 November 2003, p. 3.

—— 'Campion fires up at "career crisis" jibes', *Sydney Morning Herald*, 10 September 1999, p. 2.

—— 'Young gun a shooting star', *Sydney Morning Herald*, 9 September 1999, p. 19.

Maio, Kathi, 'The Piano', *Ms. Magazine*, vol. 4, no. 5, 1994, p. 84.

Mangiarotti, Chiara, *Figure di donna nel cinema di Jane Campion: una lettura psicoanalitica*, Milan: F. Angeli, 2002.

Margaroni, Maria, 'Jane Campion's selling of the mother/land: restaging the crisis of the postcolonial subject', *Camera Obscura*, no. 53, 2003, pp. 93–123.

Margolis, Harriet (ed.), *Jane Campion's The Piano*, Cambridge: Cambridge University Press, 2000.

——, and Janet Hughes, 'Jane Campion's *The Portrait of a Lady*', in R. Barton Palmer (ed.), *Nineteenth-Century American Fiction on Screen*, Cambridge: Cambridge University Press, 2007, pp. 161–74.

Martin, Adrian, 'Losing the way: the decline of Jane Campion', *Landfall*, vol. 200, no. 2, 2000, pp. 89–103.

Maslin, Janet, 'A spiritual tug of war in the Australian outback', *The New York Times*, 3 December 1999, p. B24.

—— 'The Portrait of a Lady', *The New York Times*, 27 December 1996, p. B1.

McBryde, Louise, *Jane Campion and the National Auteur Industry*, thesis (MA), University of Queensland, 2001.

McCarthy, Todd, 'Campion's elegant, chilly *Portrait*', *Variety*, 9–15 September 1996, p. 114.

McFarlane, Brian, '*An Angel at My Table*', *Cinema Papers*, no. 81, 1990, pp. 52–3.

McGlothlin, Erin, 'Speaking the "mind's voice": double discursivity in Jane Campion's *The Piano*', *Post Script: Essays in Film and the Humanities*, vol. 23, no. 2, 2004, pp. 19–32.

McGrann, Molly, 'Holy Smoke', *The Times Literary Supplement*, no. 5025, 1999, p. 21.

McHugh, Kathleen, *Jane Campion*, Urbana: University of Illinois Press, 2007.

—— '"Sounds that creep inside you": female narration and voiceover in the films of Jane Campion', *Style*, vol. 35, no. 2, 2001, pp. 193–218.

McMahon, Thomas (ed.), *Artists for Young Adults*, vol. 33, Detroit: Gale Research, 2000.

Mellencamp, Patricia, *A Fine Romance: five ages of feminism*, Philadelphia: Temple University Press, 1995.

Meyer, T., 'Töne für die Augen. Filmmusik für Jane Campion', DU, no. 10, 1996, pp. 50–3.

Modleski, Tania, *Old Wives Tales and Other Women's Stories*, New York: New York University Press, 1998.

Molina, Caroline, 'Muteness and mutilation: the aesthetics of disability in Jane Campion's *The Piano*', in David T. Mitchell and Sharon L. Snyder (eds), *The Body and Physical Difference: discourses of disability*, Ann Arbor: University Of Michigan Press, 1997, pp. 267–82.

Muench, Holger, *Nur die Rabenmutter ist eine gute Mutter. Vergleichende Analyse der Mutter–Tochter Beiziehung in Jane Campions Das Piano*, Munich: GRIN Verlag, 1996.

Murphy, Kathleen, 'Jane Campion's passage to India', Film Comment, vol. 36, no. 1, 2000, pp. 3–36.

—— 'Jane Campion's shining portrait of a director', in George Plimpton (ed.) and Jason Snider (series ed.), *The Best American Movie Writing, 1998*, New York: St Martin's Griffin, 1998.

—— 'Jane Campion's shining portrait of a director', Film Comment, vol. 2, no. 6, 1996, pp. 28–33.

Murray, Scott, 'Women in film: what's wrong with this picture?', Cinema Papers, no. 3, 1995, p. 2.

—— *Australian Cinema*, Sydney: Allen & Unwin in association with Australian Film Commission, 1994.

—— (ed.) *Australian Film 1978–1992: a survey of theatrical features*, Melbourne: Oxford University Press in association with the Australian Film Commission and Cinema Papers, 1993.

Nadel, A., 'The search for cinematic identity and a good man: Jane Campion's appropriation of James's portrait', Henry James Review, vol. 18, no. 2, 1997, pp. 180–3.

Najita, Susan, *Decolonizing Cultures in the Pacific: reading history and trauma in contemporary fiction*, New York; Abingdon, Oxon: Routledge, 2006.

—— 'Family resemblances: the construction of pakeha history in Jane Campion's *The Piano*, Ariel, vol. 32, part 1, 2001, pp. 81–118.

—— *Pacific Literature as Local Opposition Trauma, Magic Realism and History*, thesis (PhD), University of California, Santa Barbara, 2001.

Natharius, David, and Bethami Dobkin, 'Feminist visions of transformation in *The Ballad of Little Jo*, *The Piano*, and *Orlando*', *Women and Language*, vol. 25, no. 1, 2002, pp. 9–17.

Neroni, Hilary, 'Jane Campion's jouissance: *Holy Smoke* and feminist film theory', in Sheila Kunkle and Todd McGowan (eds), *Lacan and Contemporary Film*, New York: Other Press, 2004, pp. 209–32.

Nicholls, Mark, 'She who gets slapped: Jane Campion's *Portrait of a Lady*', *Metro Magazine*, no. 111, 1997, pp. 43–7.

Norgrove, Aaron, 'But is it music? The crisis of identity in *The Piano*', *Race and Class*, vol. 40, no. 1, 1998, p. 47–56.

O'Neill, Eithne, 'Briser les gaines Eros dans l'oeuvre de Jane Campion', *Positif*, no. 521/522, 2004, pp. 32–5.

—— 'Voile blanc dans un arbre: Jane Campion, anthropologue de l'âme', *Positif*, no. 466, 1999, pp. 19–21.

Ozick, Cynthia, 'Cinematic James', in *Quarrell & Quandary: Essays*, New York: Knopf, 2000, pp. 147–58.

—— 'What only words, not film, can portray', *New York Times*, 5 January 1997, p. H1.

Paolillo, Marcello, *Il cinema di Jane Campion*, Alessandria: Falsopiano, 2004.

Park, Douglas, and Dietrich, Dawn, 'In the Cut', *Film Quarterly*, vol. 58, no. 4, 2005, pp. 39–46.

Paskin, Sylvia, 'Peel', *Monthly Film Bulletin*, vol. 57, no. 678, 1990, pp. 210–11.

Peitz, Christiane, 'Identifikation einer Frau. Das Kino der Jane Campion', in *Marilyns starke Schwestern: Frauenbilder im Gegenwartskino*, Hamburg: Klein, 1995, pp. 99–159.

Perez Riu, Carmen, 'Two gothic feminist texts: Emily Bronte's *Wuthering Heights* and the film, *The Piano*, by Jane Campion', *Atlantis: Revista de la Asociacion Espanola de Estudios Anglo-Norteamericanos*, vol. 22, no. 1, 2000, 163–73.

Perkins, Reid, 'Imag(in)ing our past: colonial New Zealand on film from *The Birth of New Zealand* to *The Piano*', *Illusions*, no. 26, 1997, pp. 4–10.

Phoca, Sophia, and Wright, Rebecca, *Introducing Postfeminism*, New York: Totem Books, 1999.

Pihama, Leonie, 'Ebony and ivory: a construction of Maori in *The Piano*', in Harriet Margolis (ed.), *Jane Campion's The Piano*, Cambridge: Cambridge University Press, 2000, pp. 114–34.

—— 'Are films dangerous? A Maori woman's perspective on *The Piano*,' *Hecate*, vol. 20, no. 2, 1994, pp. 239–41.

Polan, Dana, *Jane Campion*, London: British Film Institute, 2001.

—— 'Auteur desire', *Screening the Past*, no. 12, 2001, http://www.latrobe. edu.au/www/screeningthepast/firstrelease/fr0301/dpfr12a.html.

Powers, John, 'Movies – Jane Campion's latest film is fierce, passionate, and brilliant, while John Irving's *The Cider House Rules* is a decidedly quieter affair', *Vogue*, Dec. 1999, p. 240.

Pullinger, Kate, 'Women directors: soul survivor', *Sight and Sound*, vol. 9, no. 10, 1999, pp. 8–11.

—— 'Jane Campion', *The Times Literary Supplement*, no. 5169, 2002, p. 30.

Quinn, Meredith and Andrew L. Urban (eds), *Edge of the Known World: the Australian Film Television and Radio School. Impressions of the First 25 Years*, Sydney: AFTRS, 1998.

Radkiewicz, Malgorzata, *W poszukiwaniu sposobu ekspresji: o filmach Jane Campion i Sally Potter*, Cracow: Wydawn, Uniwersytetu Jagiellońskiego, 2001.

Raw, Laurence, *Adapting Henry James to the Screen: gender, fiction, and film*, Lanham, MD: Scarecrow Press, 2006.

Redding, Judith, and Victoria Brownworth, *Film Fatales: independent women directors*, Seattle: Seal Press, 1997, pp. 179–84.

Reid, Mark A., 'A few black keys and Maori tattoos: re-reading Jane Campion's *Piano* in post-negritude time', *Quarterly Review of Film and Video*, vol. 17, no. 2, 2000, pp. 107–116.

Riley, Vikki, 'Ancestor worship', *Metro Magazine*, no. 102, 1995, pp. 57–60; 61–4.

Robson, Jocelyn and Zalcock, Beverley, *Girls' Own Stories*, London: Scarlet Press, 1997.

Romare, Ingela, *Dialogue with an Angel: reflections on film and analytical psychology with the example 'An Angel at My Table', a film by Jane Campion*, Malmö: Myt & bild, 1997.

Rönnberg, Sylvia, *Die Frauenfiguren in den Filmen 'The Piano' und 'Portrait of a Lady' von Jane Campion*, Mainz: Univ. Magisterarb, 2000.

Roscoe, Jane, and Hardy, Anne, 'Scratching the surface: *The Piano*'s post-colonial veneer', *Span: Journal of the South Pacific Association for Commonwealth Literature & Language Studies*, nos 42–43, 1996, pp. 143–57.

Rosenbaum, Jonathan, *Dead Man*, London: British Film Institute, 2000.

—— *Movies as Politics*, Berkeley: University of California Press, 1997.

Roth, Bennett E., 'The Piano: a modern film melodrama about passion and punishment', *Psychoanalytic Psychology*, vol. 17, no. 2, 2000, pp. 405–13.

Rothstein, Edward, 'A piano as salvation, temptation and star', *New York Times*, 4 January 1994, pp. 15–19.

Rottenberg, Josh, 'Sex ed – the erotic adventures of Meg Ryan? Director Jane Campion wagers that the peaches-and-cream actress can get steamy with Mark Ruffalo for the sexy thriller In the Cut', *Premiere*, November 2003, p. 86.

Routt, William D., 'Misprision (note version), *Screening the Past*, no. 20, 2006, http://www.latrobe.edu.au/screeningthepast/20/misprision.html.

Rueschmann, Eva, 'Dislocations of home and gender in the films of Jane Campion' in Ian Conrich and Stuart Murray (eds), *New Zealand Filmmakers. Contemporary approaches to film and television series*, Detroit: Wayne State University Press, 2007, pp. 289–303.

—— 'Out of place: reading (post)colonial landscapes as gothic space in Jane Campion's films', *Post Script*, vol. 24, no. 2/3, 2005, pp. 8–21.

Ruhland, Claudia, *Die Spielfilme der neuseeländischen Regisseurin Jane Campion unter desonderer Berücksichtigung der nonverbalen Kommunikation*, thesis, University of Frankfurt, 1996.

Sarmas, Lisa, 'What rape is', *Arena Magazine*, no. 8, 1993–4, p. 14.

Schaefer, William, *Mapping the Godzone: a primer on New Zealand literature and culture*, Honolulu: University of Hawaii Press, 1998.

Schaffer, Kay, *Women and the Bush: forces of desire in the Australian cultural tradition*, Cambridge: Cambridge University Press, 1988.

Schembri, Jim, 'Me Jane', *The Age*, 8 August 1993, p. 13.

Schickel, Richard, 'Divine entertainment: Holy Smoke is surprising, inspiring, and funny', *Time*, 31 January 2000, vol. 155, no. 4, p. 73.

Schoenholtz, Stephan, 'Maoriland und Mittelerde. Neuseeländische Landschaften in The Piano und The Lord of the Rings', *Augenblick*, no. 37, 2005, pp. 111–25.

Scott, A. O., 'A mystery of language, a mystery of murder', *The New York Times*, 22 October 2003, p. E1.

Segal, Naomi, 'The fatal attraction of The Piano', in Nicholas White and Naomi Segal (eds), *Scarlett Letters: fictions of adultery from antiquity to the 1990s*, London: Macillan, 1997, pp. 199–211.

Seguin, L., 'Jane Campion: *In the Cut*', *Quinzaine Litteraire*, no. 869, 2004, p. 24.

Seiffe, Viola, *Die Filme von Jane Campion*, thesis, University of Frankfurt, 1997.

Sesti, Mario, *Jane Campion*, Rome: Dino Audino Editore, 1993.

Sharp, Helena, and Garry Gillard, '"A path of great courage": *The Piano*', *Australian Screen Education*, no. 35, 2004, pp. 109–112.

Shaw, Daniel, 'Isabel Archer: tragic protagonist or pitiable victim', *Literature/Film Quarterly*, vol. 30, no. 4, 2002, pp. 249–55.

Simpson, Catherine, 'Suburban subversions: women's negotiation of suburban space in Australian cinema', *Metro Magazine*, no. 118, 1999, pp. 24–32.

Sklar, Robert, 'A novel approach to movie making: reinventing "The Portrait of a Lady"', *The Chronicle of Higher Education*, vol. 43, no. 23, 1997, B7.

Sklarew, Bruce H., 'I have not spoken: silence in *The Piano*', *International Journal of Psycho-Analysis*, vol. 79, no. 5, 1998, 1011–13.

Slavin, John, 'The films of Jane Campion', *Metro Magazine*, no. 95, 1993, pp. 28–30.

—— '*An Angel at My Table* and *Santa Sangre*', *Metro Magazine*, no. 84, 1990–91, pp. 2–8.

Smelik, Anneke, 'Forces of subversion: on the excess of the image', in *And the Mirror Cracked: Feminist Cinema and Film Theory*, Basingstoke: Macmillan, 1998, pp. 123–51.

Smith, Krista, *Between Sound and Silence: the language of amorous exchange in The Piano*, thesis (MA), Radford University, 1995.

Smith, Mark Chalon, 'A disturbing but uplifting *Angel at My Table*', *Los Angeles Times* (Part F), 7 May 1992, p. 2.

Sobchack, Vivian, 'What my fingers knew: the cinesthetic subject, or vision in the flesh', in *Carnal Thoughts: bodies, texts, scenes and screens*, Berkeley: University of California Press, 2004, pp. 53–84. (A shorter version of this essay has been published online as 'What my fingers knew: the cinesthetic subject and vision in the flesh', *Senses of Cinema*, no. 5, 2000, http://www.sensesofcinema.com.au.)

Staiger, Janet 'Authorship approaches', in David A. Gerstner and Janet Staiger (eds), *Authorship and Film*, New York: Routledge, 2003, pp. 49–52.

States, Janel, *Confronting the Forbidden: reshaping cultural identity with Bluebeard*, thesis (MA), Utah State University, 1996.

Stiles, Mark, 'Interview with Jane Campion', *Cinema Papers*, no. 49, 1984, pp. 434–5.

Stratton, David, '*An Angel at My Table*' (Review), *Variety*, 20 June 1990, p. 32.

Strain, Ellen, 'Reinstating the cultural framework', *Spectator*, vol. 11, no. 2, 1991, pp. 32–43.

Stuart, Jan, 'Up in smoke', *The Advocate*, 1 February 2000, p. 49.

Suckfüll, Monica, *Film erleben: narrative Strukturen und physiologische Prozesse – "Das Piano" von Jane Campion*, Berlin: Sigma, 1997.

Taubin, Amy, 'In the Cut' *Film Comment*, vol. 39, no. 6, 2003, p. 51.

Thomas, Philip, 'Dig yourself out of this one', *Empire*, no. 54, 1993, p. 16.

Thomas, Stephanie Ann, *Underneath and In Between: interpretations of Jane Campion's Sweetie*, thesis (MA), University of North Carolina at Chapel Hill, 2006.

Thornley, Davinia, 'Duel or duet? Gendered nationalism in *The Piano*', *Film Criticism*, vol. 24, no. 3, 2000, pp. 61–76.

Tulich, Katherine, 'The big screen', *Sydney Morning Herald*, 20 September 1990, p. 31.

Twemlow, Stuart, 'Maori and pakeha images and their interrelationships in Jane Campion's *The Piano*', *Journal of Applied Psychoanalytic Studies*, vol. 3, no. 1, 2001, pp. 85–93.

van den Berk, Tjeu, *The Piano: 'boeiende' klanken : een beschouwing. Zin in film*, Kampen: Kok, 1994.

van Leeuwen, Theo, 'Emotional times: the music of *The Piano*' in Rebecca Coyle (ed.), *Screen Scores: studies in contemporary Australian film music*, North Ryde, NSW: Australian Film, Television & Radio School, 1998, pp. 39–48.

Verley, Claudine, *The Portrait of a Lady: Henry James, Jane Campion*, Paris: Ellipses-Marketing, 1998.

Vigderman, Patricia, *Images of Absences: nineteenth-century British novels as film, history, and autobiography*, thesis (PhD), Tufts University, 1998.

Villasur, Belén Vidal, *Textures of the Image: rewriting the American novel in the contemporary film adaptation*, Valencia: Biblioteca Javier Coy d'estudies nord-americans, 2002.

—— (Re)reading is (Dis)remembering: the pleasures of adaptation in postmodern film. A critical reading of Martin Scorsese's The Age of Innocence and Jane Campion's The Portrait of Lady, thesis (MA), Georgetown University, 2000.

Walton, Priscilla, 'Jane and James go to the Movies: post-colonial portraits of a lady', *Henry James Review*, vol. 18, no. 2, 1997, pp. 187–90.

Wark, McKenzie, 'Antipodality', in *Angelaki: Journal of the Theoretical Humanities*, vol. 2, no. 3, 1997, pp. 17–28.

Warrack, Christoph, 'Kathleen McHugh's *Jane Campion*', *The Times Literary Supplement*, no. 5453, 2007, p. 33.

Weinstein, Steve, 'Critics: now she's a sweetie', *San Francisco Examiner-Chronicle*, 23 June 1991, p. 28.

Wevers, Lydia, 'A story of land: narrating landscape in some early New Zealand writers or: not the story of a New Zealand river', *Australian and New Zealand Studies in Canada*, vol. 11, 1994, pp. 1–11.

Wexman, Virginia Wright (ed.), *Jane Campion: Interviews*, Jackson: University Press of Mississippi, 1999.

—— 'The portrait of a body', *Henry James Review*, vol. 18, no. 2, 1997, 184–6.

White, Devon, *Toward Alternative Resolutions for Women or, Her Score Rewrites the Script: Jane Campion's The Piano*, thesis (MA), University of North Carolina at Wilmington, 1995.

Williams, Donald, '*The Piano*: the isolated, constricted self', *The Jung Page*, 14 December 2005, http://www.cgjungpage.org/index.php?option=com_content&task=view&id=730&Itemid=40.

Williams, Sue, 'The portrait of a certain lady', *The Weekend Australian*, 7 December 1996, pp. 55–61.

Wilson, Emma, 'Isabel's child: the portrait of a lady', *Film Studies: An International Review*, no. 3, 2002, 18–30.

Wood, Robin, *The Wings of the Dove: Henry James in the 1990s*, London: British Film Institute, 1999.

Wrye, H., 'Tuning a clinical ear to ambiguous chords of Jane Campion's *The Piano*', *Psychoanalytic Inquiry*, vol. 18, no. 2, 1998, 168.

## ARCHIVAL SOURCES

Biographical cuttings on Jane Campion – held at the National Library of Australia, Canberra

Early Campion films and scripts, student essays – held at the AFTRS Library

Films, film stills and promotional materials – held at the National Film and Sound Archive of Australia

Films, television and audio interviews, promotional materials – held at the NZ Film Archive

Media clippings on Jane Campion and her individual films – held at the AFI Research Collection, RMIT University, Melbourne

# GLOSSARY

**academic–fan** a scholar who also claims, often proudly, to be a fan

**'adapteur'** my phrase referring to filmmakers who are distinguished
   for their adaptations of pre-existing material (literature, other films)

**AFC** Australian Film Commission

**AFI** Australian Film Institute

**AFIRC** Australian Film Institute Research Collection

**AFTRS** Australian Film Television and Radio School

**AFTS** Australian Film and Television School (later AFTRS)

**ancillary market** film media outlets that occur after theatrical release
   (DVD, TV)

**art film (art house)** usually low-budget films, often focused on style
   and characterization, intended for specific, sophisticated audiences

**artbuster** combination of art house and blockbuster. A highly
   successful art house film

**artplex** a small cinema that screens specialized (art) films

**ASDA** Australian Screen Directors Association

**ATOM** Australian Teachers of Media

**auteur (auteurism)** French word for 'author', usually referring to a
   director with a distinctive 'signature' style. Coined in the 1950s to
   recognize the creative contributions of directors, particularly those
   working in Hollywood. Expanded by later critics, the theory gave

overall responsibility and credit for the vision of a film, its identifiable style, themes and techniques, to the director, rather than to a collaborative effort

**auteurprint** evident signs of a filmmaker's authorship found in their films; their signature

**AWGIE** Australian Writers Guild Awards

**box office** theatre ticket sales (aka BO or 'gross')

**cameo** a bit part (usually non-speaking) in which an uncredited director, actor or celebrity appears in a film

**chick flicks** films considered popular with women

**cine pragmatics** term coined by William D. Routt to describe 'the recognition that what is shown on the screen is the result of countless apparently minute or trivial practical decisions'

**cineaste** especially enthusiastic film audience member, often well versed in art cinema

**crossover film** (appeal) a film that is successful in audience segments other than its intended audience

**culture jamming** the act of transforming existing media to make a commentary on itself, for example, altering advertising banners to undermine the original brand message

**distributor** a person or company that resells or rents films to exhibitors; usually responsible for promoting film titles

**exhibitor** a person or company responsible for showing films to audiences

**fan–academic** a fan who uses academic theories and language in their fan writing

**FFC** Film Finance Corporation of Australia

**flop** a film that fails at the box office

**FTO (NSWFTO)** (New South Wales) Film and Television Office

**high concept** film containing an unusual idea that can be promoted simply for its uniqueness

**greenlighting** final financing that enables a film to go into production. Opposite to *redlighting*

**IMDB** internet movie database

**indie** in the US, any film production company that is not one of the seven major studios based in Hollywood; a film company that is not an industry heavyweight. Can also refer to a director or film distributor not associated with a studio

**limited release** a film screening at a few venues in a given location

**major (studio)** in the US, large film producer–distributor companies: Columbia Pictures/Tri Star (part of Sony Pictures Entertainment); Dreamworks SKG; MGM; Paramount; Twentieth Century Fox; Universal; Walt Disney Studios (including Buena Vista); Warner Bros. In the UK, the term might also refer to EMI or Rank at different historical moments.

**mash-up** a media entity or application that combines elements from multiple sources, for example, merging two different styles of music into one song or a webpage that combines information from two different sources to create a new service

**megaplex** a multi-screen cinema venue with more than 20 screens

**metteur en scène** often used disdainfully to refer to directors whose work is creatively unremarkable

**MIFF** Melbourne International Film Festival

**miniplex** a cinema venue limited to three to five screens

**multiplex** a cinema venue with more than five screens (but fewer than 20)

**new auteurism** revival of auteurism but that accounts for industrial changes in film production and distribution and the theoretical limitations of traditional understandings of the director's agency. See also *post-auteurism*

**NFSA** National Film and Sound Archive of Australia

**NZFC** New Zealand Film Commission

**OFLC** Office of Film and Literature Classification (Australia)

**pakeha** New Zealanders of predominantly European ancestry, a non-Maori

**platform release** a film release strategy that has a film opening in a small number of venues and then increasing to a larger number of venues if the film receives a favourable reaction

**post-auteurism** revision of classical auteurism that proposes the author as a multivalent identity best understood from a pluralism of approaches to authorship. See also *new auteurism*

**press kit** (media kit; EPK) folders of information about a film provided to the media by distributors. More recently, these are provided electronically and may include film clips (hence EPK).

**redlighting** when a film that has been in production loses its financial backing (aka the film is in turnaround). See also *greenlighting*

**rentals** money returned to the distributor after the exhibitor has deducted their take

**saturation release** a film screening at between 2000–2999 venues

**SBS** Special Broadcasting Service

**secondary circulation** the use of a star's image in media other than cinema (e.g. television, magazines and so on)

**smart cinema** identified by Jeffrey Sconce in 2002, both a production and marketing descriptor for a type of disaffected and ironic form of art cinema popular with 'X generation' audiences

**soft money** film investment drawn from public subsidy and other government incentive schemes (such as rebates and tax concessions)

**SPAA** Screen Producers Association of Australia

**tent pole release** key film used to build the studio's broader distribution strategy; the film around which other films in the slate will hang

**territory** the geographical area in which a distributor owns the rights to show a particular film

**theatrical rights** the distribution of films to cinemas

**turnaround** a waiting period before a developed film project is 'greenlighted'

**vertical integration** in which companies involved in various aspects of the production, distribution and exhibition business are financially linked

**Web 2.0** second generation of internet use and services that facilitate collaboration and sharing between users

**wide release** a film playing at 600–1999 venues

**WIFT** Women in Film and Television

**window** time gap between various stages in a film's release

# INDEX